The Transformative Power Of Learning

THE TRANSFORMATIVE POWER OF LEARNING

*50 years of Lifelong Learning at
Fielding Graduate University*

Edited by
Elena I. Nicklasson and Jean-Pierre Isbouts

Associate Editors:
Kaylin R. Staten and Luca Belloiu

TABLE OF CONTENTS

Preface

Karen S. Bogart
Chair of Fielding's Board of Trustees

Like many alums before me, my introduction to Fielding Graduate University was nontraditional. Professionally, I came to Fielding in 2009 with two master's degrees and 25 years of human resources and global business management experience at Eastman Kodak Company. When I left Kodak, I was the Chairperson of Asia based in Shanghai, China. I also was serving on several company boards. Personally, I had recently remarried, and we were blending our family in California. As a lifelong learner, I was attracted to Fielding. I believed that I could integrate learnings at Fielding with my professional and personal interests and aspirations including consulting, teaching, and company board leadership. I welcomed the opportunity to shape my doctoral journey in the Human and Organizational Systems program while collaborating with others in the learning process.

I enjoyed being a student again. I also appreciated the shared learning process between Fielding students and faculty. My dissertation process was stimulating and energizing. It focused on a topic close to my heart. It considered the influence of company boards of directors on Corporate Social Responsibility in U.S. public companies that are recognized as sustainability leaders. I was fortunate as I had a broad interest in ESG. I also had a great dissertation committee that encouraged me while pushing me to think strategically and systemically. I have since used my doctoral learnings in research and professional board applications with companies and nonprofit organizations, as well as in director educational processes. My experience is much like those of alums and students. Fielding seems to find us when we need it. Fielding encourages adult learners to study what they are interested in through appreciative and unprescribed patterns. The Fielding faculty and university leadership recognize that adult learners must balance their ongoing life demands with scholastic commitments. They encourage a vibrant excitement for learning and the will to keep going during challenging moments. They provide the support, systems, and tools to enable adult student success.

Every doctoral student's experience is unique. It shapes us as a learner, scholar, and practitioner. Fielding's founders had that vision and commitment. Fielding enriches the collection of our life experiences, stretches our thinking, and transforms us.

While Fielding's lifeblood is its scholarship and practice, its heart is the interwoven relationships you build while you are at Fielding. If you have ever been to an in-person or virtual Fielding commencement ceremony, all three components are on display. New graduates share their personal journeys and explain their dissertation work. I am always inspired by their diverse interests, heroic pursuits, support systems, resilience, and success. My hope for Fielding is that it will thrive in the education of adult learners, scholarship, and impact. This will integrate the founders' mission, Fielding's values, and diverse capabilities, as well as the growing partnership with Rowan Education Partners. Ensuring an ongoing learning relationship for our students, faculty, alums, and friends will be critical as we try to shape a more just, sustainable world. We have a bond, and we often refer to ourselves as the "Fielding family." We must collectively work together to ensure that Fielding excites, nurtures, and supports adult learning success. As both an alum and Fielding's board chair, I continue to be inspired by our community. This monograph, aptly titled "The Transformative Power of Learning," weaves inspirational narratives into a tangible collection as we celebrate Fielding's 50th Anniversary. Published by our own Fielding University Press, it contains testimonials of scholarship and experiences of our Fielding community and how Fielding has supported transformational learning. We learn more about the individual and collective impacts, from scholarly research to personal testimonials and enriching conversations. While each chapter has a unique take on what Fielding means, the core remains through the uplifting vignettes of how people encouraged and sustained them as they pursued their passions and work. Fielding is a place where transformation is the norm!

This is the dawn of a new beginning, and it's an opportunity for us to continue to move forward in a robust way. I encourage you to reflect on these stories of transformational learning so they can live outside of these pages and in your own scholarship and practice. May these narratives invigorate your own delight for Fielding and the transformative power of a learning journey in higher education.

*Fielding faculty and staff on the steps of the De La Guerra apartments,
where Fielding was based until 1983.*

Foreword

Katrina S. Rogers
President, Fielding Graduate University

I like to say that my parents raised me by aphorism. "Quickly done is twice done." "Many hands make light work." "Work is its own reward." "A burden shared is a burden halved—a joy shared is a joy doubled." "Make haste slowly." "If it were easy, everyone would do it." Growing up, I didn't understand many of their sayings as I was at the tail end of a much older family, and their ways of speaking seemed old-fashioned and irrelevant. Over time, though, I have come to appreciate the importance of how their past shaped my present at the time, and now shape my future as I carry their wisdom within me. The enterprise of graduate education is very much an endeavor that takes the accumulated wisdom of those that went before us, that we then carry on, adding to it with our research and practice, knowing that those that come after will do the same. This continuity is critical to a civil and civic society. After all, it is original research and scholarly practices that help to provide the foundations of an educated world. Within this understanding of the higher purpose of education, Fielding Graduate University was born.

An anniversary is a time to look both backward and forward. As we are often reminded by eastern philosophy, the past is behind us, the future as yet unknown, so we only have the present. Yes, and (as we say at Fielding) the past does guide both our present and future. We are a university that sees itself as a purveyor of a set of timeless values, and as an institution that is both steady and adaptive. Our enduring values come from our founders and the early faculty who believed that graduate education was a vehicle for positive social action. Furthermore, they thought it was important to create an educational experience specifically for people who wanted to have a strong voice in co-creating their topics within a chosen discipline. Raising their voices not only honored the experience and autonomy of learners, but their voices would also provide the perfect environment for the adult learner who wanted to contribute to society—or as our motto states, "change the world; start with yours."

There are three legs of this stool upon which our education models sit. The first leg is community. We strive to reduce the transactional needs of education by forming strong bonds amongst faculty and students, students and students, students and staff, students and alumni, and alumni and faculty. Underpinning Fielding's idea of community are our values of transformational learning and learner-centered education. We strive to place our graduate learners at the center of our university life, offering courses, dialogical spaces, and other educational opportunities to forge common ground and build relationships. Fielding faculty subscribe to the humanistic principles of learning, that we as humans need the relational— both social and emotional—that propels us to be the greatest version of ourselves.

The second leg of this stool is the element of flexibility. We think of flexibility in two ways: the first is to provide as much flexibility as possible in the learning modalities. Some examples are synchronous and asynchronous virtual courses; learning opportunities conducted as independent studies; in person professional development seminars; and many other forms of engagement such as one on one with Fielding faculty as well as spaces that students may create for themselves. This flexibility is both created for and by learners. The second aspect of flexibility concerns the pedagogical intent of a good graduate education—the ability to build the skills that accompany a flexible mind. As human beings, we all have greatness within us. We know from human development that to release that greatness within us, we need to draw on a reservoir of skills that allow us to manage ambiguity, complexity, and paradox. These skills add up to a flexible mind. A Fielding graduate education is unique in this regard—it is not just mastering content in one's field of expertise, but also developing the habits of mind that, long after graduation, we can use in navigating our modern world and creating positive change for ourselves and others.

The third leg of this stool is quality. Quality means an education that meets the high standards of accreditors, which we have done consistently within years of our founding. But it means much more as well. Quality is also about designing curricula that is intellectually challenging, aligned with disciplinary norms, and forward thinking in orientation. Academic excellence is a core value at Fielding and necessitates a vigilance to inquire consistently about what our students are learning, and how they are learning. Diversity, Equity, and Inclusion (DEI) are also a part of quality in that we seek to foster an environment internally that mirrors the external needs of society. A value orientation of DEI educates us all to be more nuanced in our thinking about what it means to belong and to foster belonging in an increasingly diverse society. When we speak of social justice, we mean that the quality of our education enhances one' ability to understand the root causes of injustice, poverty, and inequality, and within these understandings we can find ways to play a part in overturning them to create a more just society for all through our professional work.

It seems just a moment ago that Fielding celebrated our 40th anniversary. As President at that time, I remember that we all were grappling with such deep issues as the lingering effects of the 2008 recession, growing economic precarity for so many Americans, and sweeping changes in higher education. We had no idea of the road ahead: such as, the rise of vitriolic politicization of so many things we as educators take as a given, such as teaching about racism, structural inequality, sustainability, social justice, and social and emotional learning. We did not see the pandemic around the corner, and the ways in which the pandemic furthered exposed the fractures in societies throughout the world.

We cannot know the future; however, we can live into using our strengths and raising our collective voices. What can do is provide the best graduate education we can in the present, so that our graduates are prepared to tackle hard things with everyday courage and resilience, equipped with the tools and capabilities to take action that improves their lives, the lives of their families, and the people, organizations, and systems that they care about and work.

One of our founders, Dr. Frederic Hudson, wrote in a speech at our 10th anniversary celebration, that Fielding was always meant to be a social experiment dedicated to and for adult learning. Whether it would continue would be up to the people that came after him. We are those people. As you read this book, it is my hope that Fielding will reveal itself to you as the human endeavor it is—a place where we continue to experiment, where we are building community with each other, cultivating the habits of mind necessary in a civilized society, and creating a sense of inclusion and belonging for all, both with Fielding and in the greater world.

The birth of Fielding's online network at the beginning of the computer revolution in the early 1980's. Note the Corona portable PC.

Introduction: The Transformative Power of Learning

Elena I. Nicklasson and Jean-Pierre Isbouts
Editors

Since its inception in 1974, Fielding Graduate University has served as an educational setting for adult learners who want to embark on a profound journey of self-discovery and transformative learning. In a society where the constant buzz of life's demands often drowns out the pursuit of knowledge, we risk losing sight of the intrinsic value that education brings. The pursuit of wisdom that was once cherished as an essential cornerstone of personal and societal growth now contends with the distractions of the digital age and the allure of quick fixes. The frantic rhythms of modern life have given rise to a culture of instant gratification, where the merits of patient, diligent learning are increasingly sidelined.

As editors of this monograph, we believe that education remains a beacon of enlightenment, a conduit for progress, and a compass that guides us through the labyrinth of an ever-changing world. We see it as our responsibility to reignite the flame of appreciation for education, recognizing its enduring importance in the broader narrative of our society, especially for adult learners. With this 50th anniversary edition, our goal is to offer English-speaking readers in North America and around the world an inspiring and highly diverse collection of testimonials illustrating the transformative power of learning in 21st-century society.

With *The Transformative Power* of Learning we will explore the annals of Fielding's history, guided by the voices of those who have contributed to its tapestry. As we traverse these pages, we are introduced to a diverse cast of individuals, each with a unique story of their journey through Fielding, and each with their own take on the transformative power of learning.

The Preface, written by Karen S. Bogart, the longest-serving Chair of Fielding's Board of Trustees, sets the stage by highlighting Karen's remarkable path, demonstrating how Fielding often finds its way to those who need it most, igniting their passion for lifelong learning and creating a space for them to shape their own educational odyssey. Fielding, at its core, embodies the spirit of empowerment, encouraging adult learners to delve into subjects they are passionate about, nurturing their inquisitiveness through appreciative and unprescribed patterns of study. This is a place where the traditional boundaries of academia yield to the desires and interests of the learners, enabling them to harmonize their life's demands with their scholarly pursuits.

Fielding's journey is an intricate tapestry woven with scholarship, practice, and relationships. The heart of this institution lies in the connections that students build during their time here, whether through in-person or virtual interactions. These relationships are the bonds that propel Fielding's mission of transformation.

In her Foreword, Katrina S. Rogers, the longest-serving President of Fielding Graduate University, discusses enduring values that have shaped Fielding over the years. She reflects on the importance of community, flexibility, and quality in the university's educational philosophy, explaining how these three principles have been vital in preparing graduates to navigate an ever-changing world and contribute to positive social action.

In our vision for this monograph, we were particularly interested in stories by alums about how their pursuit of a Fielding degree had a transformative impact on their lives. For example, some have leveraged their degree to reach or change their career goals; for others, the degree may have enabled them to positively change their personal later-life journeys, communities, or society at large.

We begin with an excerpt from Keith Meville's book *A Passion for Adult Learning* about Fielding's foundation in 1974. It reveals the revolutionary quality of Fielding's vision in the mid-1970's, not only in terms of its focus on adult learners but also given its concept of a distributed network of learners across the country—and eventually, the world.

In "Pursuing my Noble Goal," Zieva Konvisser discusses her research journey into the lives of individuals who have faced trauma and adversity, beginning with a deep desire to understand Holocaust survivors. She draws inspiration from Viktor Frankl's teachings on finding meaning in the face of hopelessness. The author's experiences in Israel during the Second Intifada prompt questions about learning from such traumatic events. She discusses the importance of providing a safe space for survivors to share their stories, which leads to her work with freed and exonerated women who faced wrongful convictions. Throughout, the author emphasizes the power of storytelling, personal growth, and the resilience of individuals in the face of tragedy. Michelle Obama's quote, "Becoming is never giving up on the idea that there's more growing to be done," aptly summarizes the theme of continual transformation in the author's life and the transformational journey of a Fielding alum.

In his chapter, Richard Yao, President of California State University Channel Islands, delves into the profound impact of his Fielding education on his personal and professional journey. He vividly recounts that at Fielding, he was introduced to a broader epistemological landscape, challenging his preconceived notions and instigating a transformative journey. He reflects on the significance of epistemological curiosity, awareness, and growth, emphasizing that these processes are continuous and require intentionality, humility, and perseverance. As he advanced into leadership roles, especially as President of CSU Channel Islands, he realized the pressing need to integrate diverse epistemologies, including transformational thinking, into his approach to ensure diversity, equity, inclusion, and access (DEIA) at the forefront of the institution. His journey, informed by his Fielding education, serves as an enduring testament to the power of learning and growth, both personally and professionally.

U.S. Representative Salud Carbajal is a graduate of Fielding's Masters program who also served on Fielding's board. In his chapter, Carbajal reflects on the profound impact Fielding education had on his leadership and commitment to effective governance. He commends Fielding's unique pedagogical approaches, emphasizing the guiding principles of social justice and transformational learning, which resonated with his mission to enhance government transparency and responsiveness. Carbajal's testimony highlights the significance of higher education in empowering today's practitioners and calls for increased accessibility to such transformative learning experiences.

In "Becoming a Network Weaver," Linda Honold's narrative centers on her transition from being a leader in a pioneering employee-centric organization to her pursuit of a Ph.D. in Human and Organizational Systems at Fielding. Her research culminated in the study of organizations that emphasize employee engagement through self-designed systems that promote a sense of ownership among employees. This educational journey not only solidified her understanding of the significance of systems thinking in her work but also helped her contribute significantly to democracy initiatives by the Democratic Party. One of the longest-serving board members and past Board Chair, Dr. Honold's experience underscores the enduring impact of lifelong learning and the unique, self-directed learning opportunities that Fielding Graduate University offers.

In the "Transformational Learning and the Hidden Curriculum," Fielding student-trustee Zabrina W. Epps chronicles her personal journey as she embarks on a challenging doctoral program at Fielding Graduate University. Despite initial self-doubt, Epps is motivated by her aspiration to become a scholar-practitioner, aiming to enhance her analytical and writing skills to effect transformative change in the education system. Her narrative is about success in academia beyond mastering course material, which involves the navigation of a hidden curriculum within educational institutions, a concept inspired by Kegan. Epps invites future Fielding students to embrace their transformative journey.

Maria V. Sanchez is a Fielding student trustee. Her pursuit of a doctoral degree is another example of a journey of personal and academic transformation. Transitioning from a career as the President & CEO of a private company to philanthropy and radio hosting, she embarked on a later-in-life quest for academic excellence. Her decision to pursue a Ph.D. in Media Psychology at Fielding Graduate University led her on an unexpected path of discovery. While initially unsure of her dissertation's focus, Maria's journey organically introduced her to the pressing issue of Female Genital Mutilation (FGM). Her groundbreaking work led to the creation of the STOP THE CUT NOW! Foundation and a deep involvement in advocacy, including testifying before legislators and supporting anti-FGM legislation. Maria's journey at Fielding ignited the scholar-practitioner within her, providing her with the tools and inspiration to make a difference in the fight against FGM, both locally and globally.

Shifting focus from a personal journey, Pauline Albert's contribution delves into the intricate nature of transformational learning within the academic realm. Albert's extensive experience as both a teacher and learner prompts her to explore the essence of transformation and how it can be measured empirically. She defines transformation as an enduring expansion of consciousness leading to increased awareness, a broader identity, and an enlarged framework for meaning-making. In her reflection on the essence of transformative learning experience, she underscores the role of love, collaboration, humility, and community in the co-creation of meaningful, lifelong learning experiences. The chapter concludes by emphasizing the importance of nurturing leaders and learners who embody a broader worldview, reflecting the transformative ethos of Fielding Graduate University.

Chris Lowell's personal narrative about his transformative experience at Fielding emphasizes that learning is not merely about understanding but about applying knowledge for better outcomes. He reflects on the diverse ways people can achieve greatness and the essential role of mentors, family, friends, and colleagues in nurturing it. Lowell contends that learning is the catalyst that transforms human potential into greatness, and he emphasizes the importance of listening, thinking, and acting to create a positive difference in the world. He acknowledges that education is not solely about acquiring knowledge but about serving others, making service the ultimate goal. As a corporate leader, he integrates his research into his leadership practices, emphasizing the importance of creating equitable structures and outcomes. Lowell's narrative serves as a testament to the power of education to enrich and inspire lives, reinforcing the idea that true joy comes not from receiving but from giving.

What role do questions play in our learning journeys? In "The Transformative Pursuit of Meaningful Answers," Tracy N. Long reflects on her life's journey, shaped by a series of questions, some routine, some profound, and some life-changing. Her fascination with human advancement from using primitive tools to building spaceships, sparked by the movie *2001: A Space Odyssey*, led her to choose a career as an anthropologist. For 30 years she managed technology transitions and observed the integration of information technology into daily life. With a desire to explore new questions, she joined Fielding Graduate University, aiming to combine social science and technology in her studies. Her journey to becoming a Ph.D. expanded her horizons and led her to a new role in creating a botanical garden with a mission centered on conservation, research, and generating new knowledge for a sustainable and socially just future. Her doctoral experience leads her to a journey where she continues to ask new questions and embrace meaningful opportunities for the future.

In "A Conversation with Students from Black Student Association," three Fielding doctoral students, Donica Harper, Nathan Smith, and Shania Greenwood, share their motives for pursuing a PhD degree in clinical psychology. Donica highlights the desire for higher levels of care for clients and the opportunity to become a professor, in support of the advanced academic and social justice focus at Fielding. Nathan discusses his long-standing dream of earning a PhD and the flexibility Fielding offers for adult learners, particularly in terms of the social justice and diversity concentration. Shania expresses her passion for helping people who look like her within the African American community, outlining the importance of resources that a PhD could provide. The interview touches upon the significance of pursuing a PhD degree in addressing current mental health crises and enhancing career opportunities. Additionally, the students provide advice for potential PhD candidates, such as the importance of knowing one's goals and reasons for pursuing an advanced degree; seeking mentorship and connecting with faculty and students; and offering themselves grace during the rigorous journey of doctoral studies.

Similarly, the "Conversation with Navajo Nation Alumni" chapter reveals their remarkable journey toward obtaining doctoral degrees at Fielding

Graduate University, all while staying deeply connected to their Navajo community and culture. Miranda Haskie, Rolanda Billy, Telletha Valenski, Viola Hoskie, and Pauline Begay show that their academic aspirations were deeply intertwined with Navajo worldviews and principles. They emphasize the importance of staying true to their traditions, languages, and teaching future generations, with strong community support serving as a critical foundation for their success. For prospective Navajo students, their message is one of encouragement, underlining the feasibility of achieving a doctoral degree and the unique opportunity to stay close to their community in their academic journey. Finally, the completion of their doctoral studies evokes a mix of emotions, including relief, happiness, and a profound sense of fulfilling their responsibilities to their culture and grandparents, exemplifying the transformative power of education and cultural preservation in the 21st century.

In "My Doctoral Degree," Miranda Jensen Haskie, a professor at Diné College, traces her educational journey, highlighting her deep-rooted connection to the Navajo Nation and the significance of higher education within her community. She recounts her personal journey, marked by homesickness during her college years away from home, and relates how Fielding's unique pedagogical approach, emphasizing self-directed learning, allowed her to continue her education without leaving her beloved community. She describes her dissertation study, focused on preserving Navajo culture and language, and how Fielding's approach empowered her to create her own theory. Her Fielding experience, both as a student and now as a professor, has had a profound impact on her. She continues to appreciate the immeasurable support from the faculty during her doctoral journey while being proud to be part of a community of education leaders dedicated to making a difference in their community.

How do the communities that we belong to define us? And how do we create our own communities? In Sergej van Middendorp's chapter, "The Perspective of a Foreign Student", he reflects on his academic journey and his choice to attend Fielding Graduate University for his doctoral degree. Along the way, he embraces metaphors, explores the communication theory of The Coordinated Management of Meaning, and discovers the worlds of opera and classical music. His journey also leads to a new approach to knowledge and an ongoing commitment to the healthcare system in the Netherlands. Sergej highlights the importance of higher education and transdisciplinary degrees. He acknowledges the sacrifices made and the challenging aspects of learning and growth. His is yet another story of the transformative power of intellectual pursuit.

In this monograph, many Navajo voices are present, a reflection of Fielding's deep connection to the Navajo Nation and the educational partnership we have formed over the years. Pauline M. Begay's educational journey, as recounted in her Fielding story, is a testament to resilience and a commitment to preserving her Navajo culture and language. Her educational path encompassed a diverse array of experiences, from B.I.A. Day schools to the Sherman Institute in California, all while nurturing her passion for teaching Navajo language and culture. Her pursuit of higher education led her to a B.A. in Elementary Education, a Master's in American Indian Educational Leadership, and a Doctoral Degree in Educational Leadership from Fielding Graduate University. It was at Fielding that Pauline embarked on her groundbreaking research, "Drum and Sing Out the Language," seeking to teach the Navajo language to children through songs. Her work resulted in two Navajo song albums for children, which have been recognized with awards and nominations. Dr. Begay's intellectual journey has expanded her horizons and professional opportunities, enabling her to serve her community and promote education. She encourages future generations, particularly Native American students, to pursue their educational aspirations. In her eyes, Fielding Graduate University's unique education model and interdisciplinary programs provide the foundation for scholar-practitioners like herself to realize their full potential.

In the pages of his chapter "My Experience at Fielding," Henry Fowler embarks on an intimate exploration of his own transformative journey. With this narrative a profound connection to Dr. Fowler's Navajo heritage becomes vividly apparent: as a proud descendant of the Bitterwater clan, he bears the weight of a cultural legacy steeped in knowledge, skills, and traditions. With unwavering devotion to the preservation and exaltation of Navajo culture, the author embarks on a formidable mission – one that seeks to bridge the chasm between tradition and modern education. It is, at its core, a visionary quest to infuse the tenets of Navajo excellence into the pedagogical arena, particularly in the domain of mathematics. This fusion of heritage and academia animates his commitment to elevating the quality of life for the Navajo community and serves as the cornerstone for his vision of a math education uniquely suited to the needs of native learners.

Past Fielding trustee and one of the early graduates, Tracy Gibbons describes her career at the Digital Equipment Corporation (DEC) and how it led her into the new field of Organizational Design and Development. When her position became redundant in 1983, she successfully petitioned the company to support her pursuit of a Ph.D. degree in Human and Organization Development at Fielding. At the time, the HOD program was still relatively knew and, as she writes, the three Fielding founders—Frederic Hudson, Hallock Hoffman and Renata Tesch—were very engaged in the student orientation at La Casa de Maria.

At Fielding, community members wear different hats. Alums may either become faculty or revert to students again in order to pursue a new kind of certification or a degree. Alternatively, a faculty member or a graduate can become a trustee or a significant donor. Pamela Rutledge's lifelong learning journey is another Fielding story of transformation. She highlights the importance of degrees, especially for women, but argues that the true value lies in the critical thinking, analytical, and communication skills acquired in the process. Fielding remains her intellectual and professional home, offering flexibility and a supportive network for lifelong learning and career advancement. She is, in fact, a top-rated Fielding media influencer, and her opinion pieces published worldwide appear weekly in Fielding's newsroom.

Leni Wildflower's journey through Fielding in the early nineties was marked by a unique and collaborative academic experience. Students were encouraged to collaborate, interact, and explore a broad range of ideas. This collaborative spirit was reminiscent of Wildflower's activist years, drawing in midlife learners who wanted to expand their lived experiences through adult learning principles. It fueled Wildflower's love for learning and instilled a sense of collaboration as she embarked on a path of the scholar-practitioner. After graduating, she continued her journey by teaching in

Fielding's online master's program, harnessing the collaborative potential of the online environment to create supportive and intimate learning communities. Wildflower's story is a testament to the strength and joy of collaborative learning at Fielding, where the spirit of collaboration and intellectual exploration prevails.

To round out this wonderful collection of Fielding alumni voices, we also included a number of testimonials previously published by Fielding University Press, including contributions by Maxine Borowsky Junge, Cliff Hurst, Gary Wagenheim, Carrie A. L. Arnold, Julie Smendzuik-O'Brien and Timothy K. Stanton.

We are privileged to share this monograph as we celebrate Fielding's 50th Anniversary. This collection brings to life the testimonies of scholarship, personal experiences, and the transformational power of individual learning within a nurturing community of scholar-practitioners. Each chapter offers a unique perspective on what Fielding means to its community members, yet the common thread remains the transformative power that defines this institution.

This monograph is a testament to the dawn of a new beginning, and it offers an opportunity for all readers to be invigorated by the stories of transformational learning. May these narratives not only inspire you but also awaken your passion for the remarkable potential of a learning journey in higher education. In the field of higher education, Fielding's impact has been felt, one learner at a time, and we hope that its commitment to fostering lifelong learning will last for many years to come.

Fielding's founders: Hallock Hoffman, Renate Tesch and Frederic Hudson

The Power of Disruptive Innovation

Keith Melville
Doctoral faculty

> "There is nothing more difficult to take in hand,
> more perilous to conduct, or more uncertain
> in its success than to take the lead in the
> introduction of a new order of things."
> – Machiavelli, *The Prince*, 1532

Soon after the Fielding Institute was started in 1974, Roy Fairfield, a professor of education at Harvard who for eight years worked in senior administrative positions at the Union Graduate School—which was one of the first efforts to offer a graduate program in an external degree format—wrote a valuable book entitled *Person-Centered Graduate Education* (1977). As Carl Rogers notes in his introduction, "Much has been written about the vision of what innovative self-directed education might be. . . But there has been no attempt to spell out what it means to implement this newer way of education in a whole school over a period of years." In his introductory comments, Rogers expressed his appreciation of Fairfield's account, which, in his words, offers "a splendidly detailed picture of the agonies and ecstasies of that pioneering venture" (Carl Rogers in Roy Fairfield, *Person-Centered Education*, 1977).

Like Fairfield's book, this chapter provides a brief profile – including "agonies" as well as "ecstasies" – of another pioneering institution that set out to re-invent doctoral education, which was initially called the Fielding Institute. This program was radically innovative in its first few decades. Because of the ways in which its principles and practices have moved into the mainstream of higher education, Fielding's story is particularly pertinent today, a time when there is growing recognition of flaws in the mainstream model of higher education and the need to address them. It is increasingly apparent that mainstream institutions have a good deal to learn from nontraditional programs that pioneered new approaches and learning models.

Re-set era in higher education

Over the past few years, higher education has come under growing criticism. Dozens of recent books with titles like *College Unbound, Academically Adrift, What is College For?* and *Designing the New American University* illustrate a rising tide of institutional scrutiny. At a time when the cost of higher education has continued to spiral upward, many are asking what students gain from their educational experience and what social benefits justify the nation's significant investment in higher education. The business model of mainstream institutions is imperiled by decreasing state support, growing resistance to ever-higher tuition costs, and alarm about rising levels of student debt.

The traditional learning model is criticized on the grounds that it has not changed to keep up with the changing needs of students, in particular older students who need programs that are more convenient and flexible. Employers increasingly criticize higher education institutions for not producing graduates with the skills needed in today's workforce. In colleges and graduate schools, educators are under growing pressure to demonstrate what students learn in the course of their studies, pressures for accountability that many educators have resisted.

A number of years ago, in 2006, a report from a federal commission that examined the state of American higher education warned against "the danger of complacency." Rather than adapting to changing educational needs, the report characterized mainstream higher educational institutions as "increasingly risk-averse, at times self-satisfied, and unduly expensive" (Spellings report). Educators are under growing pressure to attend to their core task of enhancing student learning, to be more innovative, and find ways to make higher education more accessible.

As Goldie Blumenstyk, a veteran columnist for the *Chronicle of Higher Education* writes, at a time that can be characterized as "higher education's era of the re-set, 'disruption' may well be the key buzzword" (*American Higher Education in Crisis*, Oxford, 2014).

The term "disruptive innovation," which was coined by Harvard Business School professor Clayton Christensen, refers to a process in which innovations introduced at the margins of an established industry work their way into the mainstream and eventually displace well-established competitors. This process of displacement, as Christensen points out, is apparent in many industries. At a time when the flaws of mainstream educational institutions are increasingly apparent and when many traditional institutions have been scrambling to innovate, creative disruption is clearly apparent in higher education. Innovations that were introduced in programs formerly regarded as outliers are now taken seriously by and have been incorporated into the learning model of hundreds of mainstream institutions. In particular, increasing attention is paid to innovative programs whose learning models feature no-frills, low-residency programs that offer convenient, high-quality education at lower cost.

Educational Pioneers

The experience of the Fielding Institute, which started in 1974 as a one-of-a-kind program, is particularly instructive in this regard. Fielding was a pioneer in important respects, and not just in the sense that it was one of the first graduate programs to recognize the potential of the internet and employ it as an integral part of its learning model. The founders anticipated and appreciated the importance of a handful of significant developments:

• They anticipated that higher education, which has traditionally been geared to young adults in their 20s, needs to be re-designed – part of it, at least -- to respond to the influx of adult, mid-career learners, who have different needs and bring a different set of experiences to their graduate education.

• Recognizing that many mid-career adults who pursue a PhD are not able to interrupt their lives to attend residential campus-based programs, they anticipated the need for distributed learning, a model now called "low-residency" programs.

• At a time when the cost of higher education was starting to increase rapidly, they recognized how important it is to pare down the amenities and accoutrements offered in campus-based programs to keep costs down and make doctoral education accessible to a broad group of students. What happened over the next few decades showed how prescient they were. Over the next 30 years the cost of tuition at public and private colleges more than doubled in inflation-adjusted dollars, which led to the current crisis of affordability and staggeringly high levels of student loan debt.

• Fielding's founders saw that a higher education system based on course credit or "seat time" is a misleading and inaccurate way to assess what students know and what they have learned. From the beginning, Fielding's model was assessment-based, which anticipated by several decades the national movement toward outcome-based learning.

• They anticipated that doctoral programs, which have traditionally been devoted to the task of preparing graduates for academic careers, do not respond to the needs of a growing number of students who seek a graduate education which they intend to apply in other ways, as practitioners in a wide variety of fields. As illustrated by the HOD (Human and Organization Development) program, one of Fielding's hallmarks has been its scholar-practitioner orientation.

• They recognized that most graduate programs, which are intended to prepare students for academic careers in specific academic disciplines and focus their curricula on discipline-specific knowledge, are not well suited to the needs of many people entering graduate programs. For this reason, Fielding's H.O.D. program was among the early inter-disciplinary Ph.D. programs.

• They recognized that learning – especially at the doctoral level –is not likely to be effective if it is faculty-centered, featuring professors as sage-on-the-stage experts. Learning is more effective when it is based on agreements that are mutually developed by faculty and students.

The shift from faculty-centered learning to student-centered learning signals a fundamental departure from the way higher education has been organized over the past century.

• Finally, the founders recognized that one of the chief weaknesses of mainstream doctoral programs is that they focus almost entirely on scholarly knowledge and concepts. What has been neglected is *competency* development, or what a well-educated person should be able to do. These include fundamental scholarly competencies such as research skills, and the ability to make critical assessments of knowledge claims, which transcend specific disciplines. As Fielding's co-founder and first president Frederic Hudson noted on various occasions, the evaluation matrix for doctoral learning should include the ability to demonstrate high levels of professional competence in applied settings, as well as what he called "developmental knowledge of oneself and others," by which he meant the ability to demonstrate "emotional skills, decisional skills, and communication skills," among others. (Hudson, "Assessment of knowledge skills in an external degree graduate school," address to CAEL, November 29, 1984). Fielding's founders envisioned a doctoral experience that enhances various aspects of a student's development, not just their scholarly knowledge, an orientation referred to as "whole-person education."

The term "visionary" is often used, sometimes quite loosely. In the case of Fielding's founders, it is accurate and well-deserved. They identified major trends and imagined the future of higher education several decades before these trends were widely recognized, and they asked fundamental questions: What is higher education's purpose? How do people learn best? What kind of learning environment is best suited to adults as they re-tool for the third and fourth quarters of their lives? Does it make sense to organize higher education according to academic disciplines? Far from being captive to traditional ideas about how doctoral students should be educated, Fielding's founders put forward a bold new approach to graduate studies.

A new kind of graduate program

Starting a new university, especially when its founders have few resources to launch the start-up, is a high-risk venture. What was readily apparent to anyone who talked with Fielding's founders in the mid-1970s was that their new university was a radically departure likely to encounter resistance of many kinds. They proposed to change not just *how* doctoral studies are done and *for whom* such programs are intended. They also redefined the *purpose* of doctoral studies.

Ever since the German model of higher education was introduced in North America at Johns Hopkins University in 1876, it has provided the template for graduate education. It has not changed much in the century since then. As the scholarly disciplines staked out their turf in the latter decades of the 19th century and the first few decades of the 20th century, doctoral programs were mainly oriented to socializing students into specific disciplines and professions, and training them as researchers. Graduate education has long been conducted by faculty members who spend their careers in the scholarly world and prepare students to do the same. In effect, graduate programs that encourage students to take on the research projects of their faculty advisors serve as conveyor belts for sustaining certain scholarly topics and conversations.

As a result, the scholarly enterprise became an "ivory tower" that is removed from the original promise and purpose of the social sciences, which was to be applied disciplines that serve a practical purpose. In graduate programs that have followed this tradition – especially the "research I" institutions that are regarded as the gold standard, the institutions that others emulate – faculty are evaluated mainly by their success in producing research and publishing it in journals that are mainly read by and relevant to the work of a small group of similarly trained scholars.

Fielding's founders—Frederic Hudson, Renata Tesch and Hallock Hoffman—set out to re-invent doctoral studies for a new generation of graduate students, many of whom enter graduate programs not as a pathway to scholarly careers but as a way to become more effective and insightful practitioners. To use a phrase that has become a key element in Fielding's approach and its brand, they aspire to become scholar-practitioners. As the founders recognized, it is no easy matter to achieve that goal. Indeed, it requires a substantially different approach to doctoral studies.

In the 1930s, the Spanish philosopher Jose Ortega y Gasset delivered a series of lectures in which he raised fundamental questions about the university model and academic culture. Arguing against the transferability of the English and German models of the university, he asserted that higher education should be designed "in view of the service it is expected to perform." "Imitation" he said, "is fatal." Arguing against what he regarded as the disproportionate emphasis on scientific research and training students for specialized professions, Ortega called for a "complete reformulation of the purpose" of academic institutions.

In each of these assertions, Ortega's critique anticipated themes that were taken up by reformers who came along several decades later, many of them under the banner of progressive higher education. Fielding was part of the most recent wave of the progressive education movement, which crested in the late 1960s and early 1970s. Most of the institutions that featured progressive ideas were undergraduate programs. Fielding's notable distinction was that it was one of the first fully accredited graduate programs to embody progressive ideas in an external degree program.

This chapter was excerpted from Keith Meville (2016), *A Passion for Adult Learning.*
Santa Barbara: Fielding University Press.

Pursuing My Noble Goal

Zieva Dauber Konvisser
Institute for Social Innovation Fellow

"Walker, there is no path, It becomes path in the walk."
~ Antonio Machado, *Border of a Dream: Selected Poems* [1]

For as long as I can remember, I have been on a journey of self-exploration, personal transformation, reflection, and growth. What began as a random walk, became a career path, then became my life path and purpose. It has forked, turned, and twisted. But with each new opportunity I have built on and strengthened my skills and my persona. At 80, who I am, and what I may yet become, as an individual, in the context of my daily life of work, family, and friends, and as a member of the community and world at large, remains paramount to all I do.

Although a clear vision and goal are needed, I have come to recognize the importance of the journey itself. It is my journey through life that has helped me define and fulfill my noble goal, my passion, as well as my purpose and my legacy. Wherever my journey has led me, whether in the laboratory, the parts distribution center, the streets of Jerusalem, the boardroom, the classroom, or sitting with a trauma survivor, I have always been driven by a commitment to make a positive difference in people's lives and the communities in which they live and work.

Throughout, my life has been guided by three questions. Does it support my noble goal to be a model for creating a context for humanity in all the domains of my life? Does it meet the criteria of passion and meaning to my life? And does it create a balance of physical, emotional, and spiritual health?

I was born in Miami Beach, Florida, in 1943, to Emanuel and Dina Dauber. My brother Eddie and I were raised in a traditional Jewish and Zionist home in Passaic and Clifton, New Jersey. During our formative years, we were surrounded and inspired by our parents' love of education, the importance of the State of Israel, family, and friends, and *tikkun olam,* Hebrew for repairing or healing the world through our good deeds. From them, I inherited my desire to leave a proud legacy for my children and future generations, and, in my own small way, to help heal the world through my good deeds and intentions.

I attended Hebrew day school, something that was still a rarity among young Jewish girls. Later, I was enrolled in an after-school Hebrew high school program along with public high school. The dual curriculum taught me to stretch my mind and make more efficient use of my time.

In 1964, I graduated with an A.B. in chemistry from Douglass College, the women's college of Rutgers State University of New Jersey. I met my husband Marc in college and, within a few weeks of graduation, we were married and went on to do graduate work at Ohio State University, where I received a M.S. in pharmaceutical chemistry in 1966. The combination of a non-traditional women's college and non-traditional science degrees for women in the 1960's prepared me for a lifetime of non-traditional roles.

My first job as an assistant editor at Chemical Abstracts Service was interrupted by my desire to be a mother and a housewife, two traditional jobs I had always expected and wanted to hold. After all, it was the 60's! A six-year sidetrack in my career path followed, during which I raised our two sons, Aaron and Joshua, to school and pre-school ages, and filled my time with organizational and charitable work and numerous arts and crafts courses and projects. But something was still missing. It was increasingly clear that I needed a sense of purpose and an identity of my own. It was time to think about getting back into the job market, even though I still had no definite career path in mind. Of course, the additional income would be welcome too!

Fortuitously, I found a position as a chemistry laboratory and recitation instructor at the University of Michigan-Dearborn. The job was posted for a part-time experienced instructor. I applied anyway, although I had never taught before, not even in graduate school where I was a research assistant, not a teaching assistant. I worked more than part-time, 30 to 40 hours a week, keeping ahead of my students and relearning chemistry. A decade and a half later, chemistry had become much more theoretical and, seemingly, more difficult than it had been as a college freshman. Most importantly, I gained self-confidence. I enjoyed working with the college students and the comfortable campus life, but, after two years, it was time to look for a full-time job.

A friend introduced me to the instructional design work being done by Performance Systems Design, a group within the Chrysler Institute that developed self-paced training programs, the precursor of on-line interactive training. That struck me as being the perfect job, combining all my previously learned and acquired skills as an analyst/chemist, writer/abstracter, and educator/instructor. I gave my resume to my friend and immediately was invited for an interview. I was able to convince myself that I was indeed qualified and could do the job. My new employer agreed. She was a former nun with a Ph.D. in instructional design and technology and understood the value of a non-traditional career path. I was lucky to have someone open the door for me, but now it was up to me to prove myself.

My 25-year automotive career followed from 1976 to 2001. It was non-traditional, evolutionary, and revolutionary and was marked by many firsts. I became the first woman to hold increasingly responsible supervisory, management, and senior executive positions in planning, operations, and marketing within the *Mopar*® Parts Division of Chrysler Corporation. I led by example, by my way of being, and by applying my strong analytical, problem-solving, communication, and interpersonal skills to each situation. I became known as a strategic thinker and for my ability to bring about positive changes in the organization, its people, its culture, and its processes. I was guided throughout by my desire to help people do a better and more effective job and to make a difference in their lives.

As a scientist during my college years, I had thought of becoming a doctor or a researcher. In my early years at Chrysler, I felt that I had attained my goal of healing my small part of the world. As the years progressed, this essence of who I am, a nurturer and healer, became subordinated to the outwardly visible thinker and doer. For so long, my heart and soul were hidden behind my businesswoman mask.

In my last few years at Chrysler, several stimulating and exciting opportunities presented themselves. These created an unplanned, but welcome, turn in my journey and in my life path.

In 1994, I began participating in systems thinking, organizational learning, and dialogue initiatives through Chrysler Corporation to learn and practice skills for personal and organizational growth. I continued to pursue this learning through my association with the Society for Organizational Learning and its member companies. My mentors and teachers were many of the leaders in the field of organizational learning theory and applications, including Peter Senge, Fred Kofman, Daniel Kim, Diane Cory, Dawna Markova, Andy Bryner, and Claire Nuer. Thus began my more formal journey of personal transformation, reflection, self-awareness, and growth. I learned much about myself and how I think and learn, and about others and how they think and learn. With this knowledge and increased sensitivity, I learned and practiced how we can better communicate with each other and work together.

I met Claire Nuer at a Society for Organizational Learning retreat in the Spring of 1995. She was born in the Jewish ghetto in Paris, survived the Holocaust as a hidden child, and later survived terminal cancer. Claire founded At the Heart of Communication International, dedicated to creating healthy communication between individuals, families, and communities and to making a difference for all humankind. I was inspired by her efforts to confront powerlessness, learn from past disasters, and look ahead to create a different future for herself and for others.

I accepted Claire's invitation to the Turning Point '95 International Leadership Intensive to be held at Auschwitz-Birkenau on the 50th anniversary of the liberation of the Auschwitz extermination camps. The invitation touched me on multiple levels. It was an opportunity to join with 367 people representing diverse religions, generations, countries, communities, and social and professional backgrounds to remember those who perished there at the hands of the Nazis. Together, we would learn to create a new context for humanity, not for destruction, within which we hoped that another Shoah would not only be unacceptable, but impossible. Furthermore, it was a way to continue my journey of personal transformation, reflection, and growth, to see what I could learn, and what I might do to transfer my business skills and efforts into support for an initiative that can truly make a difference in the world.

I went to the Turning Point and to Auschwitz, with my husband to support me. We toured the camps with three survivors, two Jews and a communist resistance fighter. The experience offered me a personal and concrete dimension to a tragedy that remains difficult to comprehend. We dialogued to confront and explore how our individual, family, and social histories interacted with the dynamics and realities that set the stage for something so evil as Auschwitz, and how we could apply the lessons of Auschwitz to our lives today. As a second-generation witness, I deeply sensed and identified with the horror and the pain. At the same time, I felt the hopes of those who had not only suffered such horrendous events, but who had thrived in spite of them. It became something that happened not just to them, but also to us. I came away with an important question: *How can we learn from our experiences to prevent genocide?*

The Turning Point '95 reawakened my heart and my soul. It reminded me of who I am and how much I could impact others through my actions and deeds. The experiences we shared at Auschwitz made a difference in both my personal and professional life. It greatly impacted the way I look at our world and react to events in a personal way. At work, I was reminded that change resided within me. That with a clear and shared vision, I believed I could make a positive difference for myself and the people who worked with me.

What was next on my journey? A few years earlier, my boss took early retirement at age 54. At his retirement party, I was struck by the thought that he had prepared himself throughout his career for this moment. While working hard in a succession of jobs and doing his best for Chrysler Corporation, he had maintained his love for and involvement in outdoor activities, ranching in Montana, hunting, and gun collecting.

I asked myself, what would I do when I retired? The healer and nurturer in me might join Claire's renamed organization, Learning as Leadership, in their personal and organizational transformation work to coach others to define their noble goals. Or I might use my strategic planning and visioning skills as a business consultant to help other businesses and companies get better. I had always gained a lot of self-satisfaction from this type of work, but now I wondered if I could take this further into my personal life, my community, the world, or the planet.

Synchronously, in June 1999, Don Mroz, a Fielding graduate and local consultant, invited me to participate in a focus group to assess Fielding's proposal to create a consulting and research arm within the automotive industry. Fielding was introduced as a distributed learning university for adult students established in their careers, granting Ph.D.'s in human and organizational development, and educating leaders, scholars, and practitioners for a more just and sustainable world. Fielding's vision, research, and learning model were based on core beliefs and values that immediately resonated with my own values: academic excellence, community, diversity, learner-centered education, social justice, and transformational learning.

Suddenly, the light came on for me. I could not douse it. It was burning even brighter. I left the meeting knowing that this was my future. My conviction was strengthened when I was warmly welcomed by Libby Douvan and Jody Veroff, Fielding faculty members and co-leaders of Fielding's Midwest Cluster in Ann Arbor, Michigan. Although Libby passed away in 2002, I would feel her presence throughout my Fielding journey and beyond. I could hear Libby's caring voice during my Fielding interview: *Now Dear, will you be able to study while you are doing all of that travel for business and pleasure?* She awakened my conscience, always reminding me to read wherever I might be. Jody was there too, telling me when to stop reading and start reflecting and how to use APA format to perfect my skills.

Despite Anaruth's advice, with very little other thought or investigation, I submitted my application and statement of purpose to Fielding in March 2000. I was accepted into the cohort that began in September 2000. Once I recognized it, the next stop felt so natural. Fielding would allow me to feed my obvious passion for learning, intellectual stimulation, making things better, and helping people. I could study theory and research, while applying what I learned to my work and daily life.

I was fortunate to be at a point in my life where I could take the time to explore new ideas and enjoy the journey. I was not limited by career advancement along my current track or by needing to set a firm direction for the future. The Ph.D. for me was an opportunity for personal growth and transformation that I believed would make a difference beyond my own life. It would help me think out of the box, become creative, experiment, be passionate, and take off the business mask. It would force me to look deeper into what makes us human. All too often, we ignore our humanity in the workplace. Ultimately, I hoped this might help me refine and fulfill my noble goal, my purpose in life, and my legacy.

And so, I became a student again at age 57 and embarked upon yet another non-traditional educational experience.

My doctoral journey began with the Orientation and Planning Session, anchored by Lenneal Henderson. The exercises and discussions were designed to bring some clarity to my goals and study preferences. I left the session with the basis for my Learning Plan. My research interests and questions were only vaguely formulated, but I knew that I would like to deepen my understanding of the Learning as Leadership personal mastery methodology and continue to apply it personally and professionally.

Within six months, I accepted an early retirement offer from my leadership role. That allowed me to fully follow my passions of learning and doing meaningful work. Both my prior work experiences and my future transition experiences into uncharted areas of opportunity could provide rich learning fields to test and practice these explorations.

Fielding provided me the freedom, framework, and faculty to explore my options. As a new learner in the field of social sciences, I had to shift my brain to social science thinking from the more fact-based natural science and business ways of thinking. The second step was coming to an understanding that there were many commonalities between research and scientific communities. Whether they are natural or social, the distinctions or biases seemed to be in the eyes of the beholders. The third step concerned my socialization as a social scientist to master the procedures of a community and some of its roles, which then allowed me to function like a member of that community. This process was evolutionary. It gave me permission to grow, expand my knowledge and experience, and appreciate my values and humanism.

I worked through the initial required Knowledge Areas or KA's, the basic building blocks of the Fielding program. Their increasing focus on overview, depth, and applied levels helped me solidify that I should be using these and further readings to find my own epistemologies. At the same time, I continued to reflect on how I think and learn and behave and how I might become a whole being with a balance of emotional, physical, and spiritual health.

By comparing what I learned from these KA's to my interests, perceived knowledge, and experiences, I soon recognized that my research interests were less around organizational learning and more around human development, and its broader focus on individual and transformational growth in personal, organizational, and cultural settings. This was, in part, due to corporate burn-out, as well as acknowledging that I could not change the organization. Instead, I could apply my human development studies and personal mastery work to help myself grow and transform and model healthy behaviors for others in the organization to follow.

Fielding's faculty represented a wide breadth of scholarship and practice. This allowed me to select faculty assessors by matching his/her overall synchronicity with my selected KA's, research and applications interests, learning style, goals, and passion. I followed a similar process to select my faculty mentor, Steven Schapiro, and, later, to select my dissertation committee chair, Miguel Guilarte, and committee members, Steven Schapiro and Thierry Pauchant.

During the next six years, the Fielding community of faculty, administration, staff, students, and alumni recognized, valued, and encouraged my research and traveled with me on this ongoing journey. I am most grateful to my amazing committee members for their caring and encouragement. Each of them enriched my learning through their mentoring, guidance, and concrete help. Through his own life experiences and research, my external reader, Mark Chesler, introduced me to the literature of posttraumatic growth and opened the door for me to discover the research perspective that resonated with who I am. Likewise, Annabelle Nelson and Barnett Pearce helped bring out my creative side and strengthened my affinity towards narrative knowing, while numerous other faculty members shared their wealth of knowledge and insights. My student readers were there for me at the different stages of my journey. We learned from each other and filled the gaps in our knowledge. I am thankful to other students, who by being their student reader, and later their alumni reader, enhanced my own learning process, as did the like-minded student members of Fielding's local cluster group during our monthly meetings and casual luncheon conversations. And I am indebted to the Fielding Graduate University for supporting, in part, my research with four student research grants.

Initially, through my proposed research into human development, I hoped to understand and know the people who have dedicated their lives to create meaning from their experiences and make a difference in the world. I wanted to learn from the voices and faces and passions of Holocaust survivors, like those with whom I had walked and dialogued at Auschwitz, as well as the stories of family members who I knew personally.

Like so many of my generation, I grew up remembering more than thirty of my relatives who were murdered in Vilna, in what is now Lithuania, and hearing the extraordinary stories of those who survived the Holocaust, in particular two of my mother's cousins who lived to tell their stories. Izaak Wirszup survived the hell of the Vilna Ghetto and Nazi concentration camps. He came out believing that he was spared in order to make a difference. Out of his struggle came a survivor's love of life. Sima Shmerkovitz Skurkovitz, a 17-year-old girl, managed to survive by never losing her humanity. Her singing gave hope to her companions in the terrible darkness of the Nazi Holocaust.

The more I studied the Holocaust, the more closely I examined my own reactions to what I learned. I noted that many survivors, resisters, and rescuers shared their extraordinary stories in the hope of creating meaning from their experiences and making a positive difference in the world.

"We must never forget that we may also find meaning in life
even when confronted with a hopeless situation, when facing a fate

that cannot be changed. For what then matters is to bear witness
to the uniquely human potential at its best, which is to transform
a personal tragedy into a triumph, to turn one's predicament
into a human achievement. When we are no longer able to
change a situation… we are challenged to change ourselves."
~ Viktor Frankl, *Man's Search for Meaning* [2]

The lessons of Viktor Frankl, the noted neurologist, psychiatrist, and
Holocaust survivor especially resonated with me. I was deeply affected by
his story of how personal strength, wellness, and other positive outcomes
can result from the struggle with a trauma or life crisis. Logotherapy, his
humanistic and existential approach to psychotherapy, stresses the freedom
to transcend suffering and the defiant power of the human spirit to make
choices and embrace life. While you cannot control what happens to you in
life, you can always control what you will feel and do about what happens
to you. In other words, while we may not all find the *why* of our survival,
there is strength to be found in the search itself, in the actions taken,
by loving another human being, and by the attitude one takes toward
unavoidable suffering. [3]

Similar lessons came from the more recent work of Richard Tedeschi and
Lawrence Calhoun, [4] who coined the term posttraumatic growth (PTG).
PTG describes the positive psychological change that can be experienced
as a result of the struggle with a highly challenging life circumstance, a
traumatic event of seismic proportions, such as a holocaust, that severely
shakes or destroys some of the key elements of the individual's important
goals and worldview. In their research, they found that reports of growth
experiences in the aftermath of traumatic events outnumber reports of
psychiatric disorders and that continuing personal distress and growth
often coexist.

The international logotherapy and posttraumatic growth communities
welcomed me, answered my conceptual questions, and encouraged me to
pursue our mutual interests.

A trip to Israel in October 2002, at the height of the Second Intifada,
helped me connect what I had learned about Holocaust survivors to Israel,

Palestine, and the Middle East conflict. My husband and I chose to visit Israel for two weeks, a trip we didn't take lightly in those days of frequent terrorist bombings. We went to show our support for peace and to observe and experience what it was like to live with the threat of terrorism.

As I talked to family, friends, and new acquaintances, and listened to government officials, tour guides, doctors, therapists, and terrorism survivors, I observed the strength of the human spirit to cope with tragedy and uncertainty. Once again, I reflected upon my earlier question: *How can we learn from our experiences to prevent genocide?* In addition, a new question began to take shape: *How can we move beyond the trauma of such an event?*

These two life-changing or transformational experiences, visiting Auschwitz in 1995 and Israel in 2002, as well as the histories of my own family and their impact on my collective unconscious, compelled me to want to examine these related areas more deeply for my dissertation concept.

To answer my questions, I knew I had to listen more. I needed to understand and know the voices, faces, and passions of ordinary people who suddenly found themselves victims of terrorism. I turned my focus to understanding through their narratives how they are or, in some cases are not, able to live next to or alongside their feelings of grief, pain, and helplessness and move forward in their lives.

I also hoped that to explore their stories lived, told, heard, and retold might help them gain a better understanding of what had happened to them and to understand the meanings they take away from their experiences. At the same time, their narratives might help all of us to personalize and contextualize historical events, humanize the people who have survived or perished, and establish real faces in the overwhelming sea of facts and statistics.

Again, I was welcomed by the experts in the field, the trauma community in Israel. These clinicians, researchers, and helping organizations recognized the importance of my work and supported me in numerous ways. They graciously helped me design and conduct the pilot interviews, introduced me to many of the study participants, and shared their insights into working with and assessing terror survivors. This was the beginning of the discovery of my passion, to provide survivors of trauma a safe space in which to tell their stories, to find their voices, and of my becoming an oral historian.

In 2004, I spoke with 24 survivors of terror acts and 17 family members, bereaved family members, and injured soldiers in Israel. I was deeply moved by their stories. These stories became the research study sample for my doctoral dissertation, *Finding Meaning and Growth in the Aftermath of Suffering: Israeli Civilian Survivors of Suicide Bombings and Other Attacks.*[5] From their stories, I discovered the individual differences in how these trauma survivors understand what has happened to them, find meaning in their experiences, and make choices that involve significant life changes, as well as common themes of resilience and pathways of growth that led them to become their fullest and deepest selves as a result of adversity. [6]

Following graduation from Fielding in 2006, I continued to pursue this work as a post-doctoral researcher and later as a Fellow of the Institute for Social Innovation at Fielding. In 2007, I revisited these individuals to engage with them in an ongoing and widening conversation, to probe for changes in levels of functioning, both positive and negative, and factors facilitating sustained or continued positive growth. In addition, I interviewed seven other survivors and bereaved family members, as well as 15 Christian, Muslim, and Druze Arab-Israelis, who also directly experienced the effects of terrorism.

Between 2004 and 2010, I traveled to Israel eight times for extended stays to collect the stories of 63 survivors and family members. In 2013, I invited the same individuals to reflect upon and describe any important and meaningful changes that they might have experienced in their family, work, health, and/or outlook in life since the earlier interviews. Their voices are published in my 2014 book, *Living Beyond Terrorism: Israeli Stories of Hope and Healing.*[7]

In my book, they speak of their remarkable life journeys from terror to hope and from grief to meaning, not just moving on with life as usual, but moving forward in their lives, contributing to society, and turning tragedy into action or activism.

Their stories strengthened my belief in the incredible power of the human spirit and brought me back full circle to my original interest in understanding and knowing the voices, faces, and passions of Holocaust survivors. Just as some stories of Holocaust survivors told of moving forward to extraordinary action, so have some of these otherwise ordinary people who personally experienced acts of terrorism shown that they too can prevail by the positive attitude and perspective they adopt in the face of tragedy. Like Sima, who found light in the Nazi darkness, they too demonstrate the power to light up the darkness of terrorism, refusing to allow the terrorists to stop their way of life.

In late 2006, my life path took a turn along another parallel path. Wayne State University Criminal Justice Professor Marvin Zalman heard me speak about the human impact of trauma on the lives of survivors of terrorism in Israel. He quickly made the connection to survivors of wrongful conviction, another understudied population. He told me that historically, most wrongful conviction studies had focused, not on the innocent persons themselves, but on the causes of miscarriages of justice that expose systemic flaws in the criminal justice system. Furthermore, those studies that do address psychological issues have focused on the psychology behind these causes. He invited me into his world and challenged me to explore the human impact of wrongful conviction on the wrongfully convicted person's life and the lives of their loved ones.

As a trauma researcher, I was intrigued by the question. I took on the important task of gathering what was known in the literature about the human impact of wrongful conviction in general, again from my perspective of the possibility of positive change alongside the lasting effects of their traumatization.[8] I then turned to the voices of wrongfully convicted and exonerated individuals to learn from them about their experiences, and to share their lessons to build public awareness.

Soon thereafter, I met a young mother who had been tried, convicted, and sentenced to 65 years in prison for the murder of her 10-year-old son. She had just been exonerated after nine long years and the confession of a serial killer. Thus, began my more specific focus on the psychological consequences of wrongful conviction in freed and exonerated women. [9]

Since helping her launch the first Women and Innocence Conference in 2010, I have been privileged to organize roundtable discussions at the annual Innocence Network Conferences as a space for freed and exonerated women to speak out and be heard and to give voice to their emotion-laden experiences. The women share their stories so that we might learn from them about their unique qualities as women and the creative and resourceful strategies that have helped them cope with their situations. They powerfully describe the physical, emotional, social, and material challenges that they continue to face and their ongoing needs to rebuild their shattered lives and productively reengage with life. Most importantly, these brave women continued to have hope throughout the long years of wrongful incarceration and their fight to prove their innocence.

I have listened to the stories of over 150 survivors of traumatic events, their families, and families of the bereaved and continue to document and share their stories of surviving terrorism, the Holocaust, and wrongful conviction. While death and distress are all too present in these stories, they also emphasize that hope and meaning can be found after struggling with and surviving any life crisis. Like a beautiful butterfly breaking free from its cocoon, and like a fragile cyclamen flower pushing up through the crack in the hard stone wall, these individuals too symbolize rebirth and new growth.

Throughout my journey, I have discovered my noble goal and my passion to give voice to the lived experiences and emotions of those who have been silenced by the trauma of such highly challenging circumstances, as both a *storylistener* and a *storyteller*. By creating safe spaces for them to speak out, listening with my heart, and looking into their eyes, the interview and storytelling process often has a positive and meaningful impact.

As the survivors share their narratives, I have learned how they are able to make sense of the traumatic event and their lives, develop a greater personal awareness and understanding of their past experiences and actions, and discover for themselves their hopes and dreams for the future. Through such encounters, we are strengthened and enlightened by each other. My life has been enriched by our ongoing relationships.

At the same time, their narratives are a gift to them and their families, as well as a legacy for others to remember and learn from their experiences to meet their own challenges, make meaning of their own experiences, and make choices that will help them live more purposeful and fulfilling lives.

Since 2011, I have volunteered as the Oral Historian at the Zekelman Holocaust Center in Farmington Hills, Michigan.[10] I honor my roots and continue to collect and share the testimonies of Holocaust survivors, in remembrance of the past and as a responsibility to the future. Their stories create a memorable record of a dark historical period.

Earlier I described my noble goal and pivotal challenges around creating a context for humanity in all the domains of my life. Retirement from my leadership role as an automotive executive and studying for my Ph.D. at Fielding allowed me to pursue not only my love for learning, but also my passion for doing meaningful, contributory work and for making a difference in my community and in the world. Over the years, I volunteered with several community, philanthropic, social justice, and innocence organizations to co-create and support their vision, purpose, goals, and action plans. I served on the National Commission on American Jewish Women sponsored by the Hadassah-Brandeis Institute and currently am on the international board of Metiv: The Israel Psychotrauma Center, the advisory board of Strength to Strength, and the board of Proving Innocence.

As a Fellow of the Institute for Social Innovation at Fielding Graduate University, I continue to research, write, speak, and advocate for survivors of trauma. My goals are congruent with Fielding's aims to build human capital and sustainable change, and Fielding provides the lifelong learning community in which to do so. As I write this, I am struck by how often I refer to communities and the important role they have played in my journey of transformation and growth. It is this deeply sensed shared feeling of *communitas*, of belonging and community, which continues to bring me back for my "Fielding fix" and the opportunity to join my academic friends for intellectual stimulation and community building. For their ongoing personal and institutional support, I am grateful to Fielding President Katrina Rogers, Director of Fielding Institute for Social Innovation Charles McClintock, and Director of Alumni Relations Hilary Lyn.

Most importantly, my community of family and friends has supported and accompanied me on my journey. Throughout, I have remained committed to my integral loving, caring, and nurturing relationships with my husband Marc, my sons, daughters-in-law, and grandchildren Aaron, Diana, Natasha and David and Josh, Julie, Maddie and Ellie, and my extended family and friends.

As I celebrate my 80th birthday, I am living my passions and purpose and savoring the joys of family and friends. I cannot predict where this life path journey with all its forks, turns, and twists might take me. I have learned to trust that my actions will continue to make a difference in my life and in the lives of others. Like my parents and their parents before them, I hope I will leave a proud legacy for my children and future generations and, in my own small way, help heal the world through good deeds and intentions.

> *Becoming is never giving up on the idea that there's more growing to be done.*
> ~ Michelle Obama, *Becoming*

End Notes

[1] Machado, A., & Barnstone, W. (Translator, Introduction) (2003, November 1). *Border of a Dream: Selected Poems.* Port Townsend, WA: Copper Canyon Press.

[2] Frankl, V. E. (2006). *Man's Search for Meaning,* trans. Ilse Lasch. Boston: Beacon Press, p. 112.

[3] Frankl, V. E. (1984). *Man's search for meaning: An introduction to logotherapy* (3rd ed.). New York: Simon & Schuster. See also Frankl, V. E. (1978). *The unheard cry for meaning: Psychotherapy and humanism.* New York: Simon & Schuster; Frankl, V. E. (2000). *Man's search for ultimate meaning.* Cambridge, MA: Perseus.

[4] See, e.g., Tedeschi, R. G., Park, C. L., & Calhoun, L. G. (Eds.) (1998). *Posttraumatic growth: Positive changes in the aftermath of crisis.* Mahwah, NJ: Lawrence Erlbaum Associates; Tedeschi, R. G., & Calhoun, L. G. (2004). Posttraumatic growth: A new perspective on psychotraumatology. *Psychiatric Times,* XXI(4), 58; and Tedeschi, R. G., & Calhoun, L. G. (2004).

Posttraumatic growth: Conceptual foundations and empirical evidence. *Psychological Inquiry*, 15(1), 1-18.

[5] Konvisser Z. L. D. (2006). Finding meaning and growth in the aftermath of suffering: Israeli civilian survivors of suicide bombings and other attacks. Ph.D. *Dissertation Abstracts International-B, 67*(09). (UMI No. 3234197)

[6] See also Mandell, S. (2015). *The Road to Resilience: From Chaos to Celebration.* New Milford, CT: The Toby Press.

[7] Konvisser Z. D. (2014). *Living beyond terrorism: Israeli stories of hope and healing.* Jerusalem: Gefen. See also Konvisser, Z. D. (2013). Themes of resilience and growth in survivors of politically motivated violence. Traumatology, 19(4), 292–302; Konvisser, Z. D., (2016). From terror to meaning and healing – A Franklian view. *The International Forum for Logotherapy, 39*, 22-27.

[8] See Konvisser, Z. D. (2012). Psychological Consequences of Wrongful Conviction in Women and the Possibility of Positive Change. *DePaul Journal for Social Justice*, 5(2), 221-94.

[9] See Konvisser, Z. D. (2015). "What Happened to Me Can Happen to Anybody"— Women Exonerees Speak Out, *Texas A&M Law Review*, 3, 303-366.

[10] The Zekelman Holocaust Center Oral Histories Index with Summaries. https://www.holocaustcenter.org/visit/library-archive/oral-history-department/index-summaries/. See also Konvisser, Z. D. (February 15, 2019). Resilience and Vulnerability in Aging Holocaust Survivors and Their Descendants. *Resilience: Navigating Challenges of Modern Life* (Fielding Monograph Series, Volume 12), pp. 13-51.

Epistemological Growth in This DEIA Moment

Richard Yao

President, California State University Channel Islands

As a proud alumnus of Fielding Graduate University, I can speak directly to the transformative power and lifelong impact of this school. It was such a catalyst for my growth and evolution and continues to impact me on many levels to this day. This is true for me as a Chinese Filipino American still navigating my own personal journey of racial identity development, and as President of California State University Channel Islands (CSUCI). At CSUCI, our students – the large majority of whom are the first in their family to attend college and are members of minoritized and historically marginalized groups – truly serve as the heart and soul of our institutional identity. We are committed to our students' success because we embrace and celebrate each and every one of them as the face of a college graduate. Many do not fit the mold historically cast for that role, but our students from every walk of life have participated in breaking that mold, replacing it with a more flexible model in which diversity, equity, inclusivity, and accessibility are the markers for and creators of excellence.

At the foundation of this work is my Fielding education.

Throughout my educational journey until then, I was thoroughly unaware of the epistemological underpinnings, assumptions, and implications of the positivistic framework that serves as the foundation of modern-day clinical psychology. While my early professional work with individuals with chronic and persistent mental illness facilitated an experiential introduction to constructivist concepts (e.g., the realities and consequences of power differentials in every realm of human endeavor, the limitations of reductionism in understanding the human experience, the value-laden nature of the diagnostic process and subsequent treatments, and the role of language in our conceptualization of reality and "universal" truths), these concepts created significant levels of cognitive dissonance for me on personal and professional levels. In hindsight, of course, such dissonance is unsurprising given the unrelentingly positivistic framing of my education from elementary through graduate school.

My doctoral education at Fielding changed all of this for me. It started in my Research Methods course with the late Dr. Nolan Penn, who introduced me to a vast literature base that upended my positivistic worldview. This was transformational for me, on so many levels. I developed newfound insight and awareness into how my epistemological alliances and assumptions impact every facet of my life. I learned how becoming aware of epistemological assumptions, and then challenging and evaluating the merits of them, is the first step in authentic growth and development at the deepest, most meaningful levels. This learning continued throughout my Fielding experience, especially under the mentorship of the late Dr. Will Kouw, leading to my internalization of the reality that epistemological curiosity, reflection, and growth are continuous processes requiring intentionality, humility, vulnerability, strength, and perseverance.

For many years after Fielding, I lived in this mix of positivistic and constructivist worlds – fully recognizing and embracing the benefits of science and the positivistic assumptions underlying it, but at the same time acknowledging and integrating their limitations. I fully incorporated this complexity into my clinical work, my pedagogy as a faculty member, and my personal life on varying levels. During this time, I believed I had developed some degree of clarity on the usefulness and limitations of both worldviews.

Then I arrived at CSUCI in 2018 as a new Vice President for Student Affairs. I immediately realized how much more work and growth I had to do. The confluence of my daily interactions with colleagues and students learning about their lived experiences, the continued and highly publicized acts of racial violence and other hate crimes, the accompanying cultural and political discourse, and my own personal reactions to it all served as a catalyst for my continued development, evolution, and growth as a Chinese Filipino American and university leader.

On a personal level, I began to realize how the turmoil and distress that characterized my childhood, adolescence, and emerging adulthood, as well as a sense of estrangement so pervasive throughout my life, was attributable to difficulties in navigating my own racial identity development. This brought me back to the literature base that I first encountered at Fielding – especially the epistemological underpinnings of racial identity theory. While I had not yet been ready to fully embrace and lean into this space during my time at Fielding, I found myself at almost 50 years of age in an executive leadership role, finally ready to embrace this process. At long last, I felt and understood the need for it. It is an ongoing challenge and continuing gift from my doctoral studies.

On a professional level, the beauty of the transformational education I experienced at Fielding is that it serves as the foundation for my continued growth and evolution to this day – integrating and evaluating the main tenets of positivistic, constructivist, and now transformational epistemologies to inform my work as President of CSU Channel Islands – to ensure that diversity, equity, inclusion, and access (DEIA) are at the forefront of everything we do.

While this epistemological integration provides me with a framework for how to approach our University's DEIA work, it does not provide all the answers. In fact, it has led to increasingly complex and critical questions for me to explore, both to better inform my work and to continue learning, developing, and growing as a leader. As a clinical psychologist, I am a firm believer in our capacity for overcoming conditioning to facilitate change, growth, and evolution at the individual, organizational, and systemic levels. While progress is being made, however, we are also experiencing resistance and backlash in varying forms across our country.

Is it conceivable to think that we can effectively lean into and better understand such resistance while concurrently ensuring movement and growth? Is it appropriate and useful to apply concepts of Motivational Interviewing and the Stages of Change Model at the organizational level to inform this work? Should our primary focus be on policy or individual-level interventions? What role does our expanded conceptualization of violence and trauma play in this process, and how do we integrate this evolution into our discussions and initiatives?

If we are doing the necessary work to examine such questions with a critical lens and high degree of intentionality, humility, and rigor, our students' success will follow – not only during their time at Channel Islands but post-graduation, as well. I am grateful for my time at Fielding which was integral to my development as an educator and as an educational leader, but more importantly, impactful to CSUCI's work in helping our students to become the leaders that we so desperately need in their chosen fields.

Becoming a Network Weaver

Linda Honold

Member, Fielding Board of Trustees and Past Board Chair

I left the public school system in 9th grade to attend a private school that employed the model of Summerhill, a "free school" in England[1]. Classes were held in small groups. Faculty were mentors and facilitators of who regularly met individually with each student developing learning goals and reviewing on progress. By the time I graduated I had the skills of a self-managed learner.

My freshman in high school year also provided my first work experience. Our family's low-income status qualified me for the Neighborhood Youth Corps, a program funded through the Federal Comprehensive Employment and Training Act (CETA). I worked for minimum wage at the local Wisconsin Job Service office filing the job seeking records of local "welfare" recipients. With a firm but nurturing supervisor, I worked two hours every day after school. I became a responsible employee and manager of my own money.

I was the first in my extended family to go to college. I attended the local University of Wisconsin campus, majored in Political Science, served in student government as the Legislative and Research Affairs Director and was a member of the Young Democrats. Whereas most 'Young Dems' were interested in hitting the campaign trail, I served as the group's representative to the State Administrative Committee where I learned how the volunteer organization worked and how it interacted with the Democratic National Committee. My involvement in the State Democratic Party led to a paid summer internship in the Washington DC office of my local Member of Congress. My Bachelor of Arts degree in Political Science with a minor in American History and extracurricular activities led to induction in the Mortar Board Senior Honor Leadership Society, graduation with honors and a first hand understanding of administrative systems and organizational structure - which ultimately became the focus of my life's work.

In the first years of my career, I moved through a series of short-term jobs. I was a receptionist/constituent relations staffer in the local office of the Member of Congress. When he was defeated in the fall of that same year, I obtained a position as editorial assistant at a magazine publishing company. The job was light on editing and heavy on proof-reading. It didn't take long for me to become bored and to dread going to work. I looked around and saw that most of my coworkers and even their bosses had similar feelings about their jobs. I wanted to understand how the workplace might be altered so that people didn't have to spend 1/4 or more of their lives doing something that had little real meaning for them. I thought there had to be a better way. This curiosity led me to seeking a Master of Science in Industrial Relations at the University of Wisconsin-Madison.

My first three jobs after completing the Master's program did not get me to a position where I could change the workplace but it did expand my understanding of organizational structure. The first was at the Vocational Rehabilitation Center at the University of Wisconsin-Stout. The Center's academic program provided students a hands-on apprenticeship assisting clients, who had been injured or by other means made unable to work, gain skills that would allow them to return to work. A federal grant through the Job Training and Partnership Act (JTPA) was to help clients move into the paid workforce. There was no model on how to do this. I developed one by systematically developing relationships with employers and identifying job openings that match with the skills of the Center's current clients. There was also an opportunity to provide partial financial assistance for companies to create a new position and give priority to a Vocational Rehabilitation Center client who fit their needs. The next year when funding for the program was discontinued, I became an Area Executive Director for the American Cancer Society and worked with volunteer boards of directors in nine counties assisting them as they developed and implemented cancer education, service, and fundraising programming.

It was while working in this position that I met the man who would become my husband for the next 38 years. I moved to eastern Wisconsin where he had his home and business and initially took a limited term position at the Hmong Mutual Assistance Association working with refugees who had provided assistance to our troops in Viet Nam and had to evacuate their country after our military left. Local churches had sponsored them to come to our community. My role was to help them find jobs that fit their skills. I visited with area companies to locate job openings and when there was a skill match between a refugee and a company and assisted in setting up interviews. I also served as "good will ambassador" to the greater community educating employers and community organizations on the history of the Hmong refugees, their service to the United States military, and their arrival in our city.

The second life changing event came about a year later, when I was hired by Johnsonville Sausage Company as "Personal Development Coordinator." The company's CEO believed that "people really want to be great." His goal was to transform his company to make that possible at work. My job was to "get people in a learning mode." Work groups met regularly to review production goals and set schedules to accomplish their work. As they began to ask questions about why the goals were set as they were, I helped design and implement the systems and processes to support that learning by employees and managers alike. The result was individual employees and work groups taking responsibility for their own performance.

As a result of this radical approach to management, Tom Peters, co-author of the best-selling business book "In Search of Excellence", featured Johnsonville in his 1987 *Thriving on Chaos: Handbook for a Management Revolution* as well as in a management video "The Leadership Alliance" where he referred to Johnsonville as the company that had "gone further than anyone anywhere at handing the reigns of control over to the front-line workers." Ralph Stayer, the owner of the Johnsonville, presented his perspective on that change with a *Harvard Business Review*[2] article "How I Learned to Let My Workers Lead". It made Johnsonville internationally famous. When Stayer co-authored *Flight of the Buffalo: Soaring to Excellence, Learning to Let Employees Lead*, demand for more information about how this change was made led to speaking and consulting engagements for him. Mid-level managers, most of whom had questions focused on specifics like "How many teams do you have?" "How many people are on the teams?" were directed to me. I gathered teams leaders to develop a process to address this interest. We knew they would not be successful if all they did was develop teams. We decided they needed to experience the difference and created a weekly day-long, a revenue generating, educational program where attendees could hear about the transition directly from members. Accompanied by a production member, I then provided a presentation and facilitated a discussion of how the systems of work were changed to reinforce goals. When requests for me to conduct follow up sessions at the participants' company interfered with my ability to do the internal member development work at Johnsonville, Stayer suggested I joined him in his consulting enterprise. Over the next few years, I consulted and delivered more than 200 speeches and workshops on four continents.

I decided to pursue an additional degree in higher education because I wanted to understand why what we did at Johnsonville was successful at engaging employees, reducing costs and increasing company profits while so many of the "teams" and TQM approaches faded out.

To inform our work at Johnsonville, I had read every book I could find on organization and human resources development. They helped my thinking in creating programs and systems to support our employee centered approach, but I wanted a deeper understanding. Recalling my high school experience where I took responsibility for my own learning, I wondered if there might be higher education institutions that used a similar approach to education. I developed a list of "must haves" – I sought an accredited program in organization development, that targeted mid-career adults who wanted to manage their own learning, and a design that would allow me to complete the program without a geographical move. Of the three programs I found, the then named, Fielding Institute best fit my needs [3]. I was invited to attend a Research Session. The experience was highly engaging and mentally challenging. Faculty asked me challenging questions about what I wanted to learn and why. Students related how, with the help of their faculty advisor/mentor, they were able to design their coursework in a way that fit their learning needs. Upon arrival home, I filled out the application and mailed it in.

My PhD is in Human and Organizational Systems. When I started the program, I had no idea what the term "systems" meant in the context of organizations. I discovered that being a "systems thinker" was something that I had done for much of my working life but that now I knew that and could consciously include it in my thinking, planning and implementing projects.

I began my study at the Fielding Institute in the fall of 1995 with a goal of developing a scholarly understanding behind the work that I had done for nearly decade, namely being a key leader in the development of what was then called "a learning organization."

"The Empowered Organization: A Consideration of Professional and Theoretical Alternatives" included case studies of organizations whose strategies resulted "in high levels of employee commitment and motivation in which employees have the capacity for and willingness to take responsibility for their own performance as it is in alignment with their own needs and goals." Finding a way to study the topic was a research project in and of itself. A literature review confirmed my suspicion that there had been very little written about companies with management practices that fit what I wanted to know. A website of the U. S. Department of Labor Office of the American Workplace, whose function was to "create better jobs for American workers and better business results for American companies", listed 51 companies who did such work. I was determined to conduct in-depth case study research to surface of what these organizations had created. I narrowed the parameters of companies to study to: privately held, for profit companies in the industrial sector, that had been using employee engagement practices for at least five years, had more than 150 but fewer than 500 employees, were not unionized as that would add a level of complexity and, for convenience, were located in the Midwest. Comparing those factors to the DOL website list resulted in three companies that fit my criteria and agreed to participate. I made multiple day site visits at each facility interviewing and observing meetings with the CEO, managers, and supervisors, as well as front line workers.

My findings revealed that all three companies had self-designed systems that fit their own environment and goals. Each did things differently from traditional organization and differently from one another…but it was the same things they did differently. Among other things, they all used teams, but the teams functioned in ways that worked for them; each had a unique compensation system specifically designed to reinforce the outcomes they sought to achieve; and each had developed their own terms, almost their own language to describe their work. My interpretation was that developing their process themselves provided a sense of ownership.

For the owners and employees of the three companies I studied, the process of going through interviews with me led them to reflect on how their work lives had changed. Later, when they had the opportunity to read the case study of their company and to speak with me about it, they enhanced the initial reflection.

While waiting for my dissertation to be approved and for the opportunity for my final oral review, I embarked upon writing two books: "Developing Employees Who Love to Learn: Tools, Strategies and Programs for Promoting Learning at Work" was based upon my experiences as Coach for Member Development at Johnsonville Sausage and as a consultant/speaker on developing empowered organizations. The book was selected one of the thirty best business books of 2001 by Soundview Executive Book Summaries and, in 2005, was selected one of the top five training books of all time by Training Magazine. My dissertation research also became the basis for a second book, "Organizational DNA: Diagnosing Your Organization for Increased Effectiveness" for which I was the lead author with Robert Silverman. Each publication was shared with the people and the companies who were the basis for my research and were another community.

Has my degree helped me to advance my career or personal interests? Has it helped me to achieve my goals? I fulfilled my goal of understanding why what was done at Johnsonville was successful and lasting (it remains in effect today) in its effort to create an employee-centric organization. I also completed my goal of publishing two books and several scholarly articles. And I realized I had also over the years of consulting accumulated an investment portfolio that allowed me the freedom to think about what

I wanted to do with the next phase of my life. That thinking brought me back to the focus of my undergraduate study and of my personal volunteer time avocation…our American Democracy. I took my knowledge and experience in systems and organizational change to creating a democracy that fulfilled the hopes and dreams of our country's founders – one where average citizens could have an impact.

I have long been a member of the Democratic Party of Wisconsin and had served as chair of my local chapter. Two years after graduation I ran for and won the position of Chair of the Democratic Party of Wisconsin. The role has made me a member of the Democratic National Committee where I served as Midwest Representative on the Executive Committee and was recruited to serve on the "Calendar Commission" that examined the way the Party selects its Presidential Candidates. Our Commission's work resulting in the addition of Nevada and South Carolina, two states with significant non-Caucasian residents, to join New Hampshire and Iowa as the earliest states to select the Party's candidate for President and Vice President.

As my second two-year term was winding down, I was offered a position by a local philanthropist to manage the selection of organizations who would receive grants to enhance our democracy. Once the grants were made, I coached them as they developed their programs and worked to weave interconnectedness with other organizations who did similar work. Three years ago, after the conclusion of a full-time consulting contract to develop that network of organizations, I chose to not seek paid employment. That doesn't mean I have retired from paid employment. If an opportunity to do meaningful systems work came along, I would consider it. At the same time, I have volunteer positions as President of the Woman's Club of Wisconsin and as a Trustee of the Fielding Graduate University that keep me quite busy.

I am continuing to research, however having reached my goal of understanding why what we did at Johnsonville worked and publishing about it, that portion of my work came to a close. Reflecting on the transition ahead of me helped me to realize that I had also been a systems thinker but had become conscious of that. In knowing that, I now actively use a systems perspective in whatever project I am involved in. One ongoing area of interest is our American Democracy. I conducted research and published articles on Redistricting Reform and on Weaving a Network of Workers for Democracy and continue to explore ways to heal the divisions that have come to the fore over the past few years.

How important is a higher education degree for today's practitioners? I graduated from Fielding in January 1999 - at the turn of the last century. So much has changed. I know that for me what I learned has been invaluable and I continue to use systems thinking in everything I do. I don't know, however, that I am in a position to judge how important a higher education degree is for others.

As far as my doctoral studies are concerned, I don't know that there is anything I would do differently. However, while serving as Chair of the Democratic Party of Wisconsin, I saw first-hand very early attempts by ultra-conservative activists to undermine the infrastructure that supports our democracy. I conducted further research and developed a preliminary paper on the topic. I then got distracted and only resurfaced the paper recently. I wish I had kept at that research and writing. It is eerie how many of the things I thought conservative activists were trying to do has actually happened.

How would I advise prospective students who are considering a degree program? Begin by developing a list of your "must haves". What do you want to do and why? Conduct a search to determine where you might learn what you seek. Talk to faculty and students who have similar interests to yours to determine if their experiences match what you are looking for. Then compare it to what you would get elsewhere. While I haven't done a complete search on this recently, I would venture to say that even today, nearly 25 years after I completed my degree, there is nothing like the Fielding Graduate University that provides an education program for mid-career adults who want to frame their own course of study with unparalleled faculty support for your learning.

Fielding is Lifelong Learning. Since my graduation in 1999, I have continued my learning by attending nearly every national session and taken advantage of sitting in on sessions and conversing with faculty and students. The cost is minimal, the reward is great. As a member of the Alumni Council from 2009–2012, I worked to bring our graduates back to National sessions. I then became a member of the Board of Trustees where I have served for a total of ten years, including three as Chair of the Board. I have taken part in unparalleled opportunities for travel in the company of other lifelong learners and under the expert guidance of Faculty Emeritus Jean-Pierre Isbouts. In every one of those opportunities, I have been enriched. I learned new things, was in new places and made new friends. Fielding Graduate University has been and continues to be a true gift.

Footnotes

[1] Neill, A.S., 1993 edition <u>Summerhill School: A New View of Childhood</u>, St. Martin's Press, New York, NY

[2] Stayer, Ralph, November-December 1990.

[3] Nova University, Fort Lauderdale, Florida and Union Institute, Cincinnati, Ohio were the other two.

Inspiring Change and Leadership in the House of Representatives

Salud Carbajal

United States Representative for the 24th Congressional District

The reason I pursued a higher education degree was to continue learning and to continue making myself more viable in terms of qualifications for future opportunities. I became acquainted with Fielding when Santa Barbara County Government and Fielding partnered on the Master's program in Organizational Management. That led me to investigate the program. The price was right and affordable. The methods, the teaching, guiding principles, and mission of Fielding were very appealing to me. The remote learning and hybrid in-person approaches were also appealing and intriguing as a mid-career professional. It just checked all the boxes. It was a good program that catered to mid-career individuals and the subject matter that I chose. It was right up my alley. I have always strived to make government more effective, transparent, and responsive, which is what I've always tried to do in local government, first as a staff person, and then as an elected official. This program tied into those values and goals, and I became an elected official as I was finishing my actual program -- going from Chief of Staff for 12 years into elected office myself as County Supervisor.

The methodologies and pedagogies utilized by Fielding were appealing to me. Of Fielding's mission and six guiding principles, two are the most important to me: social justice and the transformational learning aspects of the Fielding program and philosophy. It's not just about equality. It's also equity. This transformational learning was the other guiding principle which provides a process and a framework by which you constantly assess your standing in the world. We can assess how traditional assumptions are made, how we view the world, how we view ourselves, and to be able to do critical analysis and how they relate to social justice. Transformational is the process by which you analyze the world yourself in the reciprocal context.

And for me, the Master's program came on the heels of wanting to do more in my chosen field. As a younger person, I finished my undergraduate degree at UCSB, which was exceptional but more theoretical quantitative and theoretical. Qualitative as well, but it was more theoretical. However, going through a program that really focuses on experiential learning and blending quantitative and qualitative pedagogy was important and helpful to me. I found that at Fielding.

What did I discover in my intellectual journey that I did not expect? How fun learning and practical application could be. Having great faculty, real-world practitioners who really challenged you. A lot of group exercises and projects allowed me to think critically and reflect about different challenges that are issues in the real world and which occur every day in organizations. The relationships and work assignments made it a fun and impactful learning experience.

Earning a Master's in Organizational Management allowed me to ask: What are the challenges, what makes organizations fail? What makes organizations succeed? What is the most important resource in an organization? People. How are you a better leader and boss? How are you a more effective individual in both your personal and professional life.

This is a lifelong process. You don't just take these courses and say, "Oh, that was great. I learned all the ins and outs about how to be a great leader, how to be a great manager." You learn a foundation that allows you to reflect and grow every day in your ongoing career. I certainly know I'm being a better leader or a better boss. I'm being more effective. But whether it's in the organization that I'm in -- my office -- or just personal development, I take those foundational tools that I learned at Fielding and apply them every day.

How I decided on the subject of my Master's thesis was what I've always have sought and observed: government is about serving the people in many ways. Not only the laws and the policies that improve people's lives, but the very essence of service. When people approach their government for a grievance or for assistance, to be able to have a responsive, effective and responsive government working for its citizenry is really what it's all about for me.

When I was five years old and came to this country with my family, and after living in Arizona for a few years, we later settled in Oxnard. My father was a farm worker, and my mother was a stay-at-home mom. She has rheumatoid arthritis and was always in pain and couldn't work. We were economically challenged. My parents didn't speak English. My siblings and I were the translators. I remember going with my mom to some of her appointments to help. We would take the bus 10 miles away, and some days, we would interface with some extraordinary public servants in the public clinic or hospital, whether it was me or her going to the doctor. When we received great customer service, people made you feel like you have dignity. They embraced you and knew they were there for a mission. Occasionally, you would come across someone who had no business in that position or in government because they let you know that you were a burden and maybe you shouldn't even be accessing the services. So, I, as a child, have those early memories of what is good government customer service and bad government customer service.

That experience always stuck with me. Even today, when I look at laws or programs, I always look at the elements of good customer service. That is paramount in my office. I have come to understand that it is essential and imperative for us to have a high-quality, functioning government. We know customer service comes naturally to some people, and some must be trained. In the private sector, good customer service means a better bottom line, so they often address customer service more quickly than in government. When there's a failure in getting the right type of people to interface with the public and the lack of training, it is a recipe for disaster. We should not shortchange our mission and goal to make government as responsive as any other institution or sector.

At my office's annual team retreats, the number one thing I tell my staff is that policies, laws, and all are important work. But, if we can't serve the very basic needs of folks who contact us via emails, letters, and phone calls, then we are failing. The rest is irrelevant. We can pass a big bill and improve people's lives in general, but if we cannot be responsive to the people who come to our office, then we fail.

Customer service is the number one issue for me both in local government and now here in Congress. My office knows it's fundamental to get consistent and responsive customer service right. My degree has certainly impacted me because I think I've become more effective. It's made me more conscientious. My work is rooted in research and in practice on how to lead certain efforts, approach certain problems, and achieve solutions more effectively.

Sometimes, we do process things, but we don't know why we do them. Research reminds you that there's a process that often has already been researched and codified that explains what makes change efforts effective versus not effective. If a company or government wants to make major reforms organizationally, getting the process right is fundamental. What I learned at Fielding is that there's a lot of research that helps with change management. You understand why change efforts succeed and fail. Your own work, as well as that of others, provides you with both a philosophical and practical framework to help you understand processes that can lead to more methodical in leading some of these change efforts.

Learning is an ongoing journey with continuous process improvements and reflection. At Fielding, the courses emphasized reflection. If you're not aware of your own strengths and weaknesses in your own personal and professional journey, then you won't go far toward achieving your goals. Anyone can get a degree and have it on a resume. At Fielding, however, you can pursue, visualize, and implement many paths, processes, and frameworks to be more effective. My courses made me aware that there is a human process by which we all learn and grow and can achieve continuous improvements. Fielding drove home the elements of self-awareness, reflection, and growth.

Am I continuing with my research? My wife makes fun of me because I rarely read for pleasure, and if I do, they're usually organizational development type books. For me, continued learning is reflecting on my daily life. What I'm doing to be effective, what I'm not doing, where I'm challenged – and how I can be better in all aspects of my daily life.

In Congress, we have the Congressional Research Service, which is an office in the Library of Congress, that provides support to members of Congress. You can conduct research on almost any subject pertaining to any policy subject matter. I take advantage of this as much as possible. I also have an extraordinary staff that I think are a lot smarter than I am. So, they keep me on my toes, and I learn a lot from them.

How important is a higher education degree for today's practitioners? I think it's essential. And again, the practitioner and mid-career approach at Fielding is tailored to those who have been in the workforce. Any higher education, no matter the path, age, or other factors, is helpful. I think higher education is regrettably less obtainable for all because it comes down to a great extent to the haves and have nots. It's still not as accessible to all as we want it to be. We need to provide more financial aid and less loan burden to more students so that they can be incentivized and encouraged to continue their higher education.

I don't think I would have done anything differently in my program. I have very little constructive criticism during my time at Fielding or any regrets with the program. It was great to see colleagues from all walks of life during this program. We were mostly in county government, but we also had folks from the private sector in our program. In my cohort, I think only one person didn't complete the program. One person -- that's unheard of! I think it speaks to the supportive nature of the faculty, the quality of the overall program, and Fielding as an institution.

I am proud to call Fielding University my alma mater. I think Fielding continues to be a great institution. Many students and faculty join remotely, and attend in-person annual sessions. It's a wonderful institution for the country and world. As a U.S. Representative, I am honored and grateful that Fielding is in my Congressional District. Fielding continues to be a resource and a treasure in the field of graduate learning.

73

Rep. Salud Carbajal represents California's 24th congressional district, a stretch of the central coast encompassing Santa Barbara County and portions of San Luis Obispo County and Ventura County.

A Co-created Moral Relationship

Pauline Albert
Researcher, Writer, and Lecturer

"What you are, the world is. And without your transformation,
there can be no transformation of the world."

J. Krishnamurti

Both Fielding Graduate University and St. Edward's University in Austin, Texas, where I spent twelve years teaching, claim to provide a transformative learning experience. Thus, I have spent the last twenty years studying and thinking about how universities and leaders can make such a claim. What is transformation and how does it happen, let alone how can we measure it. While there is an extensive literature on effective pedagogical methods, how can universities make this empirical claim? Is it simply an advertising slogan, or how can transformation effectively be measured? Based on my personal experience as a teacher, leader, and learner, these are my experiences and insights on the phenomena of transformative learning.

What is Transformation?

Human transformation implies a change in consciousness. While consciousness and transformation are both highly debated constructs, this is a definition seemingly applicable to transformational learning. By transformation, I mean an enduring *expansion* of consciousness that expresses itself in increased awareness; a broader, more inclusive identity; and a larger framework for meaning-making. Together, these things result in a changed way of experiencing and being in the world. (Benner, 2017, p. 23)

At Fielding the journey begins with a class on epistemology exposing students to how we know what we know, and different ways of knowing. The standard text written by two brilliant Fielding faculty (Bentz & Shapiro, 1998) provides a foundation for becoming a social science researcher. *Becoming* something implies a change in consciousness should take place, but research methods are tools like hammers and screwdrivers, and beginning to know what tools to select is a first step, but it does not yet mean that transformation is taking place. Transformation implies a change in ontology, an actual change in one's *being* or consciousness. That will take more work.

For most of my life my motivation in any school situation had been fear. Fear of failure, fear of disappointing the teacher, parents, or sponsors. I love learning, but school was always about assessment, ambition, and downright fear of failure. I will say more about Temple Grandin later in this essay, but my recent encounter with her helped me to connect a few more dots about my experience with learning in an academic setting. The visceral experience I had with Temple was about my older brother, but it also informs my own experience.

I spent a year in a body cast beginning at 9 months of age. The child development psychologist Piaget (Piaget & Inhelder, 1969) would likely conclude that this delayed my development. I did not speak until about the age of two, though my mother would later report that I started speaking in complete sentences and haven't stopped talking since. While in kindergarten I struggled to learn my colors. I could sing the song easily but struggled with matching the colors with their symbolic representations. Standing in our family living room, struggling with this task, my father wondered whether I might "be retarded." He then claimed for all my years in student life that "I wasn't too bright, so better work hard." In my forties I realized that this was a projection of his own mother's evaluation of him, but as a teen this mantra became my modus operandi. I had to work hard, or I would fail. All this to say that I desperately wanted my Fielding experience with formal education to be different.

Like all Fielding students, I attached a statement of purpose with my application. It included a Venn diagram on areas I wanted to explore. At my first research session in Houston, Texas I asked for a meeting with Barnett Pearce. He agreed to meet with me, was then excited to hear that I had a car, and asked to travel away from the hotel, so we found a coffee shop. I have such a vivid memory of that first encounter. True of that first meeting, and every other engagement I had with Barnett is that he seemed fully present. I showed him my diagram and asked for counsel on how to use it for developing my learning plan. Over time, Barnett became my role model for great teaching. He fully embraced the Socratic Method and used questions to prod my learning. I don't think that Barnett ever answered an academic question that I posed to him. He would say, "you're on the right track, now go look at this other literature."

Social constructionism (Burr, 2003; Pearce, 2006) was one of the main literatures undergirding his own communications theory called The Coordinated Management of Meaning (CMM) (Pearce, 2007), so I dug deeply into these constructs. Theories are sense-making devices; tools for better understanding the world, tools for meaning-making. CMM and its underlying literature, integrated with Barnett's loving patience, changed my life because they opened doors to a completely different way to look at human development and my own way of *being* in the world. I became less afraid of failure, and increasingly thirsty to dig further into all the things that I could correlate to CMM's worldview.

A Co-Created Moral Relationship

While at St. Edward's this notion of the student as customer became popular. I disliked this construct and found it distasteful because for me education was not a transaction, it was about relationship and transformation. Parents and students at both undergraduate and graduate levels sometimes treated faculty like people delivering a product for which they had paid, and therefore should receive a grade and experience acceptable to them. Increasingly, the faculty and administration seemed to receive less and less respect for our knowledge or process for delivering said product, i.e., curriculum and pedagogy. The product became about facilitating the acquisition of a job upon graduation, not about what was learned or the transformative process that we made available. One MBA graduate even sued the university when she did not receive a six-figure job she felt she had earned and paid for upon completing her degree.

I spent five years studying leadership while at Fielding and I pursued the topic because I had been a leader, been managed by capable leaders, and I wanted to understand how leadership should work. I was dissatisfied with the how-to nature of the leadership literature because leadership for me was not about a set of *traits* or *to-do lists*, but rather about something that happened between people. I read many books on leadership theories and I even found a book that discussed the many definitions of leadership (Bass, 1990; Rost, 1991). Most definitions were about influence *over* others and the sociology literature focused on leadership as the acquisition of power (Weber, 1921/1946).

Burns (1978) introduces the topic of transformational versus transactional leadership, but in the hands of Bass (1997) transformation becomes about the follower becoming transformed to meet the goals of the leader. For me that smelled of manipulation and a sort of conspiracy theory, not leadership. After studying what felt like all the literature, and then diving deep into the lives of Francis and Clare of Assisi I derived my own definition of leadership. Like CMM it is not something that rolls off the tongue, but I feel strongly that *leadership is a cocreated moral relationship*.

Thinking further about transformational learning, my definition of leadership may apply. Transformation involves deep learning and a change in one's worldview. As noted earlier, it involves a change in consciousness about what is and what could be. Transformation is not something one can buy; it is phenomenological and occurs in conjunction with a teacher who engages in partnership. The teacher also needs to be open to learning from the student. I have seen university faculty intimidated by the work experience of students; another concept I did not understand because the student is always vulnerable to the teacher, just as one is vulnerable to a parent. CMM and social constructionism teach us that all relationships are cocreated through exchange and our attentive presence with one another.

My dissertation study also led me to a belief that everyone is a leader, as leadership begins with how we lead our lives. Thus, both the student/ teacher and employer/employee roles are moral in nature because there is a power dynamic involved. A commitment to collaboration and in turn co-creation can soften that dynamic. Fielding's processes support student-centered learning, and this requires flexibility, responsibility, and openness from both the student and the teacher.

Valerie Bentz is a Fielding faculty member with whom I did extensive work on human development. I remember a walk in a small park in Alexandria, VA when I was frantically trying to complete the final requirement for a Fielding Knowledge Area (KA). I'm yacking away about all the reading I've done and what I've learned, and Valerie says, "what would serve you" for completing the KA? I had never had a teacher ask me such a question. I told her I wanted to draft a short article for an academic journal in which I hoped to be published. She said "terrific." I wrote the article, completed the KA, and submitted it to the journal that in turn rejected the submission. Disappointment is a key ingredient for transformation, as is *beginner's mind*.

She Persisted and Beginner's Mind

I was familiar with Temple Grandin's story outlined in an HBO movie that depicts her struggles with learning and eventual diagnosis of autism based on her autobiography (1995/2006). The movie depicts her as persistent in pursuing knowledge and skills despite her unique approaches. Temple is now 75 years old, with a PhD and serving as professor of Animal Science at Colorado State, and a consultant on livestock equipment and animal welfare. Most interestingly, she has written numerous books, and her most recent is entitled *Visual Thinking: The Hidden Gifts of People Who Think in Pictures, Patterns, and Abstraction* (2022). She was a dynamic, humorous, and forceful speaker at the 2023 Tucson Festival of Books.

I found tears running down my face when she described the difference between visual, verbal, and mathematical thinking, and the struggles she has had in a verbal-centric world. Most of us are a combination, but Temple is primarily visual oriented. I suddenly understood the struggles of my older brother, a prodigy in art and a person who could fix anything, but struggled writing papers. Dennis was labeled as brilliant (unlike me who was labeled as possibly mentally retarded), but his grades would fluctuate wildly as there were always more interesting things to do than write those required papers. He worked best in partnership, and my mother and I helped with papers, while he could do anything mechanical or structural and helped me with science projects and physical challenges. Even today, neither of us would be diagnosed as *on the Autism Spectrum*, but we had different strengths and limitations. For example, I cannot draw and am not at all mechanical. We both were strong verbally and award-winning debaters, but after completing a second bachelor's degree in architecture at Rhode Island School of Design, he was never able to pass the written exam to become a licensed architect.

Dennis was born the same year as Grandin but died at 62 because of cancer related to the agent orange chemicals he was exposed to in Vietnam. My tears during Grandin's talk were of sadness about losing my beloved brother, and about how our educational and medical systems label, categorize, and often place us in ticky-tacky boxes rather than understanding how we are all unique and gifted in different ways.

Teachers, leaders, and educational systems need to be more flexible. Why must we label people as *neuro-typical or atypical*, when in the end we are all on some type of spectrum. I realize that these diagnoses are the route to support for some children's special needs, but I fear that these labels may create identities and lower expectations. We no longer use the word *retarded,* but *intellectual disability* is not much better in terms of decreasing one's personal and societal expectations. Might we all be honored for our unique differences and potential. Transformational learning is about teachers and students honoring each other's uniqueness and supporting each student's goals and achievement, and this is true at all levels of education.

Temple Grandin was adamant that our educational systems needed technical programs, such as autobody works, for students with more visual skills. She also thought that young people were overly pampered, and persistence and hard work were required for success. She has adapted with techniques such as working with an editor on her many books or writing down and then memorizing a sequence of steps when required to execute certain tasks. Grandin (2022) wrote:

The first step toward understanding that people think in different ways is understanding that different ways of thinking *exist*. The universally accepted belief that we are all hardwired for language may be why it took me until I was nearly thirty to understand that I am a visual thinker. I am also autistic, and I didn't have language until I was four. I didn't read until I was eight, and that was only with considerable tutoring in phonics (p.2).

Transformative learning is cooperative. The student needs to approach academics with a *beginner's mind*. "The mind of the beginner is empty, free of the habits of the expert, ready to accept, to doubt, and open to all the possibilities" (Suzuki, 1987, pp. 13-14). Beginner's mind is not a one-time requirement. It is needed at all stages and phases of life. It requires humility and an openness to doing what is requested. Benner (2017) wrote how this openness may be difficult, but transformation is a heart-felt phenomena.

There is nothing we can do to engineer either the awakening or transformation. Our role is simply to respond with consent to the invitations to awakening that life brings us. We offer this consent through our openness and emptiness... The heart thrives in the spaciousness of emptiness and invites us to let go of all the things that fill us up and weigh us down (p. 25).

Transformation requires respect and compliance with the teacher's direction. I was not happy when my dissertation chair asked me to revise the final chapter of my treatise. I had worked hard, and my committee had approved my work and formal oral review. I was tired and not excited about yet more work. But I complied and I persisted without whining. The irony is that I have used this additional work extensively in teaching leadership over the last fourteen years. Those extra steps improved the final work, and they have served me well in practicing the lessons learned from my research. I am grateful for this extra work.

Transformation, Mystery, Love

An element of CMM that is not widely written about is the concept of *mystery*. As someone seeped in the mystical journey, I was particularly attracted to this notion that there are ineffable factors when engaging and communicating with others. CMM's central tenet that we are *making something together* attests that communication is cocreated and when it goes bad or goes well there is a certain level of mystery associated with what is happening. How can one explain why we *connect* or *feel seen* by some people and not others? There are instances in which we can explain why, but others that seem like magic; or might I dare to say grace. It is like trying to explain why two people fall in love.

At one point in my work as an assistant dean all students on academic probation were assigned to me for probation counseling. With their academic file before me, I would pray for the student before he or she entered my office. I would begin with a bit of rapport building then ask for their stories. Why had he or she ended up on probation? I would then respond with, "You are not your grades; you are so much more than that." We are too often defined by our successes and failures, yet they do not define who we are; our essence is more than that. Transformational learning is cocreated with presence, love, collaboration, humility, and the rest is mystery.

While writing this chapter I picked up Barnett's book *Making Social Worlds: A Communication Perspective* (2007) and the inscription put a lump in my throat. Barnett wrote, "Dear Pauline, I've learned so much from you and I've enjoyed all of our work together – and the best is yet to come." Signed: W. Barnett Pearce. Shortly after Barnett's retirement in 2009 he was diagnosed with a cancer of unknown origin. Shortly thereafter, he sent me a 1978 article entitled "The Ineffable: An examination of the Limits of Expressibility and the Means of Communication." The email noted that he had hoped to work with me on some type of follow-on to this work, but that this project would now not happen. Mysteriously, this 1978 article was written by Barnett with a colleague from Bates College in Lewiston, Maine where I grew up and where I studied my senior year in high school and freshman year in college.

I had little contact with Barnett after that, though I posted a few times on the blog that he wrote in the last years of his life. While teaching for a semester in France, I had this feeling that the end was near for Barnett. I wrote him a letter in November 2011 thanking him for all that he had done for me and how he and his work had changed my life. I wrote, "The irony is that by never answering my questions, you have taught me more than anyone that I have ever known. Now, that is mystery!"

So What?

As noted in the epigraph that opened this chapter, transformation is not solely a personal change; it is required for global change. Our social and political challenges are dependent on leaders who live out of a bigger worldview than their own personal desires and goals. Change in the world requires a *we* perspective rather than a *me* orientation. Transformation is a lifelong meaning-making enterprise requiring community and love. Porath (2022) opens her book *Mastering Community: The Surprising Ways Coming Together Moves Us from Surviving to Thriving* with a summative epigraph from another social scientist.

A deep sense of love and belonging is an irresistible need of all men, women, and children. We are biologically, cognitively, and physically, and spiritually wired to love, to be loved, and to belong. When those needs are not met, we don't function as we were meant to. We break. We fall apart. We numb. We ache. We hurt others. We get sick. – Brené Brown (p. ix).

Those who engage with the Fielding community usually find like-minded people who are passionate about making a difference in the world. The stimulating engagement found at in-person Fielding sessions is often referred to as getting one's *Fielding fix,* because the opportunity to continue learning and being transformed is ongoing if one is willing. Attending Final Oral Reviews (FORs), I am constantly impressed with the research of Fielding Graduate University students. Because of its student-centered commitment, learners are encouraged to seek out answers to problems that have long troubled them and the larger world. Research is less about going through hoops, and more about discovering new ways of approaching big hairy societal issues. Fielding graduates seek to change the world, and opportunities for transformative learning are key to making that happen. The world certainly needs more Fielding graduates.

References

Bass, B. M. (1990). *Bass & Stogdill's handbook of leadership: Theory, research, and managerial applications* (3rd ed.). New York: Free Press.

Bass, B. M. (1997). Does the transactional-transformational leadership paradigm transcend organizational and national boundaries? *American Psychologist, 52*(2), 130-139.

Benner, D. G. (2017). The heart of deep change. *Oneing: An Alternative Orthodoxy, 5*(1), 21-29.

Bentz, V. M., & Shapiro, J. J. (1998). *Mindful inquiry in social research.* Thousand Oaks, CA: SAGE.

Burns, J. M. (1978). *Leadership.* New York: Harper & Row.

Burr, V. (2003). *Social constructionism* (2nd ed.). London: Routledge.

Grandin, T. (1995/2006). *Thinking in pictures: My life with autism.* New York: Vintage.

Grandin, T. (2022). *Visual thinking: The hidden gifts of people who think in pictures, patterns, and abstractions.* New York: Riverhead.

Pearce, W. B. (2006). *Claiming our birthright: Social constructionism and the discipline of communication.* Conference presentation/paper. Fielding Graduate University, Public Dialogue Consortium, Pearce Associates.

Pearce, W. B. (2007). *Making social worlds: A communication perspective.* Malden, MA: Blackwell.

Piaget, J., & Inhelder, B. (1969). *The psychology of the child* (H. Weaver, Trans.). New York: Basic Books.

Porath, C. (2022). *Mastering community: The surprising ways coming together moves us from surviving to thriving.* New York: Balance.

Rost, J. C. (1991). *Leadership for the twenty-first century.* New York: Praeger.

Suzuki, S. (1987). *Zen mind, beginner's mind.* New York: John Weatherhill.

Weber, M. (1921/1946). Politics as a vocation (H. H. Gerth & C. W. Mill, Trans.). In H. H. Gerth & C. W. Mill (Eds.), *From Max Weber: Essays in sociology* (pp. 77-128). New York: Oxford University Press. (Reprinted from *Gesammelte Politische Schriften*, pp. 396-450, 1921, Munich: Dunker & Humblodt).

A Conversation with Students from the Black Students Association

Donica Harper, a fourth-year student in the clinical
psychology program; **Nathan Smith**, a third-year student in
the clinical psychology program; and **Shania Greenwood**, a fourth-year
student in the clinical psychology program.

Why did you decide to pursue a PhD degree?
Donica
I'm licensed at the Master's level and I realized that there were still things I
wasn't able to do at that level. This was an opportunity to get into a higher
level of academia, in terms of being a professor, but I'm also able to do
assessments [and] I'm able to do higher levels of care for clients.

Nathan
I've always wanted to pursue my PhD. I've always known that since I was a
kid. Then as I was finishing up my master's in social work, I've been doing
my research on various programs. While I pursued my master's in social
work, I was actively working. I was working at DOE—not a typical learner
in a sense. I was looking for the flexibility within a doctorate program.
Then I came across this learning model that could accommodate my
lifestyle as an adult learner. One of the things that piqued my interest was
the social justice and diversity concentration, and the representation of
African American faculty, one of whom was an African American male,
were factors that really contributed to my passion for wanting to pursue
Fielding.

Shania

I wanted to get a PhD because I wanted to help people that look like me. I think the work that I've done at the master's level is really important. But there's so much more that I can provide to the African American community with a PhD and provide resources that we really need—As a community.

How did you settle on Fielding Graduate University?
Donica

Fielding was the only option that I had. At the time, I was working full time to take care of a sick parent and so it was tailored to adult learners who already had careers and were really looking to just continue to advance those. As well, there was a social justice focus, so it allowed for that to also be a central part of my training.

Shania

I didn't want to feel like I had to choose between helping people and achieving my goals. Fielding gave me the flexibility to do that.

Who are some of the faculty that you work with?
Nathan

Dr. Anthony Green—his face is on the website—and I've had the privilege of taking courses with him. He's actually one of the advisors to the Black Student Association. He and I work closely together, and he's my dissertation chair. Very inspirational, he provides a lot of mentorship outside of being my dissertation chair.

Has there been anything about this journey that surprised you?
Donica

I think more so the balance that you need to have to be successful. As a parent, I was really focused on how to finish the studies I needed while also making sure I was showing up in those spaces. The resilience and the balance that's required for that was a little bit different at this kind of caliber of education.

Shania

It's interesting. I've been in online programs and long-distance programs, let's just say, before. It's really nice to come out to sessions and meet people that I've been seeing online. For the last couple of weeks, I've been religiously catching up with friends that I've met over the last four years.

You're a practitioner, right? What do you do?

Shania

I'm a licensed clinical professional counselor at the Master's level in Maryland and I'm a board approved supervisor. I do a lot of supervision. I see my own patients and provide culturally sensitive care for people that look like me, and people who don't look like me. I do a lot of work in community mental health so really meeting people where they are and giving them the services and resources that they need to be healthy.

Did you have a particular strategy for managing both personal life and work?

Donica

Yeah, I'm a very Type A person. But I'm also neurodivergent. It was really big for me to have calendars and planners, and I have tons of spreadsheets of what are all the requirements, and when should they happen. Really creating a system that made sense for me—I have like four calendars that are all on my phone and my MacBook, and so I can be anywhere and have access to the things that I need.

It was definitely difficult. I have a parent that has cancer. There was a space of time through the pandemic where my parent had four surgeries—so there was a lot of transitioning that occurred in that timeframe. So, it's difficult, but I think it also reminds me why I came here and the long-term benefits of having a degree.

Shania

Making sure that I have boundaries between my own work and then schoolwork and really taking intersession seriously when you're not in school—taking time off to not do anything at all.

It's been a challenge, but I will say that it has made me a better person in a way that I recognize that this is something that I can do and if you have the tenacity and the determination that you could do it too, if need be.

How did you settle on your subject for your dissertation?
Donica

My dissertation is about microaggressions, and supervision and the resilience of black, queer graduate students. It was an experience of a microaggression that I had in a supervisory relationship that kind of solidified that I always knew I wanted to look at microaggressions.

I have a passion for supervision. But that kind of is what ties it together. Then having a dissertation committee that had individuals that were Black and all of them being supervisors at some point and graduate students—it really allowed it to kind of form and shape into what it's become.

Shania

I'm looking at the meaning behind the experiences of African American women as it relates to body image on social media. My goal is to lessen the gap of literature around African American women and body image.

I'm a qualitative researcher at heart. I get right down to the interviews, and I really look for what it is that you're seeing on social media. How does that make you feel? How does that then change your perception about how you see yourself based on societal standards?

Nathan

I wasn't really sure what—right at first—but within my first term, I had a general idea. Now, in my third year, I'm sticking with Community Violence Exposure. I'm going to do a qualitative dissertation centered around black, identifying males, exposed to community violence.

I'm planning to do semi-structured interviews and I'm still deciding on what type of location that I might like. These have to be specific to my home state of Connecticut or maybe the Tri-State area, or I could possibly open it up to recruiting black males throughout the United States. It will be adult males who just get a better understanding of how they find meaning and how they have experienced direct and indirect community violence.

Community violence? What specifically are we thinking about?
Nathan

For example, with direct victimization of community violence— either being shot at or being shot, police brutality, any type of gang violence or physical assaults—those type of direct impacts. Then from an indirect perspective, whether it's hearing of someone being shot, hearing of shootings, hearing about killings, or witnessing violence in the media— those type of examples. Like having a family member pass away and you hear about it. Those types of indirect situations, where you're not directly impacted.

What impact do you hope for your dissertation to have on your career?
Shania

My goal is to create a framework based on the work that I do with my dissertation. This is just the beginning for me, with this work. My plan is to then take the research, or the data that I find from my research, and really let it influence my clinical experience with working with individuals with body image issues that have eating disorders. To just lay a foundation, because I think that there isn't a lot of research around Black women and body image and eating disorders.

Nathan

Community violence is a particular interest of mine, even before I started my journey here, kind of given my own personal experiences, which also drew me towards that particular topic. Whether it be direct impact of negative interactions with certain authority figures, like police, or more indirectly, with my experience, with friends and family being killed, based off community violence and those types of factors. I have a personal passion for this particular topic. My clinical interests and my clinical passions and research interests are primarily centered around African American males. I'm hoping that the results that come on my dissertation can provide its base. Whenever the experiences of Black males go unheard, this can provide a space for them to be able to share their stories.

Then with the sharing of those stories, I want to be able to provide insight into the lived experience of how practitioners can work with individuals that have been exposed to community violence and help treat symptoms of trauma or any type of mental health consequences from being exposed to committee violence, given the unique needs of African American males with that particular type of treatment. Then I'm just hoping that my qualitative study can contribute to the pool of literature surrounding community violence.

How important is it to pursue a PhD degree?
Donica
I think we have been in a mental health crisis. In terms of psychiatrists, and psychologists at that higher level, there is a deficit, whether it's military, whether it's schools, and so I think the biggest part of it is knowing that there's more you can do.

For me, it was very important as a Black female graduate student. There are psychologists that don't look like me and some that do. I think at the master's level, I realized that I wanted to do more, which included teaching the new generation of graduate students, which included doing research and things I wasn't necessarily able to do at the master's level. I think it really depends on what that person's *Why* is. Their reason for needing that advanced degree—because it is expensive, and it is time consuming. There are tears to my career but there's a prestige that comes with getting a doctorate degree.

Shania
It's going to allow me to reach people who I haven't been able to reach before. I can provide assessments and other tools that I have learned over the last couple of years here at Fielding—to really service people holistically.

Nathan
I am looking at completing my degree to take my career to the next level of being a licensed clinical psychologist. I am looking to stick to working

with individuals that have experienced trauma. A lot of the way that I conceptualize individuals and human nature—behavior and personality—is through a psychoanalytic, or psychodynamic lens. That factors into a lot of my work. I'm looking to continue practicing with that perspective and providing some psychological and personality assessments—but really emphasizing culturally sensitive psychological assessments.

When do you hope to graduate?
Nathan

I'm planning to graduate in 2025. I'm pretty focused, even at this session—that's the benefit of the sessions—where we have that opportunity to meet in person with our faculty. I was able to meet with my mentor [and] talk about my dissertation during downtime so that I can be on track to graduate in '25.

What would you advise people who are considering pursuing a PhD degree at Fielding or any other higher learning institution?
Nathan

I definitely would encourage them to try to think through some of their interests, maybe put their interests down on paper just so they can have a list of potential options. One of the benefits of Fielding is having access to so many faculty all over the United States. You have a wide range of faculty with experience. You can touch base with different faculty and connect with them, to see if your interests align with theirs, so you can get that mentorship. If you go one particular route and you're finding that you're not really as passionate about it, you have the opportunity to explore another route. Also, to try to look for community within Fielding.

Shania

I think the biggest thing that I would say is to utilize the faculty wisely. I think that they have an array of specialties that you can really hold on to and get close with them and build relationships with not only faculty members, but also the students here too. They're really going to be the only people that understand what it is to be in a doctoral program, especially in a program that is very unique, as compared to other brick and mortar programs that exist in the United States.

Donica

For me, it just meant there was another level. I think it really is based on what their goals are, and where and what they'd like to do. I think it's important, but it's also not for everyone. So, really having that discussion with yourself to figure out, why do I need an advanced degree? For me it was because I wanted to do things that weren't just clinical, I wanted to teach, I wanted to supervise at a graduate level, and I couldn't do that as a master's clinician.

Just knowing *why*. That's the motivator, going through this whole program is *why do I want to do this*, right? I want my nephew to be able to see that he can do whatever he wants. I also want to be able to show people that there is more that we're able to do and then also giving yourself grace. This is hard, building a different type of model. Which means that you're doing this while you're home with your families at all hours of the night and different time zones, and so grace, understanding your *why* and then just balancing as much as you can balance. I think that's where that grace comes in. It's being able to stay on top of it, but also know if you can't, that's okay too. You can still make it to the end.

TRANSFORMATIONAL LEARNING AND THE HIDDEN CURRICULUM

Zabrina W. Epps
Student Member, Fielding Board of Trustees

Initially, the thought of becoming a scholar-practitioner seemed daunting and elusive. Although I performed relatively well in college and had earned a master's degree, I wasn't quite sure whether I was disciplined enough to maintain the grueling and all-consuming demands of a doctoral program. It would be ten years before I had the confidence to apply to a doctoral program. My goal was to bolster my analytical and writing skills in preparation to launch a scholarly practice that integrates leadership development, strategic foresight, systems design, activism, and advising to create paradigmatic shifts in education systems throughout the United States. I understood how bold my ambitions were, but after working in higher education for over a decade and having served on a local board of education, I believed public education systems were in dire need of future (and emancipated) thinking.

How I got here

During the new student orientation (NSO), we were asked to create an illustration of our knowledge journey. Despite possessing a vivid imagination, I was not skilled at drawing images. I began to draw myself as a little girl growing up in suburban Queens, New York in a large house with a loving family consisting primarily of my mother and maternal grandmother. I attended a private school that was affiliated with an Episcopal Church from kindergarten through the eighth grade. I attended a high school for business careers, located in Lower Manhattan, and majored in computer science. The school was designed to expose the students to businesses throughout New York City.

I experienced many successes at a small historically black college in South Carolina, but I struggled in graduate school at a large university in Maryland where I eventually settled. Now that I have completed my doctorate at Fielding, I realize that my successes and failures had nothing to do with how well I grasped the course material. What propelled me through those learning institutions wasn't in the subjects listed in the course schedules. Instead, I learned to navigate the invisible aspects of the systems in which I matriculated. There was a hidden curriculum at each institution that was embedded deeply within the education paradigm. Mastering Fielding's hidden curriculum was the most transformative experience of my life.

The hidden curriculum

Kegan (1994) describes the hidden curriculum as, "what the culture demands of our minds and our mental capacity to meet these demands" (p. 9). This hidden curriculum is what institutional cultures consider normal and the expectations for one to thrive within the context of social systems. My life's journey has been characterized by a great love of learning, strong feminism, playfulness, and a dogged tenacity toward reaching new goals. However, my confidence and sense of self were constantly challenged by authority figures. These included an elementary school headmaster, a high school social studies instructor, several graduate program faculty members, and work supervisors. I did not experience these types of encounters as an undergraduate at the HBCU and all of the previously mentioned teachers and administrators were White. Those educators and managers were quick to inform me that I lacked academic ability and made no effort to teach or expose me to different perspectives or new knowledge. Each encounter initially left me feeling discouraged, as if I lacked intelligence. However, because of supportive parents, I was able to refocus with a renewed determination to succeed.

As I reflect on how I navigated through each developmental stage of life and learning, which required negotiating family, friends, school, work, politics, and my inner development, I am reminded of the need to cultivate self-efficacy, self-determinism, self-regulation, and self-reflection (Mezirow, 2000, 1994). It has also meant becoming keenly aware of the systems of which I was a part. Each learning organization had its own structural and cultural design and to succeed, I had to identify where and how I fit into those systems without losing my sense of self.

More than doctoral competencies

I started Fielding with my NSO group learning about doctoral competencies: how to conduct research, understand what the authors were offering to us as readers, critically analyze each piece, and ultimately understand how to develop our own arguments. However, those weren't the only lessons. We had begun a process of learning that many of us had never experienced, and for which I wasn't at all prepared.

The first was self-directed learning. Fielding was founded on this principle from its inception in 1974. At that time, the founders thought it was important to acknowledge how postsecondary institutions had not allowed for adult learners. Colleges and universities were designed to accommodate students in their late adolescence who were expected to stay on campus and conduct their studies within campus classrooms and libraries. However, more adults were returning to school as the economy shifted from the industrial age to the advent of the information age, punctuated by the financial, healthcare, and technology sectors.

The founders were students of adult learning theory and anticipated the coming proliferation of educational technologies. They envisioned a learning space that honored adult learners and saw life experiences as a point of departure for scholarship. An essential cornerstone of the Fielding learning model was self-directed learning that was supported by caring and accomplished faculty. This was in sharp contrast to the sage-on-the-stage or scholar's apprentice learning models at prestigious research-based graduate schools at the time (Melville, 2016). Fielding's learning model was also steeped in its core values, which were established by its founding board, which included the scholar, civic rights activist, and educator Dr. Marie Fielder (Johnson-Riley, 2022).

My first year at Fielding wasn't characterized by the high-touch framework that Melville (2016) described. That is, not until the end of the term. But by then, my initial enthusiasm had deflated, and I found myself ruminating on the experiences from the master's program. But I knew that my faculty mentor cared about me, so I reached out to inquire about how to salvage the term. Luckily, unlike my previous encounters with educators, my mentor submitted an incomplete and set a new deadline to complete the coursework, without judgment.

Past messages, past behaviors

The second hidden lesson emanated from within. After descending from the NSO cloud and shopping for the perfect home office furniture and supplies, I realized that I was still grappling with old negative messages about my worthiness to embark on this life-altering pursuit. Suddenly, reading, posting meaningful responses to my fellow students, and submitting final papers became incredibly overwhelming. Despite all the talk about feedback during NSO, initially, there wasn't much of it.

I admit that this pattern persisted for years. Fortunately, I attended the summer and winter sessions where I met more students, alumni, and faculty. Hearing about other people's learning journeys and gleaning wisdom on how to approach coursework in one-on-one talks with faculty proved to be a lifeline. But, when I returned home, work, school board meetings, and the politics of both left me with no energy or motivation to read, research, or write. Instead of progressing through coursework, I did what I'd always done in learning spaces, which was to get involved. People knew me to be outspoken and were impressed by my professional background. So I joined HOD governance, where I worked closely with the faculty and administration on university and program policies. I attended regional cluster meetings, research practice weekends, topical intensives, and winter sessions in Santa Barbara. I was everywhere, talking to everyone. But, I was not progressing towards my degree and my tab was growing.

By the summer of 2018 (and four years at Fielding), I had completed coursework and had taken an incomplete to defer the submission of my comprehensive essay (Comps). By now, many of the cohort members I started with had either graduated or withdrawn. Had it not been for my involvement with HOD governance, I would have felt totally abandoned.

Understanding the pivotal role of the comprehensive essay to achieving doctoral candidacy, I enlisted a local dissertation coach whom I met with weekly until submitting the comps essay just shy of the fall term deadline. What happened next could only be described as the overcoming step of the hero's journey. After all that lag, I passed the comprehensive essay, assembled my dissertation committee, and was finally progressing toward the dissertation phase. I told my committee chairperson that I needed to meet regularly, and we did. I rode the success of passing comps through my pilot study, but I knew that this wouldn't be enough to propel me to complete the dissertation and graduate. I told myself, "You have come this far but to finish strong, you must lean in and make everyone care about your success" (Baker, 2018).

With the news that my committee chair was soon retiring, my methods faculty was leaving for a new opportunity, and that the other core committee member had already retired from Fielding, I most certainly felt pressured. But I parlayed my service in HOD governance and applied to the Marie Fielder Center with the hope of finding new camaraderie and support from Vice President Dr. Orlando Taylor, and other fellows. Then, in 2019, I was tapped to join Fielding's Board of Trustees.

It took six years before I experienced consistent academic progress at Fielding, and I now see many instances where I could have squared my shoulders and got on with it. However, my expectations had been set by the videos of faculty and alums on Fielding's website, the blurbs about a community of support, and the personal invitations I received from faculty to apply. While I wasn't the model student, I was an adult learner with real-life experiences and a commitment to become a change agent in the world. I am appreciative of the faculty who did not judge me, those who nudged me, and those who listened to and encouraged me to pursue my ideas. However, I was also disappointed by the faculty who ignored email requests for feedback or time to explore new topics of interest. In some instances, the lack of responses extended my time to completion.

The hidden curriculum that required me to adapt to doctoral studies on my own almost led me to give up on Fielding and myself. The key element of self-directed learning (Melville 2016, Shapiro, 2003) is for faculty to mentor doctoral students until they build confidence in themselves. Shapiro further explains, "Although one of the meta-goals of the program is to help learners to develop their capacity as self-directed lifelong learners, it cannot be assumed that learners enter the program with that capacity" (p. 159). I knew I possessed the aptitude for doctoral studies. What I needed was the support to help me acknowledge my attitude towards the learning systems that previously hurt me.

Liberty and justice
Another complex aspect of navigating a doctoral program is the fact that despite its uniqueness, Fielding is beset by the hegemonic baggage inherent in all social systems within the United States. Education institutions are inherently hegemonic as they are undergirded by the socio-cultural, economic, and political systems that created a dominant culture based on Western European/Colonial values and social norms. Without conscientious educators and administrators who compensate for inequitable policies and practices, experiencing transformative learning will continue to be an exception for some learners but not for all.

Although Fielding was founded by people who set out to create more liberated learning spaces for adult learners to engage in knowledge generation in a supportive environment, it was not designed in a vacuum. If one were to review our success indicators, one might find lower completion rates, or more years to degree completion, among students from marginalized communities. While Fielding is enjoying a much more diverse student body today, many of these students are hard-pressed to see themselves and their experiences represented among the faculty and within the curricula. I am reminded of a recent conversation about preparing for Fielding's future, in which a faculty member lamented the perceived decline in the quality of students. That is a past sentiment that we cannot afford to take into our future.

As we continue to monitor COVID–19 and observe political debates about culturally relevant curricula throughout the United States, as Trustee Keith Early often admonishes, Fielding has also found itself at an inflection point. While providing feedback on my final paper for a knowledge area on transformative learning, Dr. Steven Shapiro asked, "What would an institution [that is] truly dedicated to transformative learning look like?" I would add, what would Fielding look like as a global, innovative, and anti-racist institution committed to the success of every student who enrolls in its programs? No cracks to slip through. Institutions like Fielding Graduate University are poised as conveners of generative discourses to create strategies and design innovative learning spaces that enable its community members to envision and become agents of social change.

I am under no illusion that I would have not been successful at any of the doctoral programs in my local area. Fielding offered several opportunities for me to "lean in." Joining HOD governance enabled me to share my professional expertise in policymaking with the program faculty and university leadership. I anchored several new student orientations and supported incoming students as they entered the HOD programs. Becoming a fellow of the Marie Fielder Center for Democracy, Leadership, and Education was a tremendous opportunity to work alongside Dr. Orlando Taylor, Fielding's Vice President for Strategic Initiatives, who remains a giant of higher education scholarship and practice, particularly in the domain of STEM leadership. Dr. Taylor was one of my most cherished champions and has continued to mentor me. Having graduated, I am also fortunate to have continued support from Fielding as a newly appointed fellow of the Institute for Social Innovation (ISI), where I will have the opportunity to shore up my work of integrating leadership development with future thinking and strategic foresight.

I am grateful to have been appointed to the Board of Trustees in 2019. In addition to fulfilling our fiduciary responsibility of monitoring the budget and sharing university priorities with President Katrina Rogers and other administrators, we engaged in aspirational discussions of how Fielding can evolve to meet the needs of students, faculty, and staff, as well as broaden the impact of the great work that we all produce. We seek to position ourselves as global thought leaders and to ignite that special flame that we have all felt at sessions, clusters, and during some courses. Fielding students are embers whose ideas and scholarship prove to be the best of what humans have offered towards sustainability and planetary thriving while scorching the status quo.

Since I have been on the board, we have grappled with how to maintain Fielding's identity as a premier institution within its program areas. We engaged with the President, Provost, and administrators on how to improve the experiences of our diverse and inclusive community. The board has grappled with how to transform Fielding into an anti-racist institution. Our most recent and most challenging work has been envisioning Fielding in the future and seeking a partner with whom to journey into the future. Envisioning and positioning Fielding for the future has been the most challenging work. We have re-examined our core philosophies and values. We also reimagined what type of institution will meet the needs of future students in terms of our programs, our business model, our global leadership, and our institutional culture. Our work continues, but I have been honored to work alongside fellow board members as we ask and attempt to answer provocative questions about who Fielding is and wants to be.

Transformed for emancipated futures

I feel affirmed by how I have been transformed. I feel affirmed by those at Fielding who were committed to supporting my doctoral goals. As my new work as a leadership coach and advisor begins to take shape, I feel affirmed that the theories and scholarly practices I have learned have led to opportunities to publish, to become an emerging fellow of the Association of Professional Futurists (APF), and to serve on two additional boards within the foresight field as I complete my service on Fielding's Board of Trustees. I feel affirmed by the belief that there are new education paradigms to be developed and I have the privilege to serve scores of students for years to come by contributing ideas backed by what I learned at Fielding.

Goldhaber (2000) paraphrased Vygotsky in stating that human development is a natural process, whereas learning is a culturally mediated one (p. 343). We know that the injustices and inequalities that exist throughout the United States (and around the globe) were socially constructed. Schools and systems of education have proselytized nationalist and ethnic ideologies which cemented social stratifications based on race, class and socio-economic status, as well as other caste systems. However, the good news is that if a group of humans can design inequitable systems, then new groups of humans can design new, inclusive learning spaces for people to focus on generating new knowledge that leads to much-needed social and global change.

As Fielding evolves into a graduate institution of the future, it ought to reveal its hidden curricula. Expose everything. Lay it all bare. There is good stuff here and anyone admitted to Fielding is entitled to it all. It should no longer be up to the doctoral students to figure it out. Doctoral programs cost a great deal of time and money.

Having been exposed to some of the hidden parts, I am hopeful. Everyone at Fielding wants those who join the community to succeed and invite others. Like me, Fielding students bring with them the problems they've observed in society, and some have burning questions about how to examine some facets of these phenomena. We also bring our burdens and insecurities, whether we realize it or not.

Fielding students will continue to learn how to become scholars in ways that they can expect to enhance their practice and transform themselves as humans. And hopefully, they will feel empowered to be transformed as creators of new paradigms, new thought leaders, new advocates, new investigators, and new instigators. Transformation is embedded in Fielding's design. It is all of us in this beloved community who make Fielding's mystique visible.

References

Baker, S (2018),   Michelle Obama on Sheryl Sandberg's 'Lean In' Strategy: 'That S--t Doesn't Work All the Time'. December 3, 2018, Entrepreneur, https://www.entrepreneur.com/business-news/michelle-obama-on-sheryl-sandbergs-lean-in-strategy/324213

Goldhaber, D. E. (2000). Theories of Human Development: Integrative Perspectives. Mayfield Publishing Company.

Kegan, R. (1994). In Over Our Heads. Cambridge: Harvard University Press.

Mezirow, J. D. (1997). Transformative learning: theory to practice. *New Directions for Adult & Continuing Education*, (74), 5-12.

Mezirow, J. D. (2000). Learning as a transformation: Critical perspectives on a theory in progress. Jossey-Bass a Wiley Company.

Schapiro, S. A. (2017). Instructional feedback on a final paper, Transformative Learning, KA, Fielding Graduate University

Schapiro, S. A. (2003). From Andragogy to Collaborative Critical Pedagogy: Learning for Academic, Personal and Social Empowerment in a Distance-Learning Ph . D . Program. *Journal of Transformative Education, 1*(2), 150–166. https://doi.org/10.1177/1541344603254145

A Conversation with Navajo Nation Alumni

**Miranda Haskie, Rolanda Billy, Telletha Valenski,
Viola Hoskie & Pauline Begay**
Alums

Why did you decide to pursue a doctoral degree?

Miranda

I always wanted to pursue a graduate degree and when I completed my undergraduate degree at the University of New Mexico in Albuquerque, I longed to return home to the reservation— Navajo Nation. I also knew at some point I wanted to return for my graduate degree. However, I was very rooted in my community at home in Lukachukai, Arizona and I knew I never wanted to leave again. Which then brought the challenge of trying to locate an accredited doctoral program/graduate program, that could allow me to stay home—rooted in my community—while pursuing graduate education, and along came Fielding Graduate University.

Rolanda

It's something that's been a lifelong passion for me, as a Diné (Navajo) educator and a woman. It's something that I had in mind as a goal ever since I left high school. I really wanted to do it for myself, my family, and [for] future educators on the Navajo Nation. I think through the grit and mindset that whatever you set your sights to, or the goals you set up, that they can be done.

Telletha

Back in my early stages after I graduated from undergrad, I went back east, to Harvard, to get my doctoral degree but it was at that time where I wasn't quite sure what I wanted to get my research in. There was rigor. It was challenging—it was not your traditional way of what you see in the educational system here. When I went there, I was challenged. At the same time, it taught me a lot of what would require me to be a critical thinker. I didn't complete it but when I came to Fielding, I was given the opportunity to do my doctorate here on [the] Navajo Nation. I was really happy that I could do it back home.

Viola

Education was always super important to my grandfather. I'll refer to him as Shicheii. It was always important to him when I was growing up. When I came home, he would always ask me what I learned in school, and I would go through my whole entire day of what I learned. The other thing that was really important to him was working hard. Those two things together— very early on I knew that I wanted to go to college. By the time I was in middle school, I also knew that I wanted to pursue a doctoral degree, because education was so important to him. It's something that I wanted to show him. I am sad that he's not here but I know that he is aware. He's been my inspiration for everything.

Pauline

To promote my own Navajo language and since I was a teacher, I wanted to teach the young students, our Navajo language, at least some Navajo, because more and more are speaking English and I wanted to use my Navajo songs to teach the language and this is what I did throughout my dissertation. I was a teacher at an elementary school so my dissertation is Teacher Action Research. I was actually in the classroom with the students, and I had about 20 students who participated, both female and male, and that's where I started, in the classroom.

What did Fielding Graduate University offer that other universities didn't?

Miranda

Well, for one, they came to me, and they allowed me to continue my career while I was pursuing my graduate studies. When I came to Fielding, the faculty were so inviting, they were the friendliest group of people I had ever encountered. I remember when I arrived, asking them, just tell me from point A to point B, what do I have to do to earn my degree? They said, "Well, what do you want to do, Miranda?" That question stumped me because nobody had ever asked me, in all of my Western education, what did I want to do?

So that was one of the challenges I encountered, and I also found one of the best aspects about Fielding—it allowed me to design my own doctoral journey, and that allowed me to become a self-directed learner.

Rolanda

I saw a couple years ago, I would say, about four years ago, I saw an advertisement in the *Navajo Times* with recruitment for students that were interested in pursuing a doctorate degree. I connected with the individual that was listed, started doing research about the university, wanting to know specifically who Fielding was or what type of higher education institute they were, what they were known for and how for me being a Diné woman, my worldview and my perspective on Indigenous education—how that would fit into their concept as a university and how accepting there were going to be and then I attended an information session at the Navajo Nation museum and I got connected with individuals who went to Fielding and who completed their dissertation processes and talked to them.

Telletha

I think what would be different was I did it at home. I didn't feel like I was in the city. I wasn't distracted by the museums. I wasn't distracted by the performance or anything like that. I was able to be in the comfort of the nation, then it wasn't too hard.

Pauline

After I finished my Master's Degree in Oklahoma City I wanted to continue and go into a doctoral program and it just so happens that Fielding University had an ad in the *Navajo Times* and I caught that. So that's where I started and joined a cohort—Navajo cohort.

Viola

Oh, my gosh, the cohort that we have. They're amazing people, they are very inspirational. They are very positive. They're very encouraging. They all have encouraging things to say all the time. I always look forward to our cohort meetings. Also, our mentors; Dr. Haskie and Dr. Fowler are amazing people too. Anytime that you felt ungrounded you could call them and say, I am struggling a little. Dr. Fowler was one. I called him and I said I'm really struggling through this. He has so much wisdom and he has gone through the same experiences too. He was able to ground me and help me through it. So, I really appreciate that.

Why is it important in the 21st century to have a doctoral degree?
Miranda
The world is changing ever more quickly and a doctoral degree can help us more easily navigate those changes that we are experiencing in our rapidly changing world. In addition, I consider myself to be a lifelong learner and at Fielding, much of their curriculum was catered toward being a lifelong learner and as a result it created this open mindedness and growth mindset in me, and as a result of of my quest to continually learn, that is helping me to navigate the changes in my environment and much of that came from my graduate studies with Fielding.

Rolanda
I think at this point, in my own research I really found it difficult to find studies out there that encompassed indigenous populations. It was very scarce when I went out to look for doctoral research, scholarly writing, in studies that were done on the reservation, with indigenous populations. So, I think that was my driving point—[it] was just the fact that for future generations that we would have to have that to build that library and to start that process for future scholars.

What was your research interest? What did you want to invest in?
Viola

Initially, I wanted to study resilience of children. There was an unfortunate event that happened at my school and that was kind of like the catapult for my studies. As I went through my first term, I knew that I wanted it to be a little bit more positive and so I thought back to what made a difference between myself and my peers growing up. I attribute my success in school to my grandparents' teachings, especially my grandfather's teachings. There are certain philosophies that he had about life. One was that you work hard for everything that you want to have. The other one is that you have the potential, and you need to realize your potential. So, using that, I knew that I wanted to transfer those same teachings to my children, because sometimes they don't have those teachings from their home. In Navajo culture, any child that enters your classroom, that's your child, too. It was my way of transferring information that was passed to me, from my grandparents, to them. I feel like that's my responsibility as well—to not just teach them academic stuff but teach them all the fundamental teachings that are important to be successful in life. The three things that I came up were grit, growth mindset, and self-efficacy.

Pauline

The title of my dissertation is "Drum and Sing out the Language." It's a Teacher Action Research. So, here's my drum and I am speaking in the Navajo language and how I help my people, my children, and our nation by singing Navajo songs in the Navajo language. After I completed my dissertation I came up with this album. In Navajo it's called *Dahwiit'ááł*, which means *we are singing*. This has been used with children and they are learning the language through singing. So that's why I brought my drum and sing out the language. This is used reservation wide, and it's also a worldview album. You can even find it on the internet.

Telletha

My dissertation was about enjoyability. How do we create environments for students to enjoy learning subjects like math, like the Navajo language, just more so looking at those nontraditional students who want to learn and have a different way of learning—targeting those students as well.

How has a doctoral degree at Fielding University affected your career path?

Miranda

We know, in the world in which we live in, the 21st century, the digital world, that our world is becoming increasingly smaller. With our ability to communicate with the click of a finger on all our mobile devices, laptops, and now with all of the new Zoom communications, Skype, and our world—that we once were nestled in—in these corners of the world, are now opened up and we're able to engage in these international relationships and partnerships with others and allow to build the human capital on Navajo and continue to help the nation in its own efforts to establish those relationships and in the process, continue to build the Navajo Nation.

Telletha

How it impacted my career is putting things into a framework. Before I was very scattered and now as a doctoral student, you really see how systematic thinking is really important. How do you put things from point A to point Z and structurally help others to see the same thing. That's what really helped me.

Viola

I know that this degree opens up other doors for me and there's other possibilities that I could pursue because of it. Right now, I am content in the classroom. It has always been my enjoyment—I don't see it as a job. So right now, I am Dr. Viola Hoskie, fifth grade teacher but I know that there's other possibilities. I want to be able to write journal articles related to grit, growth mindset, and self-efficacy, particularly in sports and then also specific to Native American students. I also am interested in writing a chapter in a book. Eventually, I would like to be an educational instructional coach because I know that I can help other teachers too. I am thinking about life after this degree.

If there is one thing that you want to change about what you experienced at Fielding, what would it be?

Rolanda

I think I wouldn't change anything because, like I said, my worldview—the perspectives were honored—as a matter of fact, it was encouraged and I wouldn't change the experience I went through, I learned a lot. I grew to extend that and give that back to the community—the community that helped pave the way and paid for the education.

Was it difficult for you to pursue a doctoral degree on top of all the other things that are going on in your life?

Rolanda

It wasn't too difficult because there's the family support system and a lot of us on the reservation, we don't grow up alone. We grew up in our family, our extended family. So, we have a great support system that could help us achieve our dreams. So, it wasn't too difficult but finding the balance, I think is a difficult part. Not the academic or the rigors that's involved in the research, but actually making it work…that's the difficult part.

Viola

I have my elderly father that I take care of and so that was challenging at some point. I was very strategic in how I did my studies. I teach a course like I taught during the day, but I always made myself do two to three hours of work after school, just on my study. I tried to be consistent about that, no matter what was going on around me. I tried to always make time for that.

Telletha

Amber Crotty, the council delegate of the eastern side of the Navajo nations, she said, "Oh, T, there's a program that's available, you should try to apply." I'm like, "I don't know if I want to, that's a lot of money." She's all like, "The Navajo nation will pay a percentage of the tuition and then you do a portion of it." It [my portion of the tuition] wasn't so much that it would have affected me financially so, I was like, "Yeah, I could do this".

What are some of the challenges facing Navajo students?
Telletha
One is the mindset. Another is that financially, it is challenging. I had to learn how to budget really tight because now you're investing in yourself. Really, what I learned in the doctoral program is I'm investing time. I'm investing the gifts that I had already and expressing it on paper. I think that would really be the biggest part because we are so invested in other people—you give to other people, but with the dissertation…you're really giving back to yourself.

Is it difficult for young people on the Nation to stay true to the Navajo traditions and language? Do they just want to leave the nation and pursue other things? Or do they still feel a strong bond with Navajo culture and Navajo language?
Pauline
I think some of them are still practicing their traditions and culture and language but that would be those who are living out in the rural area on the reservation. If you are in an urban setting, then you are more into English or other languages. It's kind of difficult for them and they're struggling to keep our language. So that is why I always want to say, teach them at an early age, or when the baby's still in the womb—speak Navajo. There are more young parents today and young parents today are the ones that speak more English as well, so the children just automatically go into it.

If you were addressing a group of young Navajo students right now, what would you tell them about pursuing a doctoral degree?
Rolanda
I would first start off by saying that a lot of our traditional teachings come with the personal philosophy of *T'áá Hó Ájí'téego*, meaning it starts within you, it starts within yourself. Our voices are something that I feel should be shared—our worldview of how we see the world, how we were brought up in our teachings and so forth. The literature to share that with an audience worldwide, I think is pivotal and to continue to be a part of that process. Diné people are just as good as anybody else out there and to put ourselves

at that limelight. I think I would tell them to do it because it's within you. Yes, it's a difficult journey at some point but it's also a rewarding journey. You learn from within, and you also learn from without and that helps you not only as an individual, but it helps you grow in a community that you're giving back to.

Miranda

They can do it. The mere fact that they've asked the question, and that they're now seeking graduate studies, and perhaps considering Fielding Graduate University as one of those options, that I would invite them to attend—that the experience that they would gain is very unique, unlike many of the traditional residential graduate programs, in which we have to leave home to earn the doctorate. With Fielding, you could stay home, continue to build your own communities, continue to invest in your own families, your career and develop both personally, educationally, and professionally—all while pursuing your graduate studies with Fielding Graduate University.

Telletha

I would tell them that it's not necessary to get a master's degree. You can go straight to a doctoral degree. You'll have a wealth of information already, based upon your culture and the history and your language. You know things from your elders, you sat down with them and they have traditional knowledge that you've taken into your daily life. That is dissertation, that you can apply it to what others would see differently.

Pauline

I think it's very important because in the future, you don't know what's coming to you, and for me, I started off and I didn't know the English language. I knew how to speak my Navajo language. So that helped carry me through my studies. The children today—some of them are learning their language, but more are into English. So, in the future, if they become a doctor, they could always come back to our Navajo Reservation, and carry on the leadership in education that we know here on the Navajo reservation, rather than go off the reservation.

When we look at the dissertations the Navajo students have written, is there something that distinguishes them from dissertations written by other students?

Miranda

Most definitely. The majority, if not all the doctoral dissertations by Navajo students at Fielding Graduate University all incorporate Navajo worldview and apply the Navajo principles of *Hózhó´*, which is harmony and balance in our world. *K'é*, establishing relationships in our world with each other, all the way to the universe, and the Navajo principles. Our educational philosophy—which is comprised of the four elements of *Nitsáhákees*—Thinking, *Nahat'á*—Planning, *Iiná*—Living, and implementation of those plans: *Sihasin*—that assurance that we build in ourselves and the self-confidence that we develop. That becomes a large part of the doctoral studies that our Navajo students engage in and are really developing a repository of knowledge. That is available in the dissertation studies at the library of Fielding Graduate University and they're certainly adding to that knowledge collectively, for the Navajo Nation, and even globally.

What does it feel like to finally come to an end of such a long program?

Viola

Oh my gosh, I think there's like an array of feelings. One is relief because you've been at your studies for so long and when you finally get your final edits back and you're like, *oh my gosh*, like it's finally finished—seems surreal, almost. The other one is happiness, and I don't really share a lot of my experiences with other people, but I found myself telling my class, "Guess what? Do you remember that paper that I showed you that I'm writing? I'm finished!" They started clapping for me. These are fifth grade students, and I was like, "Whoa." Their reaction was awesome and that's how I felt… I felt really happy.

I think another emotion that I feel is [that] I fulfill that responsibility to my grandparents. That's a huge part of it. I'm trying not to be super emotional… but it really means a lot to me.

My Experience at Fielding

Kevin Lowell
EVP, UScellular and Alum

My experience at Fielding was transformative. I was challenged, delighted, encouraged, surprised. I found differences and I explored them. I found similarities and I leveraged them. I learned from others, and I developed my own ideas. My experience with Fielding started the day I interviewed as part of my application process. The interview was a telephone call with a Fielding professor. I remember feeling nervous. I remember pacing. I can't say that I remember the content of my interview, what I was asked or how I answered. What I do remember is this: how *excited* I was. I was excited to have a conversation about scholarship. I was excited to talk about a program for learning, for really immersing myself in a field I felt passionate about. I felt on the verge of a beginning. An opportunity was unfolding before me.

Much as Fielding seeks to integrate scholarship with practice, I integrated the pursuit of my Fielding degrees into my professional and my personal life. I didn't enroll at Fielding intending to become a professor. I applied to Fielding to indulge a passion for leadership and to improve my leadership abilities. I knew that by bettering myself, I could better serve. I enrolled to integrate scholarship with practice.

With time enough, I would read most everything. I would study most everything. I would seek to learn all I could learn. But the gift of limited time caused me to be selective, to discriminate and differentiate among all that was possible, to find what mattered most for me.

T.S. Eliot wrote that knowledge can impose a pattern. Knowledge *will* impose a pattern if we seek only to understand but not to apply. Knowledge can limit us, it can constrain us, if all we do is gain that knowledge and keep it to ourselves. If we only learn what someone else has learned, we're replicating what is already known. There isn't value in a simple recitation.

We can gain knowledge, we *must* gain knowledge, but it's the application of this knowledge that creates value. *Knowing* isn't the objective; *applying what we know to cause better outcomes*, that's the objective. Gain knowledge and break the pattern with new thinking.

By its charter, the Fielding education reinforced for me not just the *expectation* that we serve, but the obligation that each of us as human beings—we who are connected at this time and at this moment on this planet Earth—that each of us serve each other. It is incumbent on each of us who has been fortunate for Fielding's investment in us.

My Fielding experience reminded me and reinforced for me that there are many ways of seeing, of thinking, of knowing, of experiencing, and of being. There are many ways to seek, and there are many ways to understand.

The transformative power of learning in the 21st century: 1

Everyone has greatness in them. Large or small, young or old, early or late, big or small, greatness exists, and it exists in each one of us. Our greatness manifests itself in different ways and at different times in our lives. We may find our greatness in the way we do our work, the way we connect to our community, or the way we live our lives with our families or with our friends. Our greatness might surprise us. It might unfold and bloom over the course of years, or it might sneak up and reveal itself when we least expect it. This way or that, greatness exists in each of us.

To *realize* our greatness is a feat that no one achieves alone. Teachers, mentors, friends, family, neighbors, classmates, colleagues, bosses—the list goes on, the list of those people in our lives who make our lives rich and who make our lives meaningful. That transformative power that converts our reading and listening and thinking and reflecting; that transformative power that converts our lived experience into our own personal greatness; that transformative power is *learning*. Learning is a catalyst that converts our potential into greatness.

There is transformative power in all types of learning: learning to listen, learning to think, learning to act. In learning, there is power to change the world. To change the world is to change one person at a time. Changing one person at a time means changing one story at a time. "The universe is made of stories, not of atoms" (Rukeyser, 1968). What are we, if not our stories?

Learning transforms the way we listen

In today's world, we're easily distracted from distraction by distraction (Eliot, 1943). Diatribes have replaced debates; squeaky wheels abound. The challenge is not to *hear*—we can hardly help but hear! The challenge is to *listen*. Learning transforms the way we listen when we seek to understand.

But seeking to understand is not enough. Seeking to understand must not be the objective. The objective is this: seek to understand so that we can *act*. Seek to understand so that we create equitable outcomes. Seek to understand so that we create a positive difference in the world. Learning transforms the way we listen. When we learn that more than 80% of workers in America are "deskless," we listen to the discourse about hybrid work arrangements differently.

When we learn that twenty million households in the United States and three billion people around the world are not connected to the internet, we listen to the debate about net neutrality and the digital divide differently. We learn to listen for the voices that are not represented. Learning has transformed the way we listen when we listen for the voiceless.

Listen. To those around you, to those who came before you, and to the murmurs and intimations of your own soul as these begin to whir and whirl, swirl and twist, and fix and condense and become the stuff that swells your heart and moves you to action. Search to understand what is not you. Seek to understand the other, the different, the surprising and the unexpected. Begin with a heightened humility, and listen. "The only wisdom we can hope to acquire is the wisdom of humility; humility is endless" (Eliot, 1943).

Learning transforms the way we think

We learn early, we learn often, and sometimes we learn too late. We learn through sight and touch and sound and taste. We learn to walk and talk. We learn through nature and books and lived experience (Emerson, 1837). The fact of the matter as a matter of fact is that we learn from the day we draw our first breath, and we learn throughout, broadly and deeply.

But to what end? What's the *value* of learning? We've heard it said that the value of the liberal arts education is to teach us to think. That's off the mark. Learning to think critically and incisively is an important skill, and the time and energy required to learn how to think critically and incisively can be well worth the effort.

But to what end? What should we think *about*? Here, we get to choose. What a wonderful gift, choice. With this opportunity to choose what to think about, with this *freedom*, comes great responsibility (Roosevelt, 2011). We can choose to think about how to nurture growth. We can choose to think about how to enable sustainability. We can choose to think about how to create equitable outcomes.

Learning transforms the way we think when we choose to learn from the past. Learning transforms the way we think when we choose to explore differences. Learning transforms the way we think when we seek to connect different domains—biology with sociology, or botany with physics. Learning transforms the way we think when we seek to understand to cause a positive change.

Think. About what has been, and why. About what isn't, and why not. And about what could be, about what is possible, and what your role can be. Identify those opportunities to take action and to make a positive difference. Find similarities, find differences, and find what doesn't work and find what does work. Seek to find the opportunity, to nurture possibilities, to turn the notion of believing only in what you see into seeing something great because you believe in what's possible. Think about what has been, and why. About what isn't, and why not. And how you can make change and play an active role in causing a healthier, more equitable, sustainable way forward.

Learning transforms the way we act

Act with kindness, with care, with vigor, with sincerity, with focused attention, with purpose, with integrity. My Fielding education helped reveal for me the opportunity that had always existed, right in front of my eyes: the opportunity to see generously and to act kindly. To lend a hand. To help.

I learned ways to serve. I learned I could make a positive difference in a single life with a single act of kindness. I learned that I don't have answers, but I did learn to see the potential that a person can realize when I help them with a word or an act or a dollar.

The structure of my Fielding program required that I set goals and do much of my work independently to reach those goals. This wasn't an undergraduate program, where there are (usually) daily classes, where I lived with my classmates, and where my life was oriented around achieving my degree. This was graduate school.

Throughout my time in the program, I learned the role and the value of a mentor. My mentor, Dr. Barbara Mink, guided me, challenged me, supported me, pushed me, encouraged me, and, most importantly, made it clear that she believed in me. I learned the discipline necessary in a rigorous self-directed program. I learned what "rigorous" meant. It meant "demanding." It meant "challenging." I learned what "supportive" meant. It meant that I chose the path, but I did not walk down it alone.

I learned what "self-directed" *did* mean, and what "self-directed" *didn't* mean. "Self-directed" did not mean that I was working alone. It meant that I was free to determine the path I would take, but it did not mean that I was alone in walking down that path. I was self-directed and free to choose my objective, but I was not alone in figuring out how to advance toward that objective. These taken together—rigorous, supportive, self-directed— inform the way I pursue my professional career. Today, I'm the Executive Vice President, Chief People Officer and Head of Communications for UScellular, the nation's 4th-largest wireless telecommunications company. I'm also an author. What I learned at fielding—both *what* I learned and *how* I learned—were invaluable to my career successes and to my successes as a writer.

I've applied what I learned about succeeding in Fielding's self-directed program not only to the way I approach my professional role, but also to the way I write books.

I've learned to create micro-habits. These are the tiny little daily habits that add up to accomplishments. The value for me? I perform micro-habits, and I know that I have done what I set out to do. Setting and achieving micro-habits sets me up for bigger successes. Another way learning has transformed the way I act: daily goals. I've just finished writing my third book. I recognized the day I signed the contract with my publisher that I would need a disciplined approach to writing the book and meeting my deadlines. I have a busy day job, so I would need to schedule writing much the same way I schedule meetings at work. I knew my book needed to be roughly 200 pages. So I did the math. I had nine months to complete it. I allowed myself two of those months for final reviews and final edits, so I reduced the number of months for writing from nine to seven. I had 214 days to write my book. I set a goal to write 500 words every day. Those 500 words didn't need to be edited. They didn't need to be exquisite prose. These 500 words simply needed to get written. The combination of micro-habits and daily goals helped me get it done.

Act. The difference between doing nothing and taking action makes *all* the difference. The technologist in me sees this difference as binary, off or on, zero or one. Leonardo da Vinci: "Being willing is not enough; we must do."

How my experience at Fielding enabled me to secure my position
My experience with Fielding and the pursuit of my degrees helped me secure my current role at UScellular. Through my work experience, I had demonstrated a capacity for leading others and developing talent. I established myself as an accomplished executive.

My scholarly research at Fielding provided an academic basis for my work as a business executive. It lent a different credibility than is established as a practitioner. My pursuit of an advanced degree demonstrated my commitment to scholarship and to learning. My learning in turn improved my performance as a leader. This commitment and this pursuit and achievement, these helped me advance in my career. Here's how:

I learned to narrow and to focus. Anyone who has pursued a Ph.D. knows the lure of exploring ideas. I found myself traveling roads that lead to yet more interesting ideas, which in turn lead to other ideas, which in turn lead to more and more and more. I could spend days and weeks – and I did! – doing research that was interesting but wasn't valuable to my objective.

I learned the difference between *doing* and *making progress*. I had a lot of fun *doing* things: reading articles and papers and books, and finding more articles and papers and books. I was having a lot of fun exploring different ideas. I convinced myself that I *had* to take the extra days and weeks to explore other ideas, because I needed to be thorough. A voice deep inside whispered to me that I was taking myself off course. I did my best to ignore that voice. Continuing with research and continuing to explore was, I realized, easier than holding myself accountable to making decisions and making progress.

I was active, I was busy, but I wasn't moving forward. Deadlines loomed, and I fell behind. I stumbled and struggled to make meaningful progress. More than once, I considered quitting the program altogether. My mentor and my colleagues at school and at work helped me regain my footing. They held me accountable in ways that I needed.

I learned perseverance. I learned that dissertations aren't written and degrees earned overnight. The same with success. It isn't achieved overnight; it's achieved every day. The daily work, the daily effort, and the daily commitment—*that's* how dissertations are written and degrees earned.

My degree added a dimension of credibility different than what professional successes demonstrate. My degree represented success in seeking out new ideas and new thoughts and developing these ideas and perspectives into new knowledge, integrating these ideas and perspectives to create new knowledge, and applying this new knowledge in unique and valuable ways. This is what innovation is. Innovation is one of the highest priorities of business leaders around the world. My Fielding degree reflected my ability to innovate—creating *new* from a broad and deep body of knowledge.

How I'm using my research in a major corporation

I apply my research to inform the way I lead. I apply both *what* I learned and *how* I learned. I apply what I learned in the School of Leadership Studies to the ways I develop talent, set objectives, and coordinate organizational change.

My research deepened my understanding of the complexity of leadership and organizational change. My research revealed for me a rich body of knowledge. As an executive, I apply what I learned to the way I work. I've developed well-informed points of view, combining and integrating scholarship with practice. I use my research in a generative fashion; that is, I synthesize what I learned as a scholar with what I do as a practitioner. My research did not cement or finalize my approach to leadership as an executive. My research informs my work.

Much as successful businesses integrate the many teams and business units that comprise the organization, I integrate the many ideas and perspectives and theories into my own leadership practice. I haven't chosen a single theory or practice as my blueprint, nor have I chosen a single scholar as my beacon. Rather, I have integrated what I learned into my own practice. I developed my own leadership voice years ago. I use my research not as my sole argument, or as my only perspective; rather, I integrate what I've learned through my research with my experience as a business leader. My ideas are more compelling and my speech more persuasive because my perspectives are informed with scholarship.

I've learned to connect seemingly dissimilar ideas from seemingly dissimilar domains. My dissertation connected a theory from the life sciences to the social sciences. I've found this skill—finding and creating connections across different fields and across different ideas and across different industries—to be exceptionally valuable in my profession. This is a source of innovation—using the materials at hand to create something new and valuable.

Fig 1. Drawing by Chris Lowell.

The transformative power of learning in the 21st century: 2

We learn in any number of ways. Do with your own learning what you will, but *do*. Emerson's 1837 essay and subsequent speech said: "The scholar must needs stand wistful and admiring before this great spectacle. He must settle its value in his mind" (Emerson, 1837). And then she, he, *we* needs *act*.

My own learning, and your own learning, and all the learning that goes on around the world: to what end is it? *Why?* Mine helped me advance in my career and attain a role that I'm excited to perform. The value of your learning? Yours is yours to answer. Everyone's? Everyone's. But the value of learning must be beyond getting a job. It must be greater than knowing answers. It's got to be greater than acquiring knowledge for the sake of acquiring knowledge. Nature and books and lived experience—yours and mine—must lead to *action*. Our learning must enable us to create more equitable structures and to help achieve more equitable outcomes. From the right to vote and the right to education, from the basic human right to enough food to eat and clean water to drink, from the rights invested in each of us as human beings, these are the rights and the outcomes that our learning and our knowledge must help manifest.

"Seek to understand." There is value in seeking, and there is value in understanding. But neither is the endgame. We don't seek simply to seek, and we don't understand simply to understand. Each is important, and each has a purpose, but neither is an end. If the endgame isn't "seeking," and if it isn't "understanding," what is it?

The end game is serving. So I'll modify the statement to read, "Seek to understand to serve." After all, it's not what we get in this life that matters, it's what we give. Service is the endgame. We seek to understand, but not to have and to hold the knowledge all to ourselves; rather, we seek to understand so that we can more compassionately serve others. Serving is the endgame.

As there are any number of ways to learn, there are any number of ways to serve. We serve by listening. We serve by encouraging. We serve when we help, when we hold, when we push from behind and pull from ahead. We serve when we bring others along. We serve when we enable others to stand. We serve when we listen. We serve when we see and accept each person for who they are, where they've been, and where they are. We serve when we demonstrate care.

One of the most empowering acts we can perform is to demonstrate to someone else that we believe in them. Give people a chance. Show faith in them. Tell someone that you believe that they *can*. Help where you're able to help, enable and assist where you can. We are all connected: me to you, us to them, today to yesterday to tomorrow.

I've seen it too often, people underestimated because of what they don't know, or because of where they're from, or what they look like, or what they haven't demonstrated. I've seen this, too, people *flourishing* when they're given a chance. I am flourishing because others believed in me and *did something about it*. My obligation now is to return the favor, pay it forward, and help the other person.

Anne Michaels wrote, "The best teacher lodges an intent not in the mind but in the heart" (Michaels, 2009). This is what the faculty at Fielding did for me: they lodged an intent. They lodged an intent to seek, to learn, to persevere. They lodged an intent in me to lend a hand and serve others. In my role as a leader, I get to create opportunities for others, much as opportunities were created for me. I get to help.

The journey of these last twenty years—a journey that started that day pacing in my basement, hoping I would be accepted into the program to join the Fielding community—this journey has been the journey of a lifetime. The twists, the turns, the wonder, the surprise, the love, the loss, the joy... If I've learned anything, I've learned this: the joy in my life comes not from the getting but from the giving.

References

Eliot, T. (1943). *Four quartets*. New York: Harcourt, Brace and Co.

Emerson, R. W. (1837, August 31). *The American Scholar*. Cambridge, Massachusetts, USA.

Michaels, A. (2009). *Fugitive Pieces*. Toronto: Emblem Editions.

Roosevelt, E. (2011). *You learn by living: eleven keys for a more fulfilling life*. New York: Harper Perennial.

Rukeyser, M. (1968). *The Speed of Darkness*. New York: Random House.

My Pursuit of a Doctoral Degree

Maria V. Sanchez
Student Member, Fielding Board of Trustees

I have lived in Westlake Village, CA (a town in Los Angeles County) for over 30 years. I raised my four children here and we consider it our hometown. We are as far away from Los Angeles as possible, as we reside one street away from Ventura County, which is on the way to the offices and campus of Fielding Graduate University. I was the President & CEO of a private company from 1999 until I sold it in 2012. Life after the sale involved lots of philanthropy, which included being on several Board of Directors and an active member of Rotary, including a Paul Harris Fellow twice.

Throughout my life, I have been a radio talk show host for decades. I love the immediacy of radio and the opportunity to respond to real-time events as the news cycles dictate. Syndication and podcasting changed the industry tremendously and I was active in various iterations over the years. I resigned from my last radio gig in 2021 for reasons I will explain later.

I decided to attend graduate school later in my life, as I thought I would reinvent myself as a Marriage & Family Therapist. I graduated from Pepperdine University with a Master's degree in Clinical Psychology in 2017. I decided to pursue a PhD and Fielding seemed like the logical choice with their Media Psychology program. I am the first Ph.D. in my family on either side. My parents both spoke English as their second language, and they did not learn how to speak English until they attended the first grade.

Earning graduate degrees is something that I am very proud of. I also earned a Master's in Media Psychology at Fielding while on the Ph.D. journey. I chose Fielding for a variety of reasons and all of them encompass the motto, "Save the World, Start With Yours." I am impressed with the caliber of the Fielding graduates who are doing just that.

I had no idea what the Ph.D. journey would look like. I have met only a few Ph.D.s in my life. I had no idea how arduous and challenging the degree would be, nor the amazing amount of learning that accompanied the pursuit. As a lifelong reader, it was wonderful to have the opportunity to read, reflect, write, and create presentations for classes, conferences, clusters, and seminars.

When I started my Media Psychology Ph.D. program at Fielding, I did not have any idea what my dissertation would focus upon. I allowed the process to unfold organically and as I created my assignments; a theme began to emerge. Social justice, equity, inclusion, women's rights, gender-based violence, and girls' rights began to inform my mission. An atrocity that I learned about while a host on National Public Radio in 1997 began to haunt me. The topic is Female Genital Mutilation (FGM) and I had hoped that over the years, someone or some entity would do something about eradicating the centuries-old procedure, which predates organized religion. Surely the United Nations, the World Health Organization, and UNICEF to name a few would have tackled this issue long ago.

Female Genital Mutilation removes all or part of a female's external genitalia and is not medically or religiously mandated. It happens all over the world, including the United States, the European Union, and the United Kingdom. Today, there are 200 *million* girls and women who are alive that have experienced the procedure. Every 11 seconds somewhere in the world a girl is being cut and the numbers aren't declining.

On average, the procedure is performed on girls between six months of age to 15 years old. There are four types of FGM and Type 3 is the most invasive and punishing. These girls experience physical challenges such as difficulty in urinating and menstruating; painful intercourse; a high infant and maternal mortality rate; and infections. The psychological harm is tremendous and often creates lifelong challenges with trusting people, as the very individuals that should be protecting a girl are often the perpetrators of the procedure. FGM is performed because of patriarchy and the desire to sublimate a female's sexual pleasure. It also guarantees the family of the groom that the bride-to-be is a virgin and often commands a higher dowry.

In the Western world, FGM exists because of culture, tradition, misguided religious observances, and control. At this moment, there are 9 states and the District of Columbia that do not yet have legislation outlawing FGM! The State of Washington just passed anti-FGM legislation in April 2023 and I was honored to testify four times before their Senate and Assembly on that legislation. A federal law was enacted on January 5, 2021. The "STOP FGM Act of 2020" clarifies and amends provisions of the underlying 1996 and 2013 FGM laws, which prohibit Female Genital Mutilation of girls in the United States and the transportation of girls outside the United States to have FGM performed.

State laws have a more direct impact on the day-to-day lives of those living within its borders. At the state level, FGM is a child protection issue that should be linked to child protection laws. Federal laws against FGM are implemented by federal agencies, whereas state laws govern activities of state-run institutions including law enforcement and courts, healthcare, social services, and other programs to address FGM. States have significantly greater capacity to reach young girls at risk of FGM and the front-line professionals that can intervene to protect them within existing child protection frameworks. Girls must be protected from child abuse and violence, including FGM, in every state and front-line professionals responsible for protecting girls must be empowered to protect girls.

As a Fielding Graduate University Doctoral Candidate, I realized that I wanted to know how we could attempt to eradicate the procedure with a Western, English-speaking audience. What could be done to make this barbaric procedure go away, and how? Researching how people might intervene in a dramatic situation I learned of the bystander effect originated by Latané and Darley in the late '60s. These psychologists were piqued by the story of a woman being assaulted and murdered in New York. As background, Catherine Susan Genovese, or to her friends, Kitty, was stabbed, robbed, sexually assaulted, and murdered in Queens, New York, on March 13, 1964. According to reports in the *New York Times*, the assault went on for about 30 minutes, during which time Ms. Genovese screamed for assistance. Nearby residents turned their lights on and off in the adjacent housing. It was reported that the neighbors heard her screams and watched from their apartments, but not one of them made a call to law enforcement. It was estimated that over three dozen neighbors witnessed or heard the assault, and yet no one did anything. This lack of bystander intervention inspired the research of Latané and Darley in 1968 and 1970 about why and how bystanders can become involved. They proposed a five-step model of bystander intervention.

I proposed the application of Latané and Darley's five-step model of intervention to engage bystanders in the FGM eradication cause. The following is an application of their research (Darley & Latané 1968a, 1968b; Latané & Darley 1970) and an approach for the bystander intervention model involving FGM and encompasses the five steps that need to occur for bystanders to get involved.

• Pay attention to a situation that needs assistance – FGM.

• Acknowledge that the circumstances are an emergency – 513,000 American females and 200 million women worldwide are affected by FGM.

• Take responsibility for intervening – acknowledge that FGM needs to be eradicated.

• Know what needs to be done – raise awareness.

• Decide to be of assistance – sign a petition, share #EndFGM/C on social media, volunteer time for the eradication cause, or donate to an entity that already has boots on the ground for the eradication efforts. Raising funds for the eradication cause is nearly essential to provide the necessary tools to the various communities in need of assistance. Donation intention was tested in my study but understanding why individuals donate is also necessary to assist with furthering the cause. Understanding what motivates donors goes hand in hand with awareness campaigns.

My study attempted to help in the eradication of FGM by having participants listen to one of two educational podcasts; one podcast utilized a traditional format and one used the Latané and Darley model of helping behavior.

The primary takeaway from my research is that I was able to change hearts and minds about FGM by creating more awareness about how serious and important FGM is and creating a willingness to act about what to do about FGM. Neither podcast was more persuasive in creating advocacy confidence about what to do about FGM and raising awareness of how serious and important an issue FGM is. They were *both* persuasive. Also, concerning which podcast created more donations towards an eradication cause, again, neither podcast was more persuasive than the other; they were *equally* persuasive! Armed with my research and my results and my frustration that global entities weren't moving the needle in the eradication campaign, I decided to create my own Foundation to do just that.

In October 2021 I created a tax-exempt California 501(c)(3) entitled, STOP THE CUT NOW! *Eradicating Female Genital Mutilation*. Our mission statement reads, "Female Genital Mutilation. Our objective is to eradicate this barbaric practice. We set out to create awareness and put an end to FGM. In addition, we support other organizations in the eradication cause, creating a unified voice worldwide to eliminate this cruel, inhuman practice. We provide education through our website, speaking engagements, seminars, and social media outreach, in hopes of raising the necessary funds needed to put an end to Female Genital Mutilation."

For more information on what we do, our website is located at https:// stopthecutnow.org/.

Since launching my Foundation, I have also been involved in governmental advocacy. I have testified before legislators in the District of Columbia, which is currently developing anti-FGM legislation. As I previously mentioned, I testified four times before the House and Senate in the State of Washington before their successful passage of SB 5453. It was signed into law by Governor Jay Inslee on April 20, 2023.

Finally, STOP THE CUT NOW! *Eradicating Female Genital Mutilation* sponsored California's AB 798, which was introduced on February 13, 2023. This legislation is meant to tighten California's already existing law. AB 798 had three Assembly Committee hearings and it was put forward to the Assembly for a vote on May 30, 2023. It passed unanimously and bi-partisan and it is now being heard in the Senate at their Committee hearings, awaiting the Senate's approval and then a vote before the full California State Legislature.

It is my opinion that my education at Fielding Graduate University stoked the fire of the scholar/practitioner within me. My dissertation, research, and results created the pathway to start my Foundation and have further fueled my activism with eradicating Female Genital Mutilation, not only in the United States but globally as well.

THE PERSPECTIVE OF A FOREIGN STUDENT

Sergej van Middendorp
Institute for Social Innovation Fellow

A good 20 years ago, just before Sterre, our first child was born, I submitted my Master of Business Administration Thesis to the Henley Business School. My assessors graded it A+. It was the first time in my educational journey that I had really enjoyed the intellectual and practical rigor required for creating such a large and coherent piece of work. And the feedback was rather surprising to me, as in all my schooling before that I had usually tried to attain my diploma's as efficiently as possible. Which - to me - meant passing with the lowest acceptable grade with the least possible effort. So, I wondered, what could this mean?

Not long after that, I was working as a strategist with e-office, a leading Dutch software services provider. And as a young father (now of two) with a fresh MBA, I was exploring the emerging fields of knowledge management, intellectual capital, and network organizations. Together with some leaders in their field, amongst whom Verna Allee, Karl-Erik Sveiby, Oliver Schwabe, and Charles Savage, I tried to apply ideas from these subjects in creating services for our company to provide to our clients, who wondered how they could make the most of their investments in portals and collaboration software. The people I worked with on this started asking if I had considered turning my quest into a PhD. So I started looking at how that might happen. I wanted to see how my newly discovered intellectual motivations and drives could be best fulfilled.

While I was exploring possibilities for a PhD position in The Netherlands, I kept following my intellectual curiosity. And I was learning that my enthusiasm for the abstract was not always conducive to getting everyone engaged in the same way I was. Charles Savage, who coached me at the time, challenged me to look at the arts as a source of inspiration to further develop my language. While alert to possibilities for doing that, I ran across a citation to Frank Barrett's (1998) article on creativity and improvisation in jazz and organization and I knew I had to work with this. I called my brother who was a professional jazz drummer at the time. We gathered a jazz band, and for several years we brought the thinking in Frank's article to practice in organizations. This did indeed change my language and way of engaging without diluting my intellectual over-excitability.

Later, Charles pointed out that Fielding might be a good place for me to pursue my PhD. I was skeptical, because I knew pursuing a PhD in the US would cost tuition whereas a position as an external PhD in The Netherlands would 'only' cost time. But I always follow-up on leads, so I went to Fielding's website, looked up who is teaching there, and there was Frank staring me in the face…I filed the experience under the category of synchronicity, and moved on as I wasn't convinced I could afford go to Fielding, yet.

A few months later, I finished reading Ken Wilber's Theory of Everything (Wilber, 2000). I really liked his approach to integrating many different theories into a coherent system, and the last page evoked an experience of wholeness in me, evoking a deep motivation to act on my insights. I thought: "if there is an integral theory, there must be an integral university!" And sure enough, when I looked it up, it existed. It was related to the Integral Institute, which collaborated with two universities to provide certificate programs, one of which was Fielding. I could no longer ignore this.

Charles connected me to Dorothy Agger-Gupta to help me learn more about Fielding. I really liked what I was learning. Later, I talked with Fred Steier, and I was convinced I wanted to go there. Encouraged by my father, who was convinced the best investments are in your children, I wrote up a proposal for supporters who would want to finance my journey. My father being the first, made it easier for others to follow, and within a few weeks, I had raised 100.000,- EUR from friends-entrepreneurs to co-finance my doctoral journey.

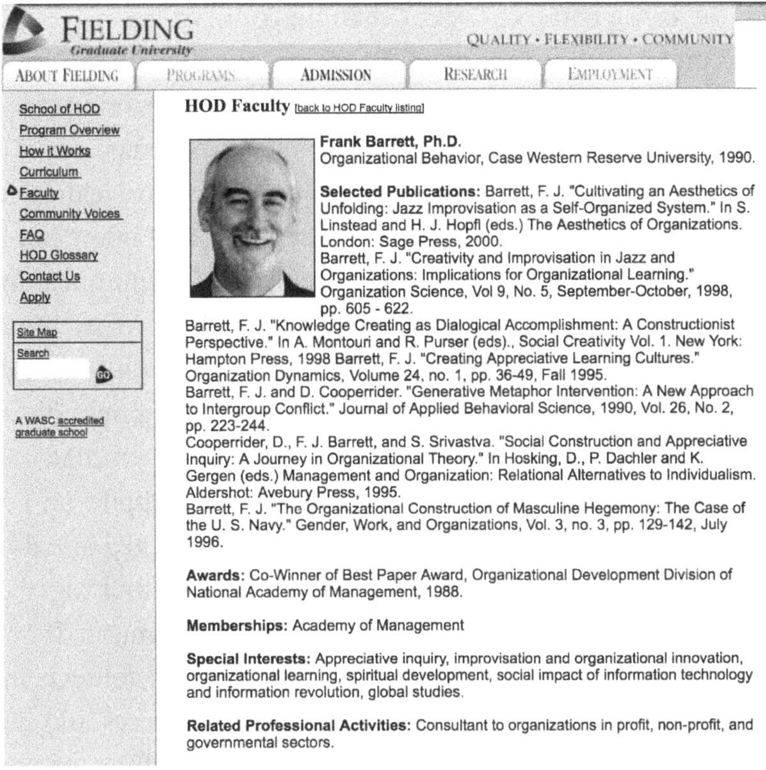

FIELDING
Graduate University

QUALITY · FLEXIBILITY · COMMUNITY

ABOUT FIELDING | PROGRAMS | ADMISSION | RESEARCH | EMPLOYMENT

School of HOD
Program Overview
How it Works
Curriculum
Faculty
Community Voices
FAQ
HOD Glossary
Contact Us
Apply

Site Map
Search

A WASC accredited
graduate school

HOD Faculty [back to HOD Faculty listing]

Frank Barrett, Ph.D.
Organizational Behavior, Case Western Reserve University, 1990.

Selected Publications: Barrett, F. J. "Cultivating an Aesthetics of Unfolding: Jazz Improvisation as a Self-Organized System." In S. Linstead and H. J. Hopfl (eds.) The Aesthetics of Organizations. London: Sage Press, 2000.
Barrett, F. J. "Creativity and Improvisation in Jazz and Organizations: Implications for Organizational Learning." Organization Science, Vol 9, No. 5, September-October, 1998, pp. 605 - 622.
Barrett, F. J. "Knowledge Creating as Dialogical Accomplishment: A Constructionist Perspective." In A. Montouri and R. Purser (eds.), Social Creativity Vol. 1. New York: Hampton Press, 1998 Barrett, F. J. "Creating Appreciative Learning Cultures." Organization Dynamics, Volume 24, no. 1, pp. 36-49, Fall 1995.
Barrett, F. J. and D. Cooperrider. "Generative Metaphor Intervention: A New Approach to Intergroup Conflict." Journal of Applied Behavioral Science, 1990, Vol. 26, No. 2, pp. 223-244.
Cooperrider, D., F. J. Barrett, and S. Srivastva. "Social Construction and Appreciative Inquiry: A Journey in Organizational Theory." In Hosking, D., P. Dachler and K. Gergen (eds.) Management and Organization: Relational Alternatives to Individualism. Aldershot: Avebury Press, 1995.
Barrett, F. J. "The Organizational Construction of Masculine Hegemony: The Case of the U. S. Navy." Gender, Work, and Organizations, Vol. 3, no. 3, pp. 129-142, July 1996.

Awards: Co-Winner of Best Paper Award, Organizational Development Division of National Academy of Management, 1988.

Memberships: Academy of Management

Special Interests: Appreciative inquiry, improvisation and organizational innovation, organizational learning, spiritual development, social impact of information technology and information revolution, global studies.

Related Professional Activities: Consultant to organizations in profit, non-profit, and governmental sectors.

Figure 2: Fielding's website in 2007 with Frank Barrett showing up unexpectedly.

Five Things I Didn't Expect

There are five things that come to mind that I discovered that were not only unexpected, but also profoundly changed me and my outlook on life.

The first is that along the journey, my focus shifted from the metaphor of improvisation to improvising with metaphors. The metaphor of improvisation offers a rich set of concepts to help us address complexity and emergence as we try to jointly make sense of it through activities like collaboration, innovation, and change. The organizations and systems that we are trying to change using these concepts however, embody metaphors that may no longer be apt for the context we find ourselves in. Those metaphors have often become non-conscious and are therefore taken literally. By shifting our attention to the metaphors themselves, and using improvisation to bring them to awareness and then creating alternatives together, we have a better chance at changing our systems.

The second is that at Fielding, I discovered the work of Barnett Pearce and the community of scholars and practitioners working with the communication theory of The Coordinated Management of Meaning (CMM). I had never heard of these, and didn't come to Fielding for this, but I immediately understood that the tools that CMM offers can be seen as ways to create minimal structures for improvised communication. This could be enormously helpful in learning how we improvise together in communication as one way to approach improvising with metaphors to make better systems. I am still active in the CMM community and the Institute that Barnett co-founded before he passed away in 2011.

The third is a course that was offered by Jeremy Shapiro on Love and Death in Modern Western Music Drama. I had not planned on taking that course, but when I saw it offered, I changed my plans and together with a small band of fellow students we watched six great music drama's and learned about the historical, philosophical, and musical contexts in which they were produced. We shared our love for these pieces and authored several reflection papers after having watched recordings of the same performances. I came away changed as a person, a growing love for opera and classical music and an expanded musical-metaphorical vocabulary.

I also discovered that knowledge, in addition to power, can be love. When I came to Fielding, I was not that aware that I tended to use knowledge as power in a way to relate to others that was informed by trauma inflicted as a child growing up. During my journey, and through shadow work, I discovered this tendency. And through its attention to diversity, equity, and inclusion, which manifested itself intellectually in the program that Fielding had to decolonize and reconstruct epistemologies, I was also made aware of the broader historical and systemic forces that had dominated scholarship and society. As a Dutchman in the time that I started my program, these discourses were completely out of sight in my country of origin. It was quite a confrontation for me to engage with this in the early years of my program. But it has taught me, through community, that there is a way to understand my personal defense in using knowledge as power and the context in which I grew up. Through becoming a PhD with Fielding, I know how to use knowledge as love and am more aware of my tendency to use it as power and know how to stop myself. Before I went, I was pretty sure about many things. Yet no-one told me these things could be discovered. And I am eternally grateful I did.

Finally, my mentor, Fred Steier, who was there with me on my journey in good times and bad, and from start to finish, I learned that I am not 'alone' in the crazy ideas that I have, and that however much I was learning, there was always more to learn and wonder about.

My Research Question

I came to Fielding with the research question "How do we make a Value Network Groove?" This question integrated my work with the group around Verna Allee, whose Value Networks approach was one of the methods we used in our practice with the experience of our jazz band going into organizations to work with the metaphor of improvisation. I wondered how we could get networks of organizations to make/find their groove just like a jazz band does when performing on stage. In the first phase of my doctoral journey, I explored these topics in my work with faculty in human development, organizations studies, and systems.

All the while, I was trying to relate what I was learning to my practice and to use what I was learning in my practice to inform my research. I was in the leadership team of a software startup in that period, where we made software that supported independent organizations to form distributed network organizations together, balancing collaboration, self-organization, and a shared purpose. Also, I was working with the financial supporters of my research to make case studies of how they were themselves part of forming network organizations. After the first phase of my Fielding program, I started crafting the first concepts of my dissertation. This I remember as a complex process of exploring, collaborating, making small steps, reflecting, and slowly shaping a coherent whole together with my committee, my business partners and my research supporters.

To support the design process of these networks of organizations, we developed a method called Embodied Making. In this method, we use principles from "designer-type" thinking to create new systems, trying to surface the embodied metaphors implicit in the current systems and generating new metaphors to help shape a new system. It was around this time that I made the shift from working primarily with the metaphor of improvisation to improvising with metaphors as a systems designer.

Then, after some preparatory work with Fred Steier, the chair of my dissertation committee, and after an eventful committee meeting, we drafted the question on a flipchart in the form that would remain the question throughout the dissertation: *How do our improvisations with conceptual metaphors become embodied in the system that a group of designers are creating?*

I designed my research as a participatory action research process with several steps and layers of reflection, each creating their own data for analysis and synthesis. Also, I kept redesigning the research design as we went through, reflecting on the outcomes of a step and then planning the next step in more detail as we integrated what we had learned. I ended up making three cycles of action and reflection before I came full circle. I used the words *stepping* and *kenning* to give meaning to the research design. Stepping refers to stepping into the Heraklitan river of the research, changing both its flow and myself as a researcher. Kenning, an old Norse word, refers to combining two concepts that together create a new knowing, referring to the metaphorical process behind how we make new meaning.

I am not sure about the impact. There was a close relationship between action and reflection in the first stages of the research, certainly impacting our own organization as we used the learning to keep designing our methods and software. But later in the process, it became more of a dialogue between our findings and the literature, resulting in a more abstract model that I am still learning how to use in my research and practice. This final synthesis within the scope of the dissertation research was very much a personal and deep journey of discovery and learning that has greatly impacted me as a person. I do bring that changed person to my work, in which I support the collaboration in a large community of organizations working together. I hope there is some impact there in how I bring what I have learned to this performance. Also, I have been presenting our work and publishing articles and chapters in differing communities of academic practice, and have been a steward on the board of directors of the CMM Institute. And now, as a research fellow, I am continuing my research guided by the question: how do we make healthy systems? All that I have learned in my research with Fielding is greatly informing this continuing journey.

My degree helped me advance my personal development. Together with complementary learning in therapy, becoming a PhD taught me to distinguish between my personality as a researcher using knowledge as a defense structure and my essence of engaging with knowledge AS knowledge. The latter form being more in tune with my higher ideals and growth potential. As a result, I feel more competent as a researcher and more humble as a person.

I am using the skills fostered in my degree program to help inform decisions and designs that may be useful in generating the collaboration needed to help transform the Dutch Healthcare System to focus on Health as its starting point. This is needed to sustain the quality of that system as it faces huge demographically driven disruption. Being able to do that using what I have learned is a great privilege and this would not have happened in the same way were it not for my journey with Fielding.

Being in a PhD program and establishing relationships with scholars in the wider community also helped me identify with people pursuing similar research and practice interests. As a result, I co-founded The Institute for Global Integral Competence, a training, education and research organization, and am serving on the board of the CMM Institute for Personal and Social Evolution. Contributing to these organizations with these like-minded individuals was one of the outcomes I hoped for when starting my PhD program.

I am currently a research fellow with Fielding's ISI and inquiring into the question how we make healthy systems. This action research project explores communication and design dynamics among participants gathered to redesign a fragmented Dutch healthcare system.

The Importance of an Advanced Degree
I think it is becoming increasingly important to be able to think for one-self, to work with others, and to bring together people from a variety of

backgrounds in communities and systems to help address the toughest challenges in our world. The complexity inherent in these challenges, combined with the amount of information being created requires skills, amongst others, in dealing with large amounts of information, critical thinking, and collaboration. A degree in higher education, especially one with a transdisciplinary focus and rooted in values like equality and community like Fielding's degree in Leadership and Change which develops those skills are sorely needed. Not least while it affords its participants to remain active in their practice where their learning can have direct impact and which ensures that what they bring to their learning is grounded in practice.

What Would I have Done Differently?
That is the most difficult question. The first thing that comes to mind is how much time I have taken for this journey that I did not spend being with Thekla, my wife and Sterre and Stijn, our kids. All in all, I took eight years for this, starting when our kids were still very young. At the same time I could not withstand the forces of motivation and synchronicity leading up to me starting this journey. It would be hard for anyone to make a rational calculation where an effort like this might fit in their lives. Would I better have done this later in life? Or earlier? Learning and growth are not only fun and fabulous. Learning and Growing also hurt, can be stressful, and take time away from others you live with and love. But the pursuit of the PhD also taught me something about love in a different way that I find is now integrated in how I am, or can be, with my family. For example, in supporting our daughter and son as they engage with their own studies and are discovering their own intellectual overexcitabilities.

When I arrived in Santa Barbara for my NSO in 2008, I came home. As I write this, I am on a flight from Amsterdam to Los Angeles to participate in Fielding's Global Session. It still feels like returning to this place that is home.

THE TRANSFORMATIVE PURSUIT OF MEANINGFUL ANSWERS

Tracy N. Long
Institute for Social Innovation Fellow

Life, in my experience, can be chronicled by a series of questions. Questions that are sometimes routine and sometimes profound, sometimes answered and sometimes only contemplated. Questions can lead us to choices that are life-changing. Today, I can look back and recognize the key questions that have defined my life. Of course, many of the questions we ask during our lives, especially when we are young and learning to navigate the world and our place in it, are of a practical nature. What are we having for dinner? Other questions, like "What do I want to be when I grow up?" will influence future questions that we ask.

I asked a question in 1968, at age 11, that seemed innocent enough at the time but would set my life on the path that has led me to where I am today. My parents drove our family to the next town to see the new Stanley Kubrick movie, *2001: A Space Odyssey*. When a pre-human primate in the opening scenes threw the bone that he was using as a tool up in the air and it morphed into a spaceship carrying humans to the moon, I was mesmerized. The question it generated for me was "How did humans advance from using bones as simple tools to building spaceships? What happened to us between then and now?" That question stayed with me. When my parents grew tired of me asking how humans developed, they gave me the Time-Life Book Series, *The Emergence of Man*. Reading those books, I decided that I would grow up to be an anthropologist.

The study of anthropology taught me to ask questions in order to understand how groups of people defined their world and their place in it. I learned how to use questions and observations to develop descriptions of group processes and requirements. I turned this skill into a successful career, helping organizations to develop better processes, define information technology requirements, and make efficient and effective use of organizational systems. The insights that I gained through the study of anthropology were a huge benefit in my 30-year career managing technology during the transition from mainframe computers to PCs on every desk. I had a front row seat as information technology became an integral, ubiquitous element of human life. While I developed my understanding of technology in the workplace, I never lost sight of the human element and continued to observe and question the behavior around me from an anthropological perspective.

I came to Fielding after years of work because I had a set of new questions that I wanted to explore. I wanted to know if other people had the same questions. I wanted to know if there were any answers to those questions. For my application to enter Fielding, I developed a series of questions related to my professional experience:

• What factors impact an individual's, a group's, or an organization's ability to adopt and incorporate new technology?

• Is there a relationship between database organization and social organization?

• Is project management an innate human skill?

• Do we organize groups, organizations, and societies around project initiatives?

• Are there universal elements in project methodology?

I wanted my graduate school experience to further my understanding of human systems but to also provide additional professional skills. I wanted to return to my social science roots, but I wasn't ready to abandon my profession. I believed that my studies at Fielding would provide me with the framework necessary to pursue a rigorous and scholarly exploration of these topics. I planned to devote the next phase of my life to the study of technology and the organizational systems and structures that have developed around it—as both a scholar and a practitioner.

My studies at Fielding gave me good opportunities to explore the questions. The graduate experience would have been worthwhile if all I had gained were the tools that would allow me to ask good questions and explore the answers. If I had only developed the means to return to my profession as a more competent practitioner and continue to explore my questions in a way that was both valid and valuable to my profession, that would have been satisfactory. What I took away, however, was much more than a few answers and a new professional toolkit.

If we are lifelong learners, we have many opportunities to add to our wealth of knowledge. These opportunities are valuable and satisfying gifts. I certainly expanded my existing knowledge while I was a student at Fielding, but the true gift of my educational experience was a complete shift in my view of our world and my place in it. From the first day in New Student Orientation, we were told that doctoral studies are not about "getting a PhD", but rather about "becoming a PhD". Those who had come before us talked about their time at Fielding as a transformative experience. It all sounded very exciting, and a little intimidating, but as I started my doctoral journey, I had no idea what those words meant. What I walked away with at the end was a personal transformation that I never would have anticipated.

The Fielding focus on asking questions from a holistic perspective and the emphasis on the fundamental values of inclusiveness and social justice quickly acted to redirect my own interests. Instead of questions about institutions and technology, I became interested in the dynamics of activism as a mechanism of social change. I asked what mechanisms lead individuals and groups to commit themselves to becoming a force for social change. What influences the adoption of a specific cause to pursue, often against personal interests? Rapidly unfolding current events led me to immerse myself in the ethnographic study of participants in the Occupy movement. My dissertation asked the question, "What are the factors that influenced the adoption of genetically modified organisms (GMOs) as a focus of protest for participants in the Occupy movement in Ventura County, California, and how is the Occupy activism situated within the larger GMO debate?" (Long, 2014, p. 12). The exploration of this question was fascinating and rewarding, but the process of pursuing the answer changed the person that I am. While becoming a PhD, I also became a more engaged and active participant in my own social system. I knew that my old profession and narrow interests would no longer be a satisfying pursuit for me, so I opened myself up to new experiences and new possibilities.

After graduation, I chose not to return to the work of managing projects and developing computer systems for organizations. It was a good occupation, and it had been both rewarding and satisfying for me for many years, but it no longer captured my imagination. Instead, I chose to join an inspired, dedicated group of people working to create a new botanical garden that sits squarely at the intersection of nature and society, both past and future. Our fundamental mission of conservation and research holds the promise of new knowledge that will promote a sustainable and socially just future. I never would have imagined myself here before I started doctoral studies. The work is challenging, all consuming, often frustrating, but always rewarding and even sometimes magical. I do continue to learn new things every day, but the experience goes beyond just learning new facts and skills. Our leadership team is continuously engaged in discussions about the questions we should be asking and the paths we should be pursuing to generate new knowledge and new understanding. This process of generative thinking is the key to who we are and what we are trying to accomplish. Fifteen years ago, when I decided it would be interesting to go to graduate school, I would not have understood or been able to contribute in a significant way to the most meaningful part of our work in the Ventura Botanical Gardens. The transformative process of becoming a PhD gave me the opportunity to start a new chapter of life that is far more personally satisfying, and hopefully more meaningful, than I ever could have imagined before starting the PhD journey. I am grateful beyond words for this gift and excited to have new questions to ask and new opportunities to pursue the answers for many years to come.

References

Long, T. N. (2014) *Making the case against GMOs: Issue adoption and adaptation by Occupy activists.* PhD Dissertation, Fielding Graduate University, Santa Barbara, CA.

My Doctoral Degree
Wódahgo Bidziilgo Ólta' Naaltsoos

Miranda Jensen Haskie
Professor, School of Business and Social Science
Diné College

I am Professor of Sociology in the School of Business and Social Science at Diné College, Tsaile, Arizona where I have taught for over twenty years. My commitment to the preservation of Diné language and culture is an enduring aspect of my work, which includes a three-week Navajo language immersion project at Diné College, and a six-year Navajo Oral History Project between Diné College and Winona State University. This collaborative undertaking led to the production of twenty-seven living histories of Navajo elders, now archived at the Smithsonian Institute Museum of the American Indian, the libraries of Diné College and Winona State University, and the Navajo Nation Museum (Shreve, 2014). I live in Lukachukai, Arizona on the Navajo Nation with my family. I earned a Doctorate in Educational Leadership and Change from Fielding, a Master of Arts in Sociology from New Mexico State University, a Bachelor of Arts in Sociology from the University of New Mexico—Albuquerque and an Associate of Arts in Navajo Language from Diné College. I did visit the campus of Fielding in February 2002, the year of my graduation. I have convened with Fielding faculty, students and school leaders across the country with one international trip at Fielding National Sessions and Fielding Research Sessions throughout my four years. My travels with Fielding took me to Santa Clara, CA, New Orleans, LA, Tucson, AZ, St. Louis, MO, Alexandria, VA, Santa Barbara, CA and Vancouver, B.C.

Fig. 3. Diné College and Winona State University Students recording Louva Dahozy for the 2015 Navajo Oral History, May 28, 2015, Fort Defiance, Arizona. L-to-R: Tobias Mann, WSU, Kaitlyn Haskie, DC, Reagan Johnson, WSU, Casie Rafferty, WSU. Image by Miranda J. Haskie and Tom Grier.

Fielding Graduate University came to the Navajo Nation in 1996 in efforts to recruit the first cohort of Navajo Nation students. Fielding began a Doctorate in Educational Leadership and Change (ELC) led by Dr. Willie DeMarcell Smith, Dean of the School of ELC. The first cohort officially began in 1998 (Witt and Four Arrows, 2005). I was a member of the first Navajo Nation cohort with Fielding. Instrumental to this important beginning was the collaboration between multiple partners—Office of Navajo Nation Scholarship and Financial Assistance (ONNSFA), Division of Diné Education (DODE), the Office of the President and Vice President of the Navajo Nation and Fielding.

My decision to pursue a graduate degree in higher education had been a personal goal since the completion of my undergraduate degree, a Bachelor of Arts in Sociology from the University of New Mexico-Albuquerque, NM

Fig. 4. 6th Annual Navajo Education Conference, July 28, 2022, Navajo Nation
Museum, Window Rock, AZ. L-to-R: Dr. Henry Fowler, Navajo Nation
President Jonathan Nez, Barsine Onyenedo, Dr. Miranda J. Haskie.
Image by Miranda J. Haskie.

in 1991. Like many Navajos, I was homesick while earning my college degree away from home, the Navajo Nation. Home for me is Lukachukai, Arizona in the heart of the Navajo Nation. There were many times that I longed to return home to the beautiful valley of Lukachukai between two mountain ranges of the Lukachukai Mountains and the Chuska Mountains.

As Diné people, we are rooted in our home community. I was rooted in my home community of Lukachukai, Arizona. In the meantime, to quell my intense homesickness, *shimasaní* (maternal grandmother), Ethnobah Sandoval would visit me periodically at my University of New Mexico (UNM) dorm room. I would help her make the flight of stairs to my second floor dorm room. We would spend the day visiting, at times present in the calming silent company of each other. *Shimasaní* would remind me that both my parents had earned their undergraduate degrees and I, too, would earn my college degree. By the end of those visits, I felt renewed in spirit and promised to trudge forward. I cannot underestimate how significant *shimasani's* visits were and the indelible memory they left about how important education was to her and my family. While Navajos were informally educated, the period of colonization mandated formal education.

Following the treaty of 1868, the Navajos were compelled to send their children to western schools. Federal boarding schools would be constructed across the Navajo reservation and the United States to carry out the mandate (Young, 1957). While the Navajo people were allowed to return home amongst the four sacred mountains (King, 2018), it was on the condition that they would compel the western education of their children. There were no schools on the Navajo reservation, and in the 1868 treaty, Article 6, the United States agreed to provide schoolhouse(s) for the Navajo children (Acrey, 1978). At first, the formal education of Navajo children would be provided by missionaries and boarding schools run by the federal government (Iverson & Roessel, 1992). Thus, many Navajo families sent their children away for a western education. That, too, had been my plight; I was sent away to school. The homesickness from being sent away for school would ensue.

Upon my return after earning my undergraduate degree, I came home to Lukachukai, Arizona. I immediately knew I never wanted to leave home again. Yet, I desired a graduate degree from an accredited university. I also recognized I did not want to move away again to attend another university in residence. In came Fielding, when the ELC program began recruiting the first cohort of the Navajo Nation. This recruitment was led by Farren Webb and Dr. Gary Knight, faculty emeriti from Fort Lewis College (Haskie, 2021). As faculty members of the Navajo Nation Teacher Education Consortium in which Navajo Nation President, Peterson Zah, made the 1991 proclamation of 1000 Navajo Teachers by the Year 2000, Webb and Knight's efforts went beyond to include Education Doctorates who could lead Navajo schools (Cabral, 1996 and Schnaiberg, 1994).

At Fielding, I discovered a unique pedagogical approach. I was accustomed to Western formal education that dictated what pupils should learn with a regimented timeline to complete—a very linear approach. When I arrived at Fielding, it was the exact opposite. I came in asking Fielding faculty what to learn. Fielding faculty asked me a novel question, "what do you want to learn, Miranda?" I was stumped; I had never been asked what I wanted to learn in my formal education experience. A paradigm shift occurred in which I was in control of my doctoral journey and my dissertation study. This pedagogical approach meld perfectly with the Navajo concept of *T'áá hó ájit'éego* (self-direction). It relegates responsibility to the individual, in this case, self-responsibility for my doctoral education. Self-directed learning was a key aspect in Fielding's distributive learning model of online education. Next, I contemplated my dissertation study.

I recalled in high school how I was periodically asked to write a research paper about my hero or role model. I would research the school library for books about Navajos. At the time, I did not find any published biographies nor autobiographies of Navajos. I soon discovered the significant contribution *shicheii* (maternal grandfather), Albert G. "Chic" Sandoval, Sr. made as an interpreter and translator of the Navajo language and co-researcher of Navajo studies with numerous non-Navajo researchers. Yet, there was no publication about his contribution. Researching his significant contribution became my dissertation study.

The design of my dissertation study was led by my discovery of the research methodology, Grounded Theory (Glaser, 1978). Dr. Odis Simmons and Dr. Toni Gregory, Fielding faculty and Research Faculty on my dissertation committee, taught the qualitative research method of grounded theory. Since my paradigm shift about self-directed learning, it made complete sense to generate my own theory as opposed to verifying existing theory. In grounded theory, researchers discover the core variable that simultaneously identifies and solves the problem the participant(s) in the study are experiencing. I utilized grounded theory to discover the problem that *shicheii* Albert G. "Chic" Sandoval, Sr. was experiencing and how he resolved that problem.

In the 20th century, colonization and the assimilationist policy thrust the Navajo people into a monolingual world of English and western education. The problem *shicheii* Albert G. "Chic" Sandoval, Sr. experienced because of the assimilationist policy was how to preserve *Diné bizaad* (the Navajo language), and culture of the *Diné* for posterity. Based upon my dissertation study, I generated the grounded theory and my dissertation title, "Preserving a Culture: Practicing the Navajo Principles of *Hózhó dóó K'é*" (Haskie, 2002). Most dissertations have five chapters, my dissertation had four chapters. Four is a sacred number for the Diné. Chapter two would be the discussion of my research methodology while chapter three would cover both the results of my study and the review of the literature. My dissertation study included data from primary sources and participant interviews as secondary sources. In the data, I identified codes and themes resulting in the grounded theory generated. The impact of my research has added to the literature on Navajo studies. I have been cited by fellow researchers on the Navajo principles of *hózhó, k'é, nitsáhakéés, nahat'á, iiná, sihasin* and the Navajo philosophy of *Sa'ah Naaghái Bik'eh Hózhóón*. I have presented the results of my dissertation study at many professional conferences including the Navajo Studies Conference, Inc. (now the Diné Studies Conference, Inc.), the School of American Research in Santa Fe, NM, southwest colleges and universities, and now with the annual Navajo Education Conference hosted by Fielding and the Navajo Nation. In addition, I have published my dissertation study results in several scholarly publications. My most recent publication was the book, *The Future of Navajo Education* (2021), published by Fielding University Press.

Earlier, I emphasized how rooted I was in my home community of Lukachukai. I have been fortunate to spend my career at Diné College, the higher education institution of the Navajo Nation. Diné College is located in Tsaile, Arizona, about twelve miles away from my home. I am a mother and grandmother. I am an educator, a lifelong learner and mentor many students in pursuit of their undergraduate and graduate education. As faculty at Diné College in the School of Business and Social Science, I have taught Sociology for over twenty years. The minimum educational credential of faculty is a graduate degree. Fielding has helped me secure a faculty position, continue my research interests, and publish my research results.

I continue to research and publish. I co-led the Navajo Oral History

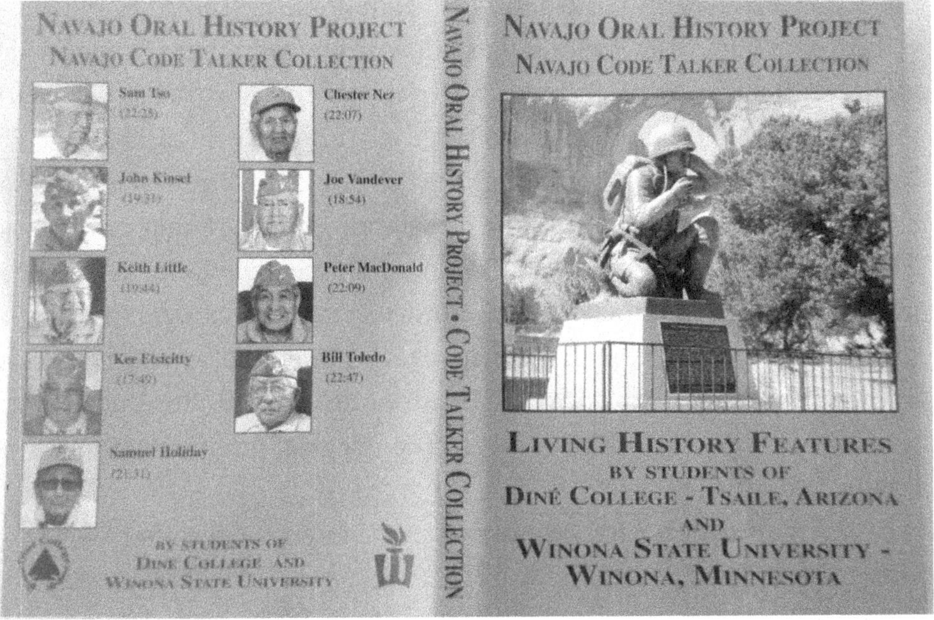

Fig. 6. Navajo Code Talker Collection, Navajo Oral History Project with Diné College and Winona State University, 2017. Image by Miranda J. Haskie.

project for six years from 2009 – 2015 in partnership with Winona State University in Winona, Minnesota. Twenty-seven (27) Navajo living history documentaries were collected by students from Diné College and Winona State University. Nine of these living history documentaries are of the famed Navajo Code Talkers (Shreve, 2014).

The significance of this research is invaluable to the Navajo Nation. In 2012, the Smithsonian Museum of the American Indian archived all of these living history documentaries (Shreve, 2014). These Navajo living history documentaries will be available for posterity. I also partnered with my colleague from Northampton Community College in Bethlehem, Pennsylvania to collaborate on an Intercultural Exchange with students from both of our campuses. Students spent one week on each campus and lived with families engaging in an intercultural exchange and building long-lasting friendships (Shreve, 2013). Recently, I co-authored a chapter with my son, Albert, entitled, "An Intergenerational Journey of Preserving the Navajo Language" in the book *The Future of Navajo Education*.

My doctorate from Fielding has allowed me to remain rooted in my home community of Lukachukai, Arizona on the Navajo Nation. With my doctorate, I transitioned into a full-time faculty position. In 2019, I was ranked Professor of Sociology in the School of Business and Social Science. My career interests are the preservation of the Navajo culture and *Diné bizaad* (Navajo language), education and research while my personal interests are family, home and community. It was especially important to raise my children at home in Lukachukai so they, too, would be rooted in their community. My doctorate in Educational Leadership and Change enabled me to pursue both my career and personal interests without ever leaving home again.

I am an advocate for education and a higher education degree. I encourage both my family and students to pursue their college degrees. The Navajo Nation increasingly requires college degrees as minimal educational credentials for employment and thus I continue to recommend a college degree. I co-facilitate with Dr. Henry Fowler, Fielding alum, the third Navajo Nation cohort pursuing their doctorate in ELC from Fielding. The dissertation studies of my Navajo colleagues and I are rich in Navajo culture, education and leadership. The book *The Future of Navajo Education* (Haskie, Mink and Tiner, 2021) is evidence of the scholarship of Navajo Fielding scholars as practitioners in the field. In the Fielding ELC program, "we use the scholar, practitioner, activist. They are using the scholarship to inform the practice, and the practice informs their scholarship, but they are going to be doing something with it. They are going to be making a difference. It is not just learning for learning sake, it is that scholar, practitioner, activist. This collaboration illustrates that" (Mink in Llewellyn, et.al., 2023, 36:09). Rogers (2022) affirms how "Research that poses new ideas or reveals insights helps us deepen our practice" (p. 1). So, too, are the dissertation studies by Fielding Navajo doctoral students. Many of these alumni continue their work across the Navajo Nation in education and leadership serving the Diné people. Like the Navajo Nation Teacher Education Consortium graduates, they are fulfilling Navajo Nation President Peterson Zah's vision "later on, they will become principals, administrators, and superintendents, and they

Fig. 7. 6th Navajo Education Conference, July 28, 2022, Navajo Nation Museum, Window Rock, AZ. L-to-R: Dr. Perphelia Fowler, Dr. Miranda J. Haskie, Dr. Henry Fowler, Dr. Michelle Tsosie, Dr. Rolanda Billy, Dr. Martha Guy, Barsine Onyenedo, Velma Hale. Image by Miranda J. Haskie.

will continue to make a difference" (Cabral, 1996, p. 1).

If I had to do it over again, I would not change a single thing. My Fielding experience has been very rewarding; first as a doctoral student and now as a professional facilitating the third cohort of Navajo doctoral students. I recall how instrumental Dr. Jenny Edwards was as chair of my Dissertation Committee. The support by faculty at Fielding is immeasurable. I strive to make similar efforts as I co-facilitate the third cohort of Navajo students of whom 30% have now graduated.

Fielding remains on the cutting edge of research and teaching, a leader in online education. I especially appreciated how the faculty at Fielding were practitioners in the field sharing their latest scholarly research and practice as they mentored doctoral students. Fielding extends a warm, inviting atmosphere to all its students as they embark upon their doctoral journey. As a lifelong learner, Fielding is a place I frequent. I feel privileged to be part of an amazing group of education leaders.

References

Acrey, B.P. (1978). *Navajo history: The land and the people.* Development of Curriculum Materials Development.

Cabral, E. (1996). "Navajo Teachers are Taking Off: From the Ford Foundation Report." *Education Digest* 62(4), 54-49.

Fielding Graduate University. (2019, Oct. 28). In honor of American Indian Heritage Month, Navajo alum Miranda Jensen Haskie, Ed.D., 2002. Retrieved April 30, 2023 from: https://www.fielding.edu/preserving-navajo-culture-an-alum-reflects-back/. Fielding University Press.

Glaser, B. G. (1978). *Theoretical sensitivity: Advances in the methodology of grounded theory.* The Sociology Press.

Haskie, M.J. (2023, Feb. 20). [Review of the book *Transforming Diné Education: Innovations in Pedagogy and Practice,* by P. Vallejo & V. Werito (Eds.)]. Tribal College Journal, Volume 34, No. 3, Spring 2023. Retrieved April 30, 2023 from: https://tribalcollegejournal.org/transforming-dine-education-innovations-in-pedagogy-and- practice/

Haskie, M.J. (2021). The Navajo Nation and Fielding partnership. In M. Haskie, B. Mink, & K. Tiner (Eds.), *The future of Navajo education.* Fielding University Press.

Haskie, M. J. (2002). *Preserving a Culture: Practicing the Navajo Principles of Hózhó dóó Ké.* Fielding Graduate University.

Iverson, P. and Roessel, M. (Eds.). (2002). *"For Our Navajo People:" Diné Letters, Speeches & Petitions, 1900-1960.* University of New Mexico Press.

King, F. (2018). The Earth Memory Compass: Diné Landscapes and Education in the Twentieth Century. University Press of Kansas.

Llewellyn, M.J., McMahon, P. and Piantanida, M. (2023, February 9). *A Partnership between the Navajo Nation and Fielding Graduate University with Guests Miranda J. Haskie and Barbara Mink.* https://podcasts.apple.com/us/podcast/speaking-of-education-podcast/id1615634116?i=1000603873943

Rogers, K. (2022). Fielding Focus Magazine: Scholar-Practitioner, July 2022

Issue. *Fielding Focus Magazine*. Fielding Graduate University. Retrieved April 28, 2023 from https://www.fielding.edu/focus-magazine-scholar-practitioner-july-2022-issue/

Schnaiberg, L. (1994). "'Homegrown' Bilingual-Ed. Teachers Take Root." *Education Week*. https://www.edweek.org/teaching-learning/homegrown-bilingual-ed-teachers-take-root/1994/03

Shreve, B. (2014). Miranda Haskie: Preserving Living History at Diné College. Tribal College Journal of American Indian Higher Education. Volume 25, No. 3. Spring 2014. Retrieved April 28, 2023 from: https://tribalcollegejournal.org/miranda-haskie-preserving-living-history-dine-college/

Shreve, B. (2013). Northampton Community College students explore culture at Diné College. Tribal College Journal of American Indian Higher Education. Retrieved April 28, 2023 from: https://tribalcollegejournal.org/northampton-community-college-students-explore-culture-dine-college/

Witt, J. and Arrows, F. (2005). Collaborative Action Learning and Leadership: A Feminist/Indigenous Model for Higher Education 3(3): 16-17. Academic Leadership: The Online Journal. https://scholars.fhsu.edu/cgi/viewcontent.cgi?article=1074&context=alj (accessed January 24, 2021).

Young, R.W. (1957). *The Navajo Yearbook*. U.S. Bureau of Indian Affairs Navajo Agency.

My Fielding Story

Pauline M. Begay
Alum

The Fielding Graduate University is a unique university. I've had a great experience while learning about the university and its faculty. It has instilled in me the opportunity to search for a goal of becoming a Doctor of Educational Leadership. I really surprised myself, going this far with my educational endeavor. Let me first explain how my educational journey began in my earlier years. My introduction will tell you where I'm coming from, who I am, and why I took this educational journey.

I will introduce myself in my own cultural way. As a Native American, Navajo, we have four clans that we introduce ourselves. The clans come from my mother, father, paternal grandfather and maternal grandfather. Therefore, I am of the Bitterwater clan, (Todich'iinii, my mother's clan), born for House in a Row clan (Kin Naazt'i'ii, my father's clan). My paternal grandfather's clan is Red Across the Forehead (Tachii'nii) and my maternal grandfather's clan is the Pueblo Hopi. I was born at home 75 years ago, at a place called Flatrock in Nazlini, Arizona. Nazlini is a very rural area between Chinle and Ganado, Arizona. I grew up without my parents because my mother passed away after she gave birth to me, and my father left for a job somewhere I did not know. My maternal grandparents, and my aunts took care of me as an infant, and as a toddler. As soon as I could walk, my paternal aunt came to my grandmother, and asked if she could take care of me. From there on, I lived with my paternal aunt. She lived in a hogan, with her husband. They had many sheep and goats. She taught me how to herd sheep and goats. As a young child, I learned a lot about animals (sheep, goats, lambs, kid goats, and horses). My younger days before starting school, was very educational to me as I learned about my environment, earth, sky, clouds, stars, plants, trees, rocks, animals, insects, lizards, dirt, sand, etc. I had the early science education per se. When I turned 6 years old, my paternal aunt enrolled me in a Bureau of Indian Affairs Day school. I had to ride in a grayish colored B.I.A. vehicle daily. There was no bus at the time. Our school was a log cabin house with wooden floor, tables and chairs. We were called Beginners, not like the Kindergarteners today. Our teacher, I remembered, was trying very hard to teach us the English language, but we did not understand her, as we were all dominant Navajo speakers, and not exposed to the English language yet. The only thing I remember learning at that time, was counting numbers, and she would punish us if we couldn't count to 100. We listened to her read a book called See Spot Run. We were unfamiliar with the characters in the book. She would tell us to speak English if we tried to speak our language. We didn't know very many English vocabulary, except what she said, we imitated her. She would hit our palms with a ruler if she caught us speaking Navajo. After a year, a school building was established for us and we started our elementary grades from first to third grade. It was a B.I.A. boarding school, so I stayed with the other children. After I completed the third grade, I was transported to Sawmill, Arizona, where my father was remarried and lived there. It was a whole new environment, but gladly, my adopted grandmother who lived there had sheep and goats. I felt happy to see the livestock and I helped herd the sheep after school and weekends.

I was enrolled in a public school, Fort Defiance Elementary School in Fort Defiance, Arizona, which was located 14 miles away from our home. I had to walk a mile to catch the school bus through rain or snow. The public school taught me more about the various subjects that entailed the Language arts, science, geography, physical education, and history. However, everything was taught in the English language. As a Navajo dominant speaker, I had to adjust to the school environment, and the students that I encountered. Most of the students spoke English, and not Navajo. I did complete my middle school years there. Thereon, my adopted grandmother enrolled me in another B.I.A. boarding school, Sherman Institute in Riverside, California. I learned about another environmental setting located in a city. There were many different tribal students such as the Hopi, Apache, Navajo, Pima, Papago, Walapai, Hualapai, and other California tribal students who attended Sherman. We graduated in 1966 as the first graduates from Sherman High School. It was no longer a 4-year vocational school called Sherman Institute. From there on, I started my higher education with various colleges and universities.

My educational journey with higher education began with a two-year attendance at Brigham Young University of Provo, Utah in 1966-68. I graduated with a B.A. degree in Elementary Education from Prescott College, Prescott, Arizona in 1995. Then, I graduated with a Master's degree in American Indian Educational Leadership from Oklahoma City University of Oklahoma City, Oklahoma in 1997. Finally, I graduated with a Doctorate Degree in Educational Leadership from the Fielding Graduate University of Santa Barbara, California in 2002. My employment began in 1971 beginning with the Headstart Program on the Navajo reservation. As I've worked with many programs, and schools, I've always continued to attend various colleges and, finally universities. I've also worked with various K-8 schools on the Navajo reservation in various capacities.

My interest has always been teaching young children our language and culture. My work experiences in various educational systems started in 1971 and have been over 41 years. I was a preschool/Head Start teacher, elementary school teacher, middle school teacher, principal education specialist, teacher/school administrator, teacher/resource instructor within the various schools on the Navajo reservation. The most prestigious job I have had was the Apache County Superintendent of Schools, overseeing 10 public school districts in the State of Arizona, Apache County. Apache County is one of the 13 counties in Arizona, located northeast of Arizona. Half of Apache County is the Navajo reservation. To this day, I am serving as a consultant to my communities, schools, and at times, called upon for meetings and conferences.

My main interest is educating young children in our Navajo language and culture. I've been a paraprofessional educator in Head Start program, in public schools and in the BIE (Bureau of Indian Education) schools. In the school systems, I have taught my own Navajo language, my culture, my tradition, my songs, history, and the arts. I was very concerned about our Navajo children not learning our Navajo language and culture as much as they would maintain and preserve, so I took it upon myself to see how I can make a difference in their learning. As I began my formal education, I had always used singing songs with children in my Navajo language. I needed to further explore ways or methods on how to teach our children, our language and culture more effectively. I wanted to make a difference in our children's learning our language and culture.

One day, I was reading the Navajo Times publication. As I read the paper, I saw the Fielding Institute (name at the time) offered a doctoral program. It was at that point, I decided to explore the offer. After submitting all the entry requirements, I was accepted to participate in a Navajo Cohort doctoral program. It was very interesting to have participated in a cohort setting with our advisors. At first, I was very curious about what the expectations were in pursuing a doctorate degree. I felt overwhelmed at first, but with the assistance of our advisors, the Fielding staff, and cohort support, I became more confident to begin my studies.

I was a teacher in a B.I.E. Elementary School, with the 2nd graders, a one room classroom with 17 students. I decided to tackle a Teacher Action Research instead of the experimental research with a control group, per se. I titled my dissertation, "Drum and Sing Out the Language." My main interest was to teach young children our Navajo language, to revitalize our Navajo language, with my second graders through singing Navajo songs. The second graders in my study were mostly Navajo students, and they spoke more in the English language. I began by designing a Teacher Action Research study by focusing on some research questions. These questions were 1. What changes will occur in the students' ability to speak the Navajo language? 2. What changes will occur in the students' attitudes toward singing Navajo songs? 3. What changes will occur in the students' attitudes toward speaking the Navajo language? 4. What changes will occur in their pronunciation of the Navajo language? 5. What changes will occur in their comprehension of the Navajo language? I gave each student a pre language assessment to determine to what extent they knew the Navajo language. I also gave the students a post language assessment at the end of my research.

The pre and post interviews were given to the parents of students, as well as the Homeroom teacher at the school. Rather than hashing out my whole dissertation, I would like to highlight some discoveries that I've found most interesting. These are: 1. Students speaking some Navajo language, 2. Students pronouncing the Navajo words, 3. Students trying to comprehend or understand the Navajo words in the songs, 4 Students attitude while singing the Navajo songs.

First, students speaking some Navajo language depended on how they were raised at home by their parents, grandparents, or guardians. Six out of seventeen parents reported they spoke Navajo with their children all the time, while others reported less Navajo language in their homes. Only one parent reported she did not speak Navajo at all. Secondly, students pronouncing some Navajo words were mostly in singing the Navajo words. Although some words were difficult to say, but when singing it in songs, the students tried to pronounce the difficult Navajo words; for an example, the word for horse (lii') in the Animal song. The first letter is slashed "l", the vowel "ii" is long, with high tone, and nasalized. At the end of the word is the glottal stop sign, much like an apostrophe ('). The Navajo language has 24 different vowel sounds. We call it short vowels (a,e,i, and o). The long vowels are double letters such as aa, ee, ii, oo. To add different sounds, there are high tones and nasalized tones with the short and long vowels. There are 15 single letters or consonants and there are at least 8 dipthongs such as hw, kw, zh, ts, etc.

The Navajo language do not have English language letters such as c, f, q, r, v and u. The Navajo language do not have English language dipthongs such as th, wh, cl and gl. When the students were learning the songs, some Navajo words were very difficult for them to pronounce at first. I used short Navajo songs with the students such as the Animal song, Moccasin song, Bluebird song, Hokii Pokii, etc. Some songs were in the tune of nursery songs that they were familiar with. Thirdly, students tried to understand or comprehend what they were singing about in the songs. In the students' home setting, some of them had animals at their homestead such as sheep, goats, cattle and horses. Those students who had livestock at their homes were more understanding of naming animals in the song while the rest who did not until it was introduced to them. The Moccasin song had to be introduced to the students using the real Navajo moccasins, both the male and female moccasins. The female moccasin has leggings that is wrapped around the legs while the male moccasins do not. This is where the students learn the words, my moccasins, (shikee'). Fourthly, the students' attitude toward singing the Navajo songs were, at first, they were shy, and embarrassed. They were puzzled whether to sing or not. However, what made their attitude changed, was the use of authentic musical instruments such as a drum, rattles or gourds, bells, and rasp; the use of the nursery song tunes but the lyrics were in the Navajo language; and finally, the students making their own short Navajo songs.

I know that my research study, *Drum and Sing Out the Language* made a difference in having the second graders learn the Navajo language through singing Navajo songs. After my studies, I had 2 song albums produced for the Navajo children to learn. It's called, 'To All Our Precious Ones' and 'Dahwiitaal' (We are Singing). I was awarded the Native American Music Award for the first album and the second album was nominated later. Therefore, the albums are made available throughout the schools on the Navajo reservation. It is also worldwide. If you google the albums, you will find it online. Today, there are reservation schools where the teachers are using the song albums to teach their students. The students are singing Navajo songs at their special programs, and community gatherings. There are also many young lady singers today, I know that there is an impact made in learning the Navajo language through songs and singing with children.

My intellectual journey began with herding sheep and goats as a young child, spoke my Navajo language, attended both B.I.A. and public schools, attended various colleges and universities. Most of all, I attended the Fielding Graduate University for my doctorate degree through a Cohort setting. Cohort meetings, and Fielding in-services were very helpful to continue to focus on my study. My doctorate degree has opened doors to see the worldwide view, instead of seeing things just under my very nose. I remembered one of my elders use to say, " Look beyond and just don't look under your nose. There is something out there." My degree has helped me in many ways such as becoming a member of the National Indian Education

Association which I served for 3 years, and other educational associations in the State of Arizona while I was a County Schools Superintendent. I know that my personal and professional career has been enhanced while studying at the Fielding Graduate University. The university has given me the opportunity that I can go beyond my potential and challenge myself to meet my goal as a professional educator. All the better to have Navajo students learn and revitalize the Navajo language one way or another that once was not allowed. My research study is the beginning and foundation for someone who can continue to study and go further into an advanced research.

I know now that obtaining a higher education degree is important, and that I would advise the younger generation students, especially our Native American students, our Navajo students to continue and strive for their goals and excellence in obtaining their educational degree. It may be financially expensive; however, I am sure there are scholarships that are available, such as the Fielding Graduate University that assisted with scholarships.

The Fielding Graduate University is a unique university based on distance educational programs. I know now that they provide an exemplary interdisciplinary programs and learning models grounded in student-driven inquiry to enhance the knowledge of scholar practitioners such as I. I feel very grateful and thankful to this university for the challenge provided me to obtain my degree. I really surprised myself that I could do this, and that there is no other way I would have done it. I thank the faculty at Fielding for their guidance, and encouragement to complete my dissertation, Drum and Sing Out the Language.

Presently, I have my family with six grown children, 15 grandchildren and 3 great grandchildren. They are all on their own, making their own living which I am proud to be a mother, grandmother, and great grandmother.

My Experience at Fielding

Henry Fowler

Professor of Mathematics,
Navajo Technical University, Crownpoint, NM

I was raised by my mother Sally Fowler who is the Navajo matriarch of our family. Her clan is Bitterwater, todích'íí'nii. I am a Bitterwater who my mother indicated it is one of four original clan group formed by the Navajo Deity, Changing Woman. The clan group of your mother side brings fruit of learning the knowledge, skills and tradition that has been passed on by generations of the Bitterwater clan group. The clan instills relations and interconnection with your environment. A clan is a family that shapes and nurtures an individual to be a whole person. I came to Fielding Graduate University to pursue my doctoral degree. Fielding Graduate University is my family clan group.

I am very grateful that I had the opportunity to experience a wealth of education through Fielding Graduate University. Fielding provided me an education that was practical, meaningful, and relevant. The Educational Leaders and Change curriculum was suitable for me and it was tailored to my needs. The schooling I received at Fielding is closely correlated with the teaching of the Navajos. In the Navajo culture, our elders illuminate their teaching based on the notion that is up to an individual to be a self-directed learner, to find balance, and to produce positive experiences that will improve quality of life for everyone. Fielding's similar emphasis on self-direction to create positive experiences has allowed me to extend my knowledge in areas of my interest to me and to explore and integrate other theories to expand my perspective in education. Fielding was open to and supportive of my cultural background. This support has allowed me to strive for more in-depth study as I had completed my graduate work in Educational Leadership and Change at Fielding Graduate University. Fielding allowed me to thrive from the comfort of my cultural environment. For this reflective paper, I will discuss my background and my journey as a learner through the curriculum of Educational Leadership and Change at Fielding. I will show how three knowledge areas, Action Research, Systems Thinking, and Leadership added new dimensions to my perspective as an educator and helped me grow as a math teacher.

Background

In 1972, I was sent to a Bureau of Indian Education (BIA) boarding school in Kaibeto, Arizona. In order to receive a formal American education, I had to leave my homestead in Tuba, Arizona, at the age of four years old. This was the only option for my family because we lived in a rural area where our life was around farming and livestock. My formal education at the BIA school was far different than my informal Navajo education I had received at home. The education I experienced at the BIA school was foreign to me and far removed from the familiarity and practicality of my home teaching. The BIA school provided basic academic classes in learning grammar, arithmetic, penmanship, and spelling. In addition, I attended a supplemental class that included correct table manners when eating. My formal education journey consisted of many challenges that included learning the English language. In grade school I was labeled as a special education student, and I was taught to leave behind my tradition and culture in order to acquire the formal American education. The concept of being bi-cultural was not an option. Today, I am using my experiences to create change in the education system, particularly in mathematics. I believe the Navajo people can acquire an excellent education that embraces the Navajo culture. I am dedicated to improving the living condition for my Navajo people and have made it my mission through the quality of re-envisioned math education for native learners.

Action Research

The action research knowledge area has expanded my knowledge in education and given me new insight into math education. As an educator, I have searched and sought new practices to improve teaching and learning in math education. The foundation of action research reminded me of a colorful art piece, which consists of colors that are intricately balanced and harmonized. This knowledge area proved significant in guiding me to look at the art of my teaching.

Fielding's focus on the art of teaching brought me back to my Native land. I was challenged to study and investigate curriculum as it related to my native population and create new approaches that could make a difference in the lives of young Navajo people. Even though I have long been motivated to teach math, throughout the years of my teaching career, I began to have mixed feelings about teaching math. My enthusiasm about teaching math had begun to lessen. Each year in my math classes, I observed my students who were quiet and unmotivated to learn mathematics. My teaching was unattractive to them and they found my questions meaningless. My daily challenge was to teach math to students who lacked knowledge of basic math facts, were unmotivated, had high absenteeism and tardiness, were unprepared for class, lacked parental support, lacked current math books, had no access to technology, had high class enrollment, and were disruptive. The sum of these reasons weighed heavily on me, and my passion for teaching began to stall. Fortunately, my enrollment at Fielding afforded me a new platform for thinking critically about my teaching experience. The application of action research and other inquiry methods has lead me to discover there are alternative methods available to improve my situation. As a direct result of my work at Fielding, I have made inquiry and gained clear insight about teaching math to Navajo students. This has set the stage for invigorated research about and development of new instructional strategies that have energized my students to learn math and me to teach.

The action research knowledge area allowed me to investigate my own challenges with teaching math and create solutions to fix the problems that I faced daily in my classroom. According to Stringer (1999), action research is a rigorous systematic inquiry through the stakeholders' own lens to study their own unique problems and phenomena. Action research allows the stakeholders to take action in creating a solution for the problem being investigated (Stringer, 1999). Anderson, Herr, and Nihlen (1994) called action research "insider" research. The stakeholders use their own setting as the center of their inquiry (Anderson, Herr & Nihlen, 1994). According to Anderson et al. (1994), action research is a reflective systematic process that allows the stakeholder to investigate a situation and take action. Action research is practical for every level of an organization and it speaks to the concerns of the local people. Action research allows an organization and stakeholders to seek improvement in their everyday activity that will enhance their situation through an alternative method of practice. Teachers can take the initiative in the action research process and search for alternative practices to improve teaching quality and student academic proficiency in the content areas.

As an educator, I am searching for better alternative math pedagogy and learning to improve my instruction and student outcome. I find myself in a situation filled with doom and gloom reports that show how high school Native American students are stagnating in their math proficiency. The accountability of No Child Left Behind (2001) has challenged schools to close the achievement gap of all demographics through standardized testing. The Arizona Department of Education (2009) reported that two of seven of the Title I (98 percent Navajo) high schools on the Navajo Reservation were 57 percent proficient on the Arizona math benchmarks, while the other five were 50 percent below proficient in meeting the Arizona math benchmarks. Furthermore, U.S. Census Bureau (2000) points out that 55 percent of the Navajos are unemployed. The performance of Navajo high school students on the math standardized test needs to be improved in order to ameliorate the situation of the high unemployment rate on the Navajo Reservation.

Fielding helped open the opportunity for me to address the dismal outlook of the Navajo high school poor performance in mathematics. As a direct result of the Fielding curriculum, I am more aware of my surroundings and how they impact teaching delivery and reception. I bring an enlivened critical thinking mindset to my intellectual endeavors, and I feel empowered as a teacher to lead efforts to change the math education on the Navajo Reservation. I am encouraged to broaden the perspective of my immediate horizon and challenged to actively pursue my interest in improving math education for Navajo students. The Fielding approach to learning engaged me and afforded me learning experiences which were was relevant and meaningful.

My area of inquiry is to change how math education is delivered to the Navajo high school students. I used action research to investigate an alternative method of pedagogy based on my perspective as a Navajo educator. My goal was to improve the math education at Navajo Reservation high schools. My inquiry was reflective and articulated to improve my situation. Mills (2003) noted that action research is a systematic inquiry conducted by teachers in using their own setting to improve student outcome. According to Mills (2003), inquiries are based on gaining insight, utilizing reflective practice, and creating a positive educational change practice to improve lives of the people involved. Stringer (1999) believed that action research helps an everyday person to realize their talent and take action by using a research based approach in addressing their problem. Stringer helped me realize that an ordinary person like me can use action research to resolve the problems that I face in my professional world. Stringer (1999) described action research as a natural extension of an ordinary person's life or activity that they are engaged in on a daily basis. Stringer (1999) also helped me clarify that action research is a spiral process of inquiry that starts with a simple frame of complexity and progresses to a more sophisticated procedure as the complexity increases through "look, think, act" (p. 18). According to Stringer, "look" symbolizes gathering all relevant data to understand the big picture; "think" is associated with analyzing, interpreting, and explaining the data and its theoretical frameworks; and "action" charges the formulation of a plan to resolve the problem, implement the activity, and evaluate the procedure. Mills (2003) and Anderson et al. (1994) point out that action research is an integral part of school systems, and that research can be initiated by a classroom teacher. Stringer (1999), Mills (2003), and Anderson et al. (1994) have helped me engage in carrying out my individual teacher action research.

Action research gave me a way to objectively look at my data. Numerous reports describe American Indians as disproportional in mathematics (Indian Nations at Risk, 1991, Cheeks, 1989, Arizona Department of Education, 2009). As a Navajo high school teacher, I witness first hand that Navajo high school students lack basic math skills. This is a barrier for student acceleration and excellence in mathematics. I heard repeatedly in staff meetings that Navajo high school students showed no interest in studying mathematics. To remedy this situation, remedial math classes were offered to improve student math skills. In addition, Arizona Instrument to Measure Standards (AIMS) math classes, which specifically target juniors and seniors students who took algebra and geometry but did not pass the Arizona math benchmark tests, were added to the math curriculum. Furthermore, after-school tutoring was offered for students who needed additional math help. Teacher in-service classes to train teachers to improve their teaching strategies were offered. Finally, the school district hired an outside consultant and math coaches to assist in aligning the math curricula to the state standards, all in keeping with the mandate to improve student learning outcomes. Even with all of this effort, math education outcomes for Navajo high school students are still showing no significant improvement.

Action research allowed me to see behind the negative portrayal of math education on the Navajo Reservation. Action research provided me the tools necessary to formulate current, onsite, research based solutions to concerns. Using the insights gained from my action research, I committed myself to take action and formulate a credible plan that would enable me to resolve the detrimental problems faced by the Navajo high school students in their acquisition and command of the Arizona math standardized tests. Corey (1953) described the situation of teachers conducting research as teachers enduring through analyzing and implementing the results of their own research. These teachers are continuing to improve their practices by questioning the entrenched curricula practices. Corey further postulates that this type of onsite research and practice is more rewarding and useful than wholesale adoption of "outside" research and practices. Implementing action research processes has allowed me to review, research, analyze, and reflect on alternative teaching and learning systems that can recharge the energy of my teaching and, simultaneously, re-engage student interest in and ability to conceptualize math principles.

Systems Thinking

Senge, Kleiner, Roberts, Ross, and Smith (1994) pointed out the importance of reflecting on my teaching practices through systems thinking. Systems thinking is the second of the three Fielding knowledge areas which impacted my personal and professional practice. Senge et al. (1994) defined systems thinking as the interrelated whole of elements wherein the elements have a common pattern that works together toward a common purpose. Capra (1996) extended my understanding of systems thinking by relating systems thinking to my background. Capra described systems thinking in the milieu as connection, relationship, and association. Capra also implied that systems thinking was related to living organisms and social systems. In my background, the Navajos view the world as a living system and have a relational connection to it as follows: Earth is "Mother Earth"; Sky is "Father sky"; Darkness is "Grandparents"; and "Sun" is "Father." According to Fowler (2003), the Navajo believe they are in balance and in harmony with the natural order of the universe through these elements (S. Fowler, personal communication, May 20, 2003). For example, the Navajos face their home in the direction of the East to greet the first sun light. The first sun light symbolizes a new beginning that is touched with a beauty from the order of the natural element.

Navajos touch the first sun ray to bless themselves and call on upon it for the wellbeing of oneself, home, family, all life, and the entire universe. Navajos view every aspect of life as a whole and themselves as an integral part of that whole. Life includes tiny insects, rivers, trees, mountains, and canyons – all of which are part of the elements that complete the natural order of the universe. For the Navajos, this phenomenon is an integral part of their life. Fowler (2003) stated that if one element does not exist, then there is no life. Furthermore, Fowler (2003) postulates the Earth is a living being and a living spirit (S. Fowler, personal communication, May 20, 2003). Capra (1996) explained this phenomenon as systems thinking, which is characterized as a whole made up of elements derived by the relationship of its parts. This is also the Navajo way. The insights gained through making the connection between Navajo life and systems thinking motivated me to pursue systems thinking with a passion.

Capra (1996) synthesized that a living system constitutes a whole. A living system is made up of a "pattern of organization and structure" (p. 158). Pattern of organization is the makeup of the relationship of a system that reveals the minutia of a system's characteristics. For example, certain trait relationships that are present in different math content, such as algebra and geometry, are the same as among different aspects of houses, animals, and people (Capra, 1996). Structure is the physical component of the system's pattern of organization. The physical component includes the shape and the nature of the chemical component. The synthesis of these approaches is illustrated in the embodiment of mathematics. The system of mathematics is defined by the configuration of relations of its pattern of organization that is recognized by math symbols as addition, subtraction, multiplication, and division. It is the underlying relationship of these patterns of organization that builds the mathematical structure. Mathematical structure is the relationship of mathematical objects of association, sets, subsets, operations, and relations. Mathematics is a system of language recognized across the globe.

The language of mathematics is referred to as numeracy, and it connects people of all backgrounds. According to D'Ambrosio (2001), mathematics and culture are intertwined systematically. Today, in the United States, mathematics is viewed primarily as the domain of European invention and is interpreted in terms of European values and experiences (D'Ambrosio, 2001). D'Ambrosio (2001), Capra (1996), & Senge et al. (1994) expanded my views on mathematics as systematically interrelated symbols used to convey reasoning to achieve a purpose in life. Their work also caused me to have new insight about looking at mathematics from the point of view of Native American values and experiences. My Navajo background conditioned me to view all aspects of any element as a whole. This was to be a new way of thinking about mathematics for me. Was there a window through which Navajo math students could view and experience math that would prove to be more meaningful and relational for them? Fowler (2003), a

Navajo elder who received no formal American education, emphasized the perspective of the Navajo belief that the system of life is a spiral process web (S. Fowler, personal communication, May 20, 2003). These theories allowed me to begin thinking more critically about the system of mathematics as a whole. D'Ambrosio (2001) studied the complexity of mathematical practice through the cultures of people around the world. His studies point out that mathematics is formed by the participation of all cultures in the world. D'Ambrosio (2001) described the discoveries and invention of mathematics as a "mosaic of cultural contributions" (p. 304). Today, the discipline of mathematics continues to evolve. Systems thinking is a platform that has given me tools to contribute to the expansion of mathematics and mathematics education.

Current mathematics education can be linked to the feedback loop. Capra (1996) described the feedback loop as a circular causal interrelated link of elements in which the first causal spawn around the loop links. Math education has gone through many changes. Souviney (1994) explained that the teaching of mathematics had been dominated by the behavioral systems point of view. The behavioral system perspective posits that learning is acquired through observable behavior which is linked with a loop of written exercises delineated by rote mental practice (Souviney, 1994). The behavioral education curricula are based on the "mechanistic view" which requires systems to be viewed in terms of their parts. Capra (1996) described this phenomena as the analytic thinking method, which "consists in breaking up complex phenomena into pieces to understand behavior of the whole" from the characteristics of the parts (p. 19).

Under the mechanistic view, the whole perspective on math education was replaced with a machine model where man and intelligence were compared to the workings of machines. The mechanistic feedback loop model has been filtering into the math classroom for decades. This model designated the teacher as the main controller and center of the learning environment. Teachers controlled learning in the form of lectures and made all of the decisions about curriculum content and student learning outcomes. They were the main dispensers of knowledge in filling student knowledge gaps. Learning was a one way loop from teacher to students.

The classroom layout reflected this loop of exchange of learning. Students faced their teacher, who was the focal point. The feedback loop model generated formal instruction that mandated students to sit quietly at their desks in straight rows. Students were expected to follow commands and listen to their teachers (Souviney, 1994). Senge et al. (1994) indicated that every system narrates a story based on each element inducing another element. The education based on the traditional model has been depicted and narrated in American education stories for decades. Today, teachers continue to use the traditional educational model to impart knowledge and skills to students and to teach academic content.

From a very young age, I was exposed entirely to the system of the traditional model of teaching. My reactions to the system were a range of emotions accompanied by fear, insecurity, and uneasiness about learning in the Western education "way." My "native" system feedback loop was portrayed very differently from the traditional feedback loop of education. The system of education I was familiar with was systematically embedded with the heritage of the Navajos. My Navajo education consisted of learning cultural values, which included storytelling and respect for the elders. The native learning model comprises 1) relationship with the order of nature; 2) history of the matrilineal clan; 3) social interaction with the surroundings; and 4) learning through modeling, observation, discovery, and doing. These social values are deeply embedded in the Navajo social pattern.

Throughout my formal education, I experienced difficulties learning in the setting of the traditional American teaching because there were no other learning alternatives. Senge et al. (1994) described this phenomenon as the "reinforcing loop" system (p. 116). The reinforcing loop system is characterized by a circle wherein each element in the circle reinforces another to make the system grow. The reinforcing loop system portrays American education as a system dominated and reinforced by the traditional teaching model. As the American education system moves around this loop, students experience their content subjects as separate parts. Teachers, with separate specialties, are drawn into practicing this model as a way to improve the student education.

Investigating Senge et al. (1994) during the course of my studies at

Fielding helped me realize I was contributing to reinforcing traditional education in my classroom. As an educator, I, as well as most teachers on Navajo Reservation, were repeating the traditional methods of instruction. This traditional approach in teaching is reinforced each year, because new teachers fresh out of college are trained in that approach. To their credit, new teachers are called to teach better and leave no child behind, but the basic model remains relatively unchanged. Senge et al. (1994) called this phenomenon the "snowball" effect which has snowballed into every level of American education. The traditional method of teaching is favored by teachers and professors from kindergarten to the university level (p. 116). This system of teaching is reinforced by the production and sales of educational materials and resources designed to support the traditional model perspective of teaching.

The systems thinking knowledge area led me to investigate innovators like Senge et al., and has helped me reinvent my practice of teaching. Through application of Senge et al.'s systems thinking processes, I realized that I needed to re-energize my practice of teaching by bringing a positive spirit of change to teaching math to the Navajo high school students. Senge et al. (1994) referred to stabilizing systems as the "balancing loops" (p. 117). According to Senge et al., balancing loops are mechanisms found in all systems. These balancing loops help "fix problems, maintain stability, and achieve equilibrium" (p. 117) in a system. In their work, Senge et al. (1994) and Capra (1996) have shown that balancing loops sustain a system through a self-regulating process. They also relate their academic systems of self-regulating or self-directing to the same systems found on earth, in life, and in the human body. These balancing loops are essential to the overall characteristics and regulations of a system. They provide a way to stop the vicious spiral phenomenon moving away from a target or goal (Senge et al., 1994).

Examination of the target compels the balancing loops to maintain the course in the range of its goal. If the balancing loops detect a system is off its course, the system generates a gap. When the gap is large, there is great pressure for the system to return to its natural state or to change for the better. As a result of understanding these concepts, I began to examine the math goals for native students in light of the results and to look for the gaps.

The institute of our math education needs a change for the better to suit the demographics of Navajo students. American education is based primarily on the traditional model of teaching and learning, which rarely draws from the perspective of under-represented minority groups. To a large measure, American education has deviated from its "No Child Left Behind" policy and currently, is not meeting the goals for its intended target, which were to close the academic achievement gaps for under-represented minority groups. Included in these goals was a focus on increasing math proficiency so that more of minority group students might have the desire to explore careers in math and science. The current educational system continues to generate achievement gaps between majority and minority students. This is most evident in the academic performance of the American Indians and Alaskan Natives. My own particular concern is for Navajo students. This negative phenomenon is a self-fulfilling process which reflects Senge et al.'s re-enforcement loop. Unfortunately, the structure of the Navajo school system is not meeting the needs of the Navajo high school students in the area of learning mathematics. The teaching methods and curricula are snowballing and creating a learning system for the Navajo high school students where it is becoming more, rather than less, difficult to comprehend the operations of mathematics, such as solving problems that contain complementary and supplementary angles, classifying real numbers, and simplifying numerical expressions using the order of operations.

Navajo schools are caught up in the process of traditional education which Senge et al. referred to as the reinforcement loop. This loop contains the following elements: a) teacher as the main dispenser of knowledge; b) students as passive learners; c) rote learning; d) teaching resources based on a Western (European) paradigm; and e) independent learning. This loop prescribes ineffective learning strategies for Navajo high school students.

Leadership

In order for a system to behave in a new way, the behavior of the system must be guided by effective leadership. Effective leadership must be based on principles of a vision, straightforward values, and belief (Wheatley, 1999). The knowledge area on leadership has broadened my capacity to lead as a teacher by creating a culturally relevant math curriculum that reflects the Navajo community and Navajo knowledge while simultaneously teaching the Arizona math benchmark standards. Gardner (1990) points out that every group in a system has a common purpose with each individual in a different role capacity. One of the capacities is the role of a leader. A leader takes the lead in motivating a group or individual to meet a common goal or to pursue objectives shared with the leader (Gardner, 1999). In my case, a leader is an individual teacher or group of teachers taking action in transforming the math education for Navajo high school students so that school and community cultures are connected with appropriate Navajo based math curriculum. Currently, for the Navajo math education, there is a math curriculum that is not congruent to the Navajo way of life. Unfortunately, most Navajo high school students are taught in a system which is led by the one-way mainstream model of education. Under this system, Navajo high school students are conditioned with a belief in an existence of only one way of learning mathematics where the realities of a native view of mathematics are not acknowledged

My instructional time spent at Fielding Graduate University has awakened in me a new educational vision for Navajo learning and a renewed vigor to carry out my vision. Instead of decrying and becoming disillusioned by the outcomes of traditional educational learning processes for native students, I am now inspired to stop the "snowballing" effect that is preventing Navajo high schools students from receiving effective math education. A new leadership that is innovative in balancing both realms of the students' worlds -- their informal (Navajo) and formal (traditional American) education is required. Senge et al. (1994) described this balancing phenomenon as the "balancing loop."

I have been educating Navajo people in mathematics at the high school level for over 13 years. I believe it is the time for Navajo educators to begin earnestly searching for effective teaching and learning strategies that will balance and harmonize the educational system for our children. During my teaching tenure, I have seen Navajo Reservation school leaders bring in outside school consultants to fix the poor performance of Navajo students in reading and mathematics. After 13 years of using outside expertise in education, the Navajo high school students are lagging even further behind in the meeting the Arizona math benchmarks (Arizona Department of Education, 2010).

The school leaders I have worked with have been pressured each school year to meet the Adequately Yearly Progress (AYP) which was enacted by the No Child Left Behind Act (2001) and now the Arizona Merit and Common Core Math Standards. The act mandated American students be 100 percent proficient in mathematics, reading, and writing by 2014. The traditional path for these school leaders has been to address the school problems by seeking outside influences to stabilize the school system in hopes of providing quality education for students and to become proficient in the common math standards. I want to be an agent for change by being part of the leadership for teachers, principals, superintendents, and community members to come together to create a high school math curricula that reflects the Navajo community, utilizes local knowledge, and creates teaching strategies that connect to real life situations and address the concerns about academic performance in mathematics.

Wheatley (1999) suggests that life teaches us lessons through emerging patterns. The need for reforming math education for native students is emerging across the Navajo Reservation. Wheatley (1999) emphasized that systems of life and organization have behavior associated with patterns. We may select to change behaviors that emerge from a system to affect a new outcome. This new outlook would support new behavior and call for new values and agreement in moving the system in the new direction. Wheatley (1999) indicated that in the new behavior, the stakeholders seek to work together toward new values. To accomplish this task, the stakeholders reflect on their daily activities to resolve any challenges that would deviate away from their change values. The stakeholders must work together to find common ground so as not to fall back into the old patterns of behavior.

May (1999) indicated Native American and Alaskan education needs to revisit how learning is acquired and the outcomes for native students receiving primarily mainstream education. Heifetz (1994) reminded me to imagine leadership as mobilizing activities to accomplish a task. He further defined leadership as an activity which mobilizes around "motivating, organizing, orienting, and focusing" all of which enable a leader to take the lead at any level of the social structure (p. 20). These leadership perspectives, which I learned about in my Fielding courses, have helped me pursue my vision to incorporate my values of teaching by creating supplemental math materials which illustrate teaching mathematics concepts for Navajo high school students. For example, I want to incorporate using Navajo cultural representations such as the Hozho model in teaching supplementary and complementary angles when solving math problems. Hozho is a way of life for the Navajos; it means beautiful, balance, and blessing. Hozho is found in art, nature, ceremony, music, and animal and human kind. It brings the essence of peace, the sacred, and complementary to the people so that they can have a supplementary good life (S. Fowler, personal communication, May 20, 2003).

The Navajos believe they are part of nature, and that this natural order gives directions for life. The Navajos agree their natural surroundings bring the energy of spirit to the people. That energy is infused with purpose and direction for the Navajo people. According to Hozho, the Navajo purpose on this earth is to keep in balance, harmony, and respect with the natural order. A good life resides in every angle of the morning light with a promising sense of beauty, hope, and determination for every individual (S. Fowler, personal communication, May 20, 2003). The Navajo understand, that with a sense of the complementary and supplementary, an individual will feel beauty above, below, around, and before him or her from every angle. The Navajo continue to practice this traditional heritage. Complementary angles are two angles whose angles add up to 90 degrees and supplementary angles are two angles whose angles add up to 180 degrees. Using the Hozho model, this phenomenon could be represented to Navajo learners as 'beauty above me + beauty below me = 90 degrees, and beauty around me + beauty before me = 180 degrees'. I believe it is time for Navajo educators to lead in creating educational math materials for the Navajo high school students to support their mathematical reasoning and communication. This approach to Navajo education would help students realize that math is part of their culture and to inspire students take an interest in appreciating and studying mathematics rather than feeling separate from it and mystified by it. According to Wheatley (1999), time will test how well the stakeholders succeed in establishing the new values. With clear agreement and commitment to purpose, the stakeholders can change the behavior of a system. Wheatley (1999) stated that "we slowly become who we said we wanted to be" (p. 130). This is my hope for the state of math education for the Navajo people.

Summary

Fielding has made a great impact on my personal life and professional practice as a math educator. The Educational Leaders and Change curriculum has broadened my awareness of the complexities and possibilities in education. It has provided me the tools to improve my own personal place of interest, which is to improve the math education for the Navajo high school students. I have humbly gotten a greater appreciation for the traditional model of learning I was exposed to and at the same time I have become awakened to how I can make a change in the math learning curriculum that could awaken and inspire Navajo learners to excel in mathematics. The learning I acquired from Fielding, especially the knowledge areas, provided me with new skills to tackle the problematic issues faced by the Navajo high school students in learning mathematics and succeeding on the standardized tests The staff provided excellent feedback for me to grow and expand my horizons in the scholarly world by recommending stellar literatures to read that related to my interests and field of study. Fielding staff made me feel special because they listened to and valued my opinions. I feel as if I have been nourished after a long draught.

Prior to my coursework at Fielding, I had become discouraged about teaching math. Now, I feel like my life has been renewed. My mind is keen to make good judgments for myself in leading the reform of math education on the Navajo Reservation. The math reform is based on my experiences, input of educators, stakeholders, and the learning I acquired through Fielding. Innovation is the key in making sure that all Navajo students receive an equity education through using cultural relevant math curriculum and motivational techniques such as cultural based math posters. Fielding allows their students to be innovative so they can contribute to the quality life of human kind and society. As a direct result of my Fielding experience, including in depth work in the knowledge areas of action research, systems thinking, and leadership, I walk away with a personal and professional transformation for the better which brings excellence and meaning to my entire life and everything I bring forth in the future.

References

Anderson, G. L., Herr, K., & Nihlen, A. S. (1994). *Studying your own school: An educator's guide to qualitative practitioner research.* Thousand Oaks, CA: Corwin Press, Inc.

Arizona Department of Education. (2009). AIMS result. Retrieved February 18, 2010 from http://www.ade.state.az.us/researchpolicy/AIMSResults/

Capra, F. (1996). *The web of life.* New York, NY: Doubleday.

Cheek, H. N. (1984). A suggested research map for Native American mathematics education. *Journal of American Indian Education, 23*(2), 1-9.

Corey, S. M. (1953). *Action research to improve school practices.* Columbia University, New York: Teacher College, Columbia University.

D'Ambrosio, Ubiratan. (2001). What is ethnomathematics, and how can it help children in schools? *Teaching Children Mathematics, 6,* 308-310.

Gardner, J. W. (1990). *John W. Gardner on leadership.* New York, NY: The Free Press.

Heifetz, R. A. (1994). *Leadership without easy answers.* Cambridge, Massachusetts: The Belknap Press of Harvard University Press.

Indian Nations at Risk. (1991). *Indian nations at risk: An educational strategy for action.* Retrieved March 10, 2010 from http://www2.ed.gov/rschstat/research/pubs/oieresearch/research/natatrisk/report.pdf

May, S. (1999). *Indigenous community-based education.* Philadelphia, PA: Multilingual Matters LTD.

Mills, G. E. (2003). *Action research: A guide for the teacher researcher* (2nd ed.). Upper Saddle River, NJ: Pearson Education, Inc.

No Child Left Behind Act of 2001. (NCLB)-Public Law 107-110. Retrieved January 30, 2008 from http://www.ed.gov/legislation

Senge, P. M., Kleiner, A., Roberts, C., Ross, R. B., & Smith, B. J. (1994). The fifth discipline fieldbook: Strategies and tools for building a learning organization. New York, NY: Doubleday.

Souviney, R. J. (1994). *Learning to teach mathematics* (2nd ed.). New York, NY: Macmillan Publishing Company.

Stringer, E. T. (1999). *Action research* (2nd ed.). Thousands Oaks, CA: Sage Publications, Inc.

U.S. Census Bureau. (2000). Census 2000. Retrieved March 12, 2010 from http://www.census.gov/

Wheatley, M. J. (1999). *Leadership and the new science: Discovering order in a chaotic world* (2nd ed.). San Francisco, CA: Berrett-Koehler Publisher, Inc.

My Journey in Lifelong Learning

Pamela Rutledge
Alum and Faculty,
Fielding Media Psychology Ph.D. Program

I grew up in Claremont, a Southern California college town at the base of the San Gabriel mountains, surrounded, in those days, by orange groves. My Dad ran a middle school program for gifted students. He was also an artist, continually conscious of the way the aesthetics of crafted spaces influenced experience. A devotee of Frank Lloyd Wright, he designed and built our houses with flat roofs, see-through rooms, and decks wrapping around trees. My stepmother was a psychologist. I grew up on Freud's developmental stages, George Kelly's personal constructs, and the therapeutic process with a folk music vibe. In retrospect, it's easy to see how I ended up in media psychology. In high school, I got my first job as a paste-up artist and designer at a local news magazine. What that job has since been replaced by software programs like InDesign, it was a harbinger of things to come.

Armed with an undergraduate degree in studio art from Pomona College, I found out that the skills I had acquired at the news magazine were more marketable than those from the printmaking studio. I worked as a graphic designer and media producer, creating recruiting materials and magazines for academic institutions. I liked the design challenge of every project—how to create media that delivered a satisfying experience within the constraints of the medium and budget. I needed to understand how media created emotion and presence.

To that end, I returned to school, convinced that learning about marketing would give me the tools I needed. I received an MBA from the Drucker Business School at Claremont Graduate University, interrupted by the births of my two girls. Ironically, marketing didn't give me the understanding I had wanted, but areas like finance and leadership gave me hints in the right direction. The most useful aspects of the business curriculum were the things that impacted human behavior. I saw that a myriad of decisions, such as the allocation of costs, leadership behaviors, and reward structures, could influence how people behave. The people who paid for the pencils rarely stole them. Parking spots based on status rather than effort often undermined respect.

Our family relocated from Southern California to Southern Connecticut, 3,000 miles away in distance and culture. I traded in my jeans for khakis and continued to design media presentations and publications part-time around raising kids. As my girls got older, I had the freedom to follow up on what had intrigued me in design and business: psychology. Inspired by my stepmother, I looked for a clinical program. I still had a full host of familial obligations, which made a traditional program that required showing up in person on a campus an hour away unrealistic. I chose Fielding because while it had some residency requirements, the program was largely asynchronous and digital, thanks to the Internet.

I began the clinical program at Fielding, worked at an eating disorders clinic to get practicum hours, and pondered potential dissertation questions. But life often takes unexpected turns, and about halfway through the clinical program, I realized that a clinical path was not compatible with my life demands and withdrew—halting my progress in the degree but not my interest in psychology.

I sometimes say that I got my PhD because of the NBA player Shaquille O'Neal. I have never met him, of course, but one day I came across a news story about Shaquille earning his EDD. It wasn't an honorary one; he actually did the work. This seriously annoyed and inspired me as, despite how busy he clearly was, he had managed to complete his degree, and I had not. In a moment of nostalgia, I revisited Fielding's website. They had just launched the media psychology program. There aren't many times in life when events provide such synchronicity. I reapplied immediately. Media psychology was the perfect blend of psychology and media design.

I graduated with a PhD from Fielding, but didn't ever leave. I taught briefly at UC Irvine Extension Business Program and in the William James College Leadership Psychology Program, but I joined the media psychology faculty at Fielding upon graduation with the launch of the Media Psychology Masters Program. My background prior to the degree was in media design and production, but I am also practical by disposition. I like to see things applied in the real world and have been focused on how media psychology can make a difference in people's lives—whether through education or media design.

The best part about Fielding, although I didn't realize it at the beginning, was not just the flexibility, but the freedom to mold the courses to fit what I wanted to learn and what I thought was important. This was true as a student and is also true as faculty. I designed and taught classes that addressed the development of marketable skills, like audience engagement and brand storytelling.

My degree from Fielding has created a lot of opportunities, but most of them happened from the changes in me, not the diploma on the wall or the Dr. in front of my name. The process of getting a PhD gave me new frameworks for critical thinking and a solid grounding in conducting and analyzing research. I acquired a depth of knowledge about psychological theory, not just one orientation—although we all have our preferred starting points--but a sense of the theoretical landscape that provides multiple lenses to approach questions and problems.

My dissertation topic looked at whether the widespread television and online coverage of the Beijing Olympics would alter Americans' negative opinions about China. Media constructs narratives that can influence our perceptions of the world, ourselves, and others. There was a significant amount of hostility toward China at the time, particularly in the media. Olympics are largely public relations campaigns for the host country to change public opinion or increase tourism. The Olympics coverage is a continual display of hero stories interspersed with personal segments to humanize the athletes, the people and the place. Given most people's lack of familiarity with Chinese culture and the rising public distrust of China as a superpower, I was curious to see if the Olympic spectacles and continual narratives would increase the sense of identification and humanity and decrease perceptions of China as a source of political conflict. The results? Taylor Swift was right. Haters gonna hate. The lesson here is that mental models are sticky, particularly when reinforced with fear.

Has my degree helped me to advance my career? While the specific topic in my dissertation was unrelated to the professional work I do or the courses I teach, the core questions are the same. They boil down to how people construct meaning out of media narratives based on core motivational drivers, from instinctive responses to needs, goals, and desires. This is the strength of applying psychology to media. Media content, tools, and applications change all the time. People, however, do not evolve quickly and are driven by fundamentals, not trends.

My degree has helped advance my career mostly through the strengths, skills, and confidence it gave me. It is fair to say that it is necessary to have a PhD to teach in most institutions of higher education and that a PhD gives you credibility in business settings (not always warranted).

Professionally, I have always had one foot in academia and the other in business. I have been faculty at Fielding since 2009 and have loved the freedom to design courses that fit my passion and have real-world applications. For me, media psychology is an applied field. Nothing makes me happier than a student telling me that a class or an assignment was something they could immediately put to use in their career, inspired a new approach to a problem, or got them a new client.

My most interesting consulting projects have been due to the ability to integrate theoretical and research skills to make sense of data and communicate it in practical terms. Some of the most fun I have had was working with the theatrical marketing team at 20th Century Fox Films for about four years, analyzing social media data in response to movie trailers. Most market research focuses on sentiment rather than narrative analysis. I evaluated the audience's comments to identify underlying narratives that might reveal expectations, intentions, and desires to flesh out the meaning and provide context to make the standard reports more usable.

I have continued research working with students, most recently looking at the impact of virtual exercise environments, such as Peloton, on the perception of belonging. I am biased toward positive media psychology—

the application of positive psychology to media and technology. My basic assumption is that since technology is not going away, we have to learn how to use it well.

While I will continue to research, my upcoming projects are focused on writing. I have contributed chapters on storytelling and narrative, media psychology, and positive media psychology to several handbooks. However, I am working with a former student and colleague, Dr. Scott Garner, to write a book based on the courses I taught on audience engagement, persona development, and brand storytelling based on a project I did with Scott for the Oprah Winfrey Network. My passion project is a monthly digital literacy webinar co-hosted with another alum Diana Graber tackling topics that support parents and teachers in helping kids successfully navigate a digital world.

Degrees are important, especially for women. Whether fair or not, they are society's validation of your effort and add credibility and social capital. The real value, however, is in gaining the critical thinking, analytical and communication skills to solve problems, make your voice heard and create value in the world. The degree may get you in the door, but the skills and knowledge get the work done.

Fielding is and has been my intellectual and professional home for many years. It is an anchor to that part of my identity, having provided a network of colleagues and friends and a host of great memories, from late nights in the bar in Santa Barbara to tearing up while hooding students at graduation. Without Fielding's flexibility and willingness to let each of us find our own lane, I would not have been able to get the PhD that opened the door to all the things that followed.

The Strength and Joy of Collaborative Learning

Leni Wildflower
Alum and Fielding faculty

Whatever the problem, community is the answer.
Margaret Wheatley

When I arrived at Fielding in the early nineties, I immediately sensed that this was like no academic institution I had experienced. To begin with, the instructors wanted to know about me—what I thought, where my learning had come from, why I wanted to embark on graduate-level work, which areas of study I was curious about. I quickly came to appreciate Fielding's unique qualities.

The face-to-face orientation occurred at La Casa Maria Retreat Center in the mountains above Santa Barbara. Accommodation was far from luxurious. We shared rooms with people we did not know. Showers were primitive, with thick paper for bath mats. We ate communally in the dining hall, cafeteria style. But the food was delicious and, more important, the conversations were exciting.

I remember thinking: Am I up to this? Can I do the level of work required? I also wondered if I would be lonely, studying on my own. There was plenty for me to do by myself, reading, reflecting and writing, but I never felt alone. From my first day, Fielding encouraged collaboration. Interactions between students and faculty members and among students, both formal and informal, were essential to the culture.

We were invited to meet up with other students in our own geographical area. I organized a Fielding cluster group in my home in Santa Monica. We met monthly, discussed our individual projects and held each other to account, providing support and hugs when needed. There were also the regular national gatherings – winter sessions in Santa Barbara, summer sessions elsewhere in the country. These were extraordinary and precious events.

Like many of my fellow students, I came to Fielding in midlife. I had spent my twenties immersed in politics, active in the anti-war movement and, later, the women's movement. For periods of time I lived in poor communities, working on issues such as welfare rights, housing, and racial discrimination. During those ten years, supporting myself by waiting tables and in other part-time jobs, I acquired a bachelor's degree from Berkeley, majoring in history, though academic work always took second place to political activism. Later, a Master's degree in Public Health led me, for the first time, aged 30, to professional employment, working for Planned Parenthood and then, as a high school teacher.

I enrolled at Fielding, driven by a desire to study and to develop intellectually. I discovered there a community that was recognizable from my activist years. I was among adult learners, many of whom had been engaged in their own ways in the progressive turmoil of the sixties and were now, like me, returning to education having raised families and had careers. Then there was that crucial collaborative spirit, a quality of shared engagement that had originally drawn me into politics, and which was now making my academic journey anything but solitary.

The theories of adult learning developed by Malcolm Knowles, Jack Mezirow and Frederic Hudson, among others, appealed to our generation. We were independent thinkers and wanted to expand on our lived experience. Adult learning principles described an approach that we were instinctively drawn to. Fielding embodied these ideas and experimented with ways of putting them into practice. With the exception of a few required courses, we were remarkably free to design what we wanted to study, how to study it, and in what form to present the evidence of our work. We were encouraged to be creative, push boundaries, be radical.

The faculty was an important factor in the excitement I experienced. Jeremy Shapiro undertook to teach us how to read a book in fifteen minutes (though it never worked for me!). Libby Douvan directed me to the inspiring writings of Fritjof Capra on systems theory and spirituality. Rich Applebaum supported my interest in sustainability. Judy Stevens-Long turned me on to adult development theories and, in particular, to the work of Robert Kegan. And Don Bushnell, in addition to his academic achievements, was a genius at helping all of us to act goofy and laugh at ourselves.

Never having devoted myself so fully to my own intellectual journey, I fell in love with learning. I gobbled up books, was eager to swap favourite passages and insights, and would get up in the middle of the night to write down a thought or a new idea. And throughout all this, it was the supportive environment that sustained me. Fielding celebrated collaboration and invented new ways for Fielding students to work together. It was through interacting with others that I learned new ways of thinking, new ideas, and the ability to see and appreciate several points of view simultaneously.

Meanwhile, there was another kind of collaboration taking place: between the part of me that was hungry for higher learning and the part that still wanted to engage with people and with the organizational structures that impacted their lives; between the theoretical and the practical.

Inspired by the concept of the scholar practitioner, I was encouraged to function at the intersection of the academy and the wider world. For any given Knowledge Area, I was required to work at three levels: overview, depth, and applied. This was the Fielding model. A journey that began in the library, poring over textbooks and scholarly volumes to get the big picture before selecting an area of particular interest, would quickly lead out into society. I found myself reflecting, in the light of my new learning, on other aspects of my life and on experiences I had had before becoming a doctoral student.

I was expected to read widely and to conform to established standards for writing and citing sources. I enjoyed this challenge. The applied projects allowed for more creative approaches and gave me space to explore established connections and to develop new ones.

A module on the process of learning led me to reconnect with the high school in Los Angeles where I had taught a course called Human Development. I interviewed students on the experience of being taught, asking them to talk about different teaching styles and to assess their effectiveness. The students had definite ideas about which strategies and approaches impacted them positively. This led to a video and then a reflection paper titled: "From the Other Side of the Desk: students talk about what they want from teachers."

As a Berkeley graduate, I was eligible for the Oxford Berkeley Program. This allowed me to spend three weeks at Worcester College, Oxford, where I enrolled in a course in Environmental Archaeology. Having travelled extensively in America, spending time in various kinds of wilderness, including the Sierra Nevada and the high desert of New Mexico, I was intrigued to discover how thoroughly domesticated the British landscape is in comparison. The Oxford archaeologist likened it to a back garden that has been repeatedly planted and replanted. There was, for me, an unfamiliar kind of richness in discovering, for example, that an ordinary looking hedgerow might be centuries old, containing a wide variety of species, and that it might provide insights into earlier social systems. I arranged with an instructor at Fielding that I could submit my final paper, written for the Oxford course, as an applied paper for one of my Knowledge Areas.

Exploring family systems, I learned about Murray Bowen and the concept of the genogram –a form of family tree that uses a variety of symbols to represent different kinds of familial relationships. One of my textbooks illustrated how a genogram might be used with reference to the Kennedys. For my depth paper, I took a different family of nine children, the one in which my husband had grown up. This was an essentially theoretical paper on how various aspects of a family's history and interconnections might be visually represented. Rather than presenting actual findings, which would have required extensive research and multiple interviews, I was playing with techniques, so I made do with my husband's insights. Suitably anonymized, his stories provided the material for a paper full of visual interest.

Among the many papers I wrote at Fielding, perhaps the ones that were most important to me personally were in the area of social ecology. I wrote an extensive review of the current literature published to date (1995) on "Saving the Planet." It included this paragraph:

"What is wrong is so fundamental that much of our basic assumptions about ourselves and the universe must be radically transformed if we are to survive. Matthew Fox calls for a re-sacralizing of nature and work; Jeremy Rifkin explores the idea of a new consciousness. Thomas Berry sees the need and the possibility of a new creation story. Paul Hawken wants business to imitate nature. And Morris Berman calls for a re-enchantment of our worldview." (Wildflower, p. 4)

The world has changed dramatically since I wrote this twenty-eight years ago and new ideas have emerged. But the need for deep structural, economic, and cultural change remains and has become even more urgent. I am moved to see that with the exception of Thomas Berry, who died in 2009, all the thinkers referenced here are still writing, speaking and campaigning in response to the climate crisis.

Before embarking on a dissertation, I wrote a paper titled: "Seven Mind Maps: Wildflower's Beliefs and Assumptions". The process of constructing mind maps yielded several insights. First, the maps encouraged me to compare and cross-reference ideas from different disciplines that had influenced my thinking. I became aware of connections between theories of human development and notions of effective leadership, organizational effectiveness, and socially responsible business practice. The exercise helped me become conscious of the extent to which my operating assumptions were oriented towards personal growth and change as an integral component of organizational change. I also discovered how important the use of metaphor is to my mode of thinking, and how often I use metaphor as a vehicle for shifting a frame of reference, both personally and in my teaching and consulting.

When it came to choosing a subject for my dissertation, I was pulled in various directions. One of my teachers suggested I explore the impact of the student movement of which I had been a part, but I was inclined to move forward into less familiar territory. I wanted to know about the more creative and responsible ways of conducting business.

Looking back, it occurs to me that I was influenced by the example of my father, a self-made businessman, who had always tried to balance making a living with expressing his values, not always with success. During the fifties, with an electronics plant in LA, he made a point of providing work in his warehouse for blacklisted screenwriters. When he himself fell foul of McCarthyism, it was not for this, but for earlier progressive activities. Excluded from the company he had founded, he started from scratch with a new company.

I decided to interview socially responsible business leaders on what motivated them. A Fielding teacher asked how I was going to assess whether they were truly as responsible as they claimed, but I wanted to focus on what I had learned to call, in my days as a community organizer, "organizing questions" such as: "What motivated you to conduct business more equitably?" I wanted to identify role models and to understand the factors—personal, political, social—that motivated an individual to become a socially responsible business leader. This led to a dissertation titled: *Defining the New Heroes: Narratives of Extraordinary Leaders in Socially Responsible Businesses.*

After graduating, I began teaching in the online master's program. Fielding was one of the first universities to offer a mainly virtual master's degree. It was an extraordinary experience. As faculty, we were exploring ways of harnessing the collaborative possibilities of the online environment. And we were learning alongside the students. With the brilliant design and leadership of Judy Stevens-Long, we developed creative, supportive, and loving communities. The technology, which might have seemed distancing, encouraged both academic and personal intimacy.

I designed Fielding's Evidence Based Coaching program because Judy suggested I should. For me, it felt like another opportunity to extend my learning, and one more chance to experience the joy and excitement of intellectual collaboration that had always been, for me, Fielding's particular gift.

If You Ask, You're More Likely to Get!

Tracy Gibbons
Past Member, Fielding Board of Trustees

I'm a retired Organization Design and Development consultant and Executive Coach. I've now lived in Silicon Valley for more than 30 years but grew up in suburban New York and spent many years in Massachusetts and other Northeast states. I had a first career with the YMCA, first in several Program Director positions and finally as a Branch Executive Director. My undergraduate school was Springfield College (formerly known as the International Training School for YMCA Workers) from which I received a B.S. in Community Leadership and Development. During this time and with financial support as a recipient of a national YMCA scholarship, I completed an M.S in Counseling Psychology (with electives in Organization Behavior and Development) at George Williams College) and then NTL's Program for Specialists in Organization Development (PSOD). These latter experiences are what first piqued my curiosity and then launched my attraction to the then-emerging field of OD, and my interest in continuing to work for the YMCA waned. Eventually I found my way to Digital Equipment Corporation (DEC) in Massachusetts.

It's 1977 and DEC is highly innovative, fast growing, and among the first companies to develop and manufacture the technology for mini (non-mainframe) computers. OD is still a relatively new field, emerging approach, and set of competencies for systemic planning, growth, and evolution of complex organizations. DEC is early to recognize and value the contributions and benefits of OD methods, expertise, and professionals to the growth and development of the company and its employees, and I was one of a growing cohort of internal OD practitioners. I'm loving DEC, loving my work, doing well. There's lots of challenge and opportunity for innovation and impact, and plenty of resources, support, recognition, and rewards.

Now it's 1983, I've been there for six years and am on my third job. Then, without any warning or even clues, there's an organization change that affects my senior level client, and I and several others suddenly find ourselves looking to find or create our next positions. (We are not the only ones who are blindsided by this change.) As a matter of DEC culture and practice, we aren't laid off, "reassigned," or left without resources and support. But it is nevertheless a veritable crash-into-a-wall experience that leaves me bereft and grieving. There's a lot of time to think.

Finding Options

This process is not unlike any job-seeking endeavor, except it's all internal and in this case, there's a lot of drama. I already know where there are officially open positions, and there aren't any that interest or suit me. I start making the rounds, thinking about what I'd like to do next, and how organizations and the field of OD have changed since I joined DEC. I am also thinking about Ph.D. programs. It's not the first time I've thought about a Ph.D., but it's not on my radar screen at that point.

I've been intellectually curious for as long as I remember. I was considered smart and did well in school. That I would go to college was instilled in me early, principally by my father, and he also encouraged me to be interested in more aspirational things and careers (e.g. as a doctor, lawyer, etc.) rather than the fields that were traditional for women at that time (nurse, teacher, librarian). When I applied for the YMCA scholarship and went on to do a Master's program, it was not because of any particular pressure or expectations other than my own: it seemed like the right and next thing to do. Getting a doctorate was more in that same realm; I didn't feel that having one was a necessity for an OD professional, and certainly not a requirement. But I had done very little professional development since completing the PSOD program. The world, our organization, and my hi-tech clients were changing and so were the contributions needed from OD people. I started to do research on Ph.D. programs that didn't require full-time residency. There were some but not many back then; the Internet isn't a thing, and most companies and people don't use or have access even to e-mail.

Then, in the midst of all of this, an issue of the OD Practitioner arrives. Inside, a succinct announcement in a 2 x 2-inch framed box jumps off the page: The Fielding Institute, located in Santa Barbara, CA, offers distance learning doctoral programs in Human and Organization Development and has been recently accredited. Without hesitation, I call them and request a catalog.

After studying Fielding's andragogical learning model and the Knowledge Areas that comprise the largely self-designed curriculum, I decide to seek sponsorship for the program. DEC's tuition reimbursement policy is very generous and available to all employees, not just principally engineers. I create a written proposal and presentation based on the Knowledge Areas that best encompass what I see as the important organization design and development needs at that time, which will maximize the ROI of my time and DEC's money most quickly; on my plan to work with actual clients on projects that have needs in those areas and that will be the basis for my In Depth and Applied Assessments; and on my ability to choose a dissertation topic that will provide learning opportunities for me as well as the corporation, and a contribution to the larger academic community. I'm anxious about going to the meeting with the two senior HR execs who have agreed to hear my proposal and make the decision: what if they say no? It occurs to me then that if you want something that requires the buy-in, cooperation, and support of someone else, you're much more likely to get it if you ask. Forty years later I can clearly recall who was there, the conversation, the office where the meeting was held —and what I was wearing that day. I also bring with me the paperwork that would need to be signed if they approved. Fortunately, in the words of a then-colleague, I'm able to turn adversity into an opportunity.

My Fielding Life

It's now 2023. As I think about my time and life at Fielding, it occurs to me that I've been part of the Fielding community for 40 years—nearly half my life! Following the completion of a detailed application, it begins in June 1983 with an invitation to the Admissions Contract Workshop (ACW). It's part orientation and part final decision-making; back then, final acceptance into the program occurred at the conclusion of the ACW. So I arrive in Santa Barbara very excited—and also a little nervous! The community is much smaller and less formal then. We are known as The Fielding Institute, the HOD program is still new and, with accreditation, it's growing. The three founders, Fredrick, Hallock, and Renata are at the helm, present at the ACW, and very engaged. Don Bushnell, an HOD founding faculty member, is Program Director; we play Pruey and other Don-inspired games. We are divided into small groups, each with a faculty member and a current student as leaders.

The other objectives of the ACW are to transmit the Fielding culture and to build community. How the system works, the educational and personal developmental objectives, and behavioral expectations are communicated clearly and frequently along with the various aspects and locations of the community. The norms and elements are modeled by the faculty and the student leaders and in the interaction between them. The fundamental operating principle of learner directed initiative and responsibility is unequivocal. Also, we're supposed to have fun! It's clear that this won't be the same sort of educational experience that most of us have had until now.

Since there is no campus, this session, like all the California-based residential sessions, is held at La Casa de Maria, a retreat center high in the hills above Montecito. The environment at La Casa, built and felt in sync with nature, is essential to the culture. Located not far from the boundary of the national forest where buildings stop, it is secluded, peaceful, and beautiful, and the energy of the spiritual community that owns and operates it is pervasive. The view to the ocean is breathtaking and awesome. The food is good. And while the sleeping spaces are short on ambiance and amenities, we joke—rather than complain—about the paper bathmats and small, thin towels. There are two outdoor pay phones, often with long lines (this is the early 80s), but the weather in California is spectacular, and there are no mosquitos. The space is comfortable and conducive to the work at hand and that which is forthcoming. The ACW experience and being at

La Casa quickly becomes an integral and fundamental part of my Fielding experience, a source of grounding and joy. Every year I look forward to being in community at Summer Session and to being at La Casa.

My Program Director is Anna DiStefano, and my Mentor and Dissertation Chair is Leo Johnson. Anna started her Fielding career at my ACW, and I know right away that I'll ask her to be my PD. Leo is the leader of the New England cluster, and I've met him previously when both of us worked for the YMCA. Both make significant, meaningful, and enduring contributions to my education, my program, and personal development. We always feel like a team, and I offer great admiration, appreciation, and gratitude to them. I'm still delighted that I was for each of them their first student to graduate.

My three years of dedication, creativity, new experiences, continuous learning, hard work, and great fun pass quickly and with relative ease. It helps that in key areas there is considerable overlap between the fundamental values and operating principles of Digital and Fielding, particularly those that require individual initiative and responsibility. The funding request that I wrote is a template for my Fielding Learning Contract which then becomes a plan that includes a process for how to utilize KA assessments to find my way to a dissertation topic and holds up well for the duration. I arrive with experience in project management, team development, and systemic change, all of which enable and enhance my experience.

I leave with the great satisfaction of having achieved my goals and plans; enormous new knowledge and a better and more nuanced understanding of how to use and apply it; the joy of being part of a like-minded, loving, and supportive learning community; and an evolved sense of self and what that means.

Then and now I feel fortunate and grateful.

Graduation!

In my era, what we called graduation is actually a celebration and a party for those whose Knowledge Area assessments are completed, and dissertations are signed off in time for that year's Summer Session, so that the recognition can come in the midst of the community as well as friends and family. There were likely a few remaining details and tasks to be completed by the celebrants—e.g. dissertation edits, and in my case the comprehensive exam. My first memories of this event are of one or two people, probably still dressed in shorts (as were the rest of us) at an informal but very exciting gathering in the lounge at La Casa. One year, the single honoree, who is on a university faculty, is adorned in the academic regalia that has been custom made in the colors of his university. These events evolve into more formal occasions when Fielding moves its offices to a large, lovely space with a formal garden on Santa Barbara Street where the gatherings are held.

The time approaches for my good friend, Kessiah, and me to graduate. Then, owing to a scheduling error, Summer Session is rescheduled and is suddenly six weeks *earlier* than planned. We both push forward to meet the new deadline and talk frequently, including about the graduation celebration—the great motivator. We agree that there are occasions in life that warrant special, even ceremonial, recognition and that graduations are one of them; we decide that we'd like to have academic regalia as part of our celebration. So we contact Don Bushnell, HOD Dean, and make our request. Not everyone on the faculty and administration likes this idea, believing that it's counter to Fielding's founding principles and identity as a non-traditional graduate school. But in the end, once again, we ask and we receive. Our group of graduates has caps, gowns, and hoods…and so do the faculty! The Class of 1986 processes into the garden to the strains of Elgar's *Pomp and Circumstance*.

The next year two close friends from my ACW cohort graduate, and they want to wear tuxes. They ask their friends, including some faculty, to wear them too. We all do. Soon after a group of grads arrives at Summer Session, only to find out that caps and gowns haven't been ordered—because they didn't ask for them. There's a scramble and by the end of the week they've arrived, but no hoods, because those are special order items. This group, all women, plus some women faculty create a way to make their event and regalia unique. Just ask around….

Each year, the number of honorees as well as the audience grow along with the size of the HOD program. The common thread—and centerpiece, then and now—of all these occasions is that each honoree is offered the opportunity to tell the story of how his/her life has been transformed by the Fielding experience. In addition to multiple HOD graduations, I attend a Master's graduation of Fielding's first on-line program, of which I am a faculty member and see the video of an early ELC graduation. I'm worried about whether this essential outcome of the Fielding experience is sustainable in the face of growth and the addition of new programs and faculty. But when I hear person after person describe life-their changing experiences, I decide that I'll worry if and when that ever ceases.

Life after Fielding

When I graduate in 1986, there are no programs or activities in place to catch those who are now in the exit chute. This matters more to HOD graduates than those from the Psychology program. We are, it is said, more group oriented and extroverted. And since HOD was launched in 1979 and accreditation was granted in 1983, there are fewer who are faced with figuring our "life after Fielding."

Nevertheless, I find ways to stay connected and contribute to the growth and sustainability of what eventually becomes Fielding Graduate University. Of course I attended many graduations of friends from my generation. Here are some examples of what I'm involved in over 30 years.

Being a Member of the Board of Trustees

For a term, I'm the alumni representative on the Board of Trustees. This requires me to think and act more broadly about Fielding and its evolution. I also pay a lot of attention to the needs of alumni and remind the other board members that alums are now the largest constituency of the organization, that most of us have had life-changing experiences while learners and are articulate about the uniqueness of the educational model, and that by not having ways to maintain their connections, we are letting an important, valuable resource drift away. At that time, Fielding is still heavily dependent on tuition as its main source of income; Board members are reluctant to divert resources from students to alums. Faculty are also reluctant to allow alumni to continue to attend Summer or Winter

Sessions because they think that participation (and perhaps even presence) will dilute the work, learning, and progress of students.

Making Space for Alumni

Led largely by HOD alumni whose numbers grow quickly, a number of opportunities are created to address wants and needs of graduates. We are invited to make presentations at sessions; a staff member with responsibility for alumni initiatives is hired; we launch the Fielding Alumni Network (FAN); and we establish an Alumni Council that meets regularly to look after alumni concerns. Eventually, we are invited to attend all events at sessions, including Final Oral Reviews, and a separate track for alums is created. At Sessions, there are receptions for alums. In 1977, for the HOD's 20th anniversary there is a reunion held at La Casa. It's well attended, and we have all the fun and none of the work!

The Advent of On-line Learning

The advent and adoption of personal computers and email begins during my student years. Because Digital is involved in the invention, design, and development of the technology that enables the internet and email, we are all early adopters.

When I arrive at Fielding most of us are still using typewriters including me, but before too long, I'm fortunate to have access to early versions of PCs. DEC has a company-wide Local Area Network (LAN) before most people know what that is, and it's possible to communicate with anyone by e-mail. But IBM and Apple are the developers of the commercialized products that enable PCs to be unique and valuable tools.

Fielding encourages us to have email accounts but that technology is still quite primitive, various platforms have different protocols for use, and they aren't necessarily cross-application compatible. The hardware most definitely is not (I wrote an assessment about this!).

By the mid-eighties the limitations of e-mail, originally intended for one-to-one or one-to few communication that doesn't require a unified response or collaboration effort, are becoming apparent. The first application that is specifically designed for group-based interaction, especially among those that are geographically dispersed, is developed, and a group of HR people at DEC are invited to learn about and start using it.

By the early nineties, this technology has evolved and improved, and HOD offers its first on-line, computer-enabled Master's program. My then-business partner and I are on the faculty, teaching and facilitating a course in Organization Design to second-year students. One of our explicit goals is to see how well the platform can be utilized to do collaborative work among teams that are geographically dispersed and whose members have similar goals and interests but different backgrounds and employment situations. We create a set of operating principles about frequency of reading and responding, and posting of assignments and individual contributions, all based on what we call Fielding Standard Time. We also require them to do peer evaluations that are factored into their grades (rewards) along with other criteria. They start out by discussing and agreeing to a process for reaching consensus and decision making—basically replicating a process that we use with face-to-face client groups. We set the expectation that they will also be learning how to use collaborative software tools as well as organization design.

As a learning experience for us as well as for HOD's emerging use of on-line technology several things are worth mentioning.

- My colleague is an early morning person, and I'm a night person. This enables us to be able between us to read and comment on all the postings that are made over the course of 24 hours. There's no way a single faculty member could have done this alone.
- One member of the class goes Radio Silent, on-line, by e-mail, and by phone. This messes with our design and causes some anxiety for the others, both because they all know each other, are worried, and there is built-in interdependence. We don't have a contingency plan or a real time solution for this problem.
- There isn't enough time in the semester to complete all the work that's required to do an organization design while also learning about it and using the technology differently.

• The next semester there are some learners who choose not to take the class because they are unwilling to have their grade impacted by peer evaluations and/or the interdependence necessary to complete the class.

My business partner and I contributed a chapter to the *Handbook of Online Learning, 1ˢᵗ ed.*, Rudestam, K.E. and Schoenholtz-Read, J., Eds., 2002, Sage Publications that describes this experience in detail.

The Power of Connections

Along the way I meet several people who aren't from my ACW cohort or even my Fielding generation who contribute to other important life experiences and/or are close friends.

On this evening, the New England Cluster is meeting at my home. There's a knock on the door, but when I answer it, I don't recognize the woman who's there. It turns out that she is a graduate of the Psych program who has recently moved to the Boston suburbs. She contacts Leo, our faculty leader, to make a local Fielding connection, and he invites her to our meeting. She lives nearby, gets a job at DEC, and we become friends. Some years later I and then she move to California and again are neighbors.

On my last consulting project with DEC, I take what turns into a temporary, full-time assignment in Silicon Valley. Having become a California Weather Wimp, I decide to stay. I know only one OD person in the area, a Fielding colleague who works at Advanced Micro Devices (AMD), a chip company, and call him. They have an opening! AMD has also recently hired a manager who's from DEC to be VP of the Network Products Division. He interviews me, and that seals the deal. My Fielding colleague and I work together for six years, along with two other alums.

At a Winter Session in the early 2000s, I meet an alumna who has recently moved to Boston. She is going to stay with friends in a medieval castle in Tuscany in the upcoming summer and asks if I'd like to come with her. How long do you need to think about that? We become travel buddies and over the years go to France, Alaska, New Zealand, Australia, and the Galapagos. Although she is in Boston and I'm in California, her son lives not far from me, she comes to visit at my home on Martha's Vineyard, and we talk and email, so we continue to be connected. Such is the power of a common experience that's based on similar values and interests and a relationship that begins with the presumption of mutual trustworthiness.

Epilogue

It's now 2018. I haven't been to a Fielding event in a long time, but I've been invited to a small gathering of alums during Winter Session who are there to honor Anna DiStefano on her retirement from her 35-year career at Fielding. She and I have known each other for all of these years and have become friends. I'm touched to be part of this group and delighted that it's small enough for us to have a conversation.

I'm also looking forward to going up to La Casa with friends with whom I shared that experience, and I plan to go to the gift shop to get a Corita-created gift for Anna. In December I'm glued to the internet to keep track of the wildfires that are invading the Santa Ynez mountains at the top of Montecito and parts of the Santa Barbara hills. Thankfully, La Casa is spared.

Three weeks later, early on the day before I'm departing, the rains come. Starting at the burn area, massive, catastrophic debris slides are triggered, carrying boulders, mud, and other leftovers from the fire all the way down to Coast Village, across the 101 freeway, the railroad tracks, Miramar Beach, and into the ocean. The pictures of the devastation are horrifying, made worse by the fact that I recognize nearly all of the places that are overrun. I know how close the fires came to La Casa, and there's a wadi that runs through the property. Most of the buildings are destroyed, or so damaged as to be red tagged. Miraculously, the chapel is still standing. There's a large hole in the uphill facing wall, and the floor is covered with mud and debris, but the boulder that hits the building remains outside. The altar, the large window behind it, and the stained glass look to be intact. The lounge and dining room building that abuts the chapel is destroyed. They will be rebuilt, but five years later that hasn't happened yet. This was the backdrop of my student years, and I miss it.

And so, as I reflect on many of the experiences I had as a learner and the ways that Fielding has affected me and continues to, I'm astonished by the enormity of the impact and the durability of this. It is woven into the fabric of my life and who I am.

The Plight of Social Justice

Tahlia Bragg, Ph.D.
Inaugural President of the Black Student Association

The plight and progress of social justice is being threatened now more than ever. As I reflect on my pursuit of health equity and justice for Black communities and the current local and national initiatives advancing and promoting every spectrum of hate and subservient oppression, I am even more grateful I am an alum of Fielding Graduate University than when I decided to attend. Allow me to elaborate, but first, I need you to imagine.

Imagine you grew up in a state that is stereotypically and somewhat accurately perceived as rural, poor, segregated, ultra-conservative, and hyper-dogmatic. The same state to date still has one of the highest rates of teen pregnancy, reading illiteracy, DUIs, mortality, and incarceration rates per capita in the entire country. The same state also has some of the nation's poorest quality of secondary education and the outcomes are worsened by race. You grow up in this state and learn that education is the *only* way to gain any economic upward mobility. Education will hopefully prevent you from the tradition of teen pregnancy, bring greater prosperity and support to the same family that encourages you to defy intergenerational family norms. Here, I could have described many places in the United States that, unfortunately, yield similar statistics. I have described an ambition that is relatable to many. In this, we have community and an understanding of the environment and what it takes to persevere and succeed in such places. However,

if you identify as a woman,
or being Black,
then all of what I just described…

may highlight endemic issues that escalate the severity of struggles experienced trying to receive an education that you and your ancestors were previously legislatively denied. This is my story—the beginning of my path to psychology, Fielding, racial justice, and beyond.

My Calling

There is something to be said about something that is your calling because if it is your calling, it will keep calling you until you answer it. That was my experience with pursuing clinical psychology. I was first seriously introduced to the prospect of a career as a clinical psychologist in high school. I decided in preschool that I was going to earn a Ph.D. when I was called "Ms. Bragg." The only way to change that was to become a doctor. My sights were geared toward becoming a computer scientist due to my passion for math, technology, and the advances in the internet at the time. Alas, fate had a different destination for me. After encountering several personal tragedies during high school, I was told by a peer that I seemed eager to help and gave great advice and should consider becoming a psychologist. I did not think that was a great career choice because mental health was a stigmatized topic in my family and surrounding community. My socialized view of anything related to mental health was regarded as negative and obscure. Then I realized that that was a problem desperate to be solved.

By my senior year of high school, I had decided that my dream of earning a Ph.D. and my passion for helping others would converge by endeavoring to become a clinical psychologist. I earned my bachelor's in psychology, and I discovered a new term, called "burnout." I was exhausted, primarily from always having to be whatever certain professors wanted me to be to meet their acceptance. I wish I were only speaking of course expectations. I often was told that I do not look them in the eyes when we talked, was told I was trying to sound smart if I used "big words," my silence was often weaponized and seen as disengagement. Meanwhile, I was often mocked or belittled in classes if I did speak. I even had a professor "accidentally" lose a handwritten final paper and threatened that I would fail the course if I did not rewrite the paper a couple of days before it was due. The "performance" led to a lot of fatigue and ultimately angst by my senior year. I decided my initial plan of going straight to graduate school would have to be on hold. The purpose of the hold was to get some rest in whatever form that meant and to really find myself. I had always said that I would wait until I was completely done with school, including graduate school, when I earned my Ph.D., to get to know who I am and really live.

That was 2008.

I met many of the political and economic turmoil of the time as a new adult in the workforce. And it was difficult. I decided to apply for graduate school the fall after I graduated. I was rejected from all five schools I applied to. I began to second-guess my calling—that getting my Ph.D. in clinical psychology was not the calling that I thought it was because there were all these issues I kept facing. I ultimately concluded that I obviously misread the *call* that I had with psychology. Alas, I made time because I tried to pursue other careers, and somehow came back to psychology, psychological and social services, things like that in some type of way and same when it came to research.

My Calling to Aging Research

My interest in clinical neuropsychology started my second year. I went to community college before I went to university, and in my second year of college, my uncle, whom I was very close to, was paralyzed in a car crash. I was already in school for psychology, and I thought about pursuing training in rehabilitation, so that by the time I was done with school I could be a part of helping him fully rehabilitate. That was a lofty ambition in my 19-year-old mind. Unfortunately, he didn't make it that far. He succumbed to his injuries and died at the end of my first year earning my master's degree. While the fire and the passion were still there for neuropsychology, they did not remain from the rehab perspective. So, I did not end up pursuing that. The other main career path I considered was aging. At the time, I didn't think that there could have been another parallel, but my grandmother was another significant influence. She just passed away at 102 last year. She was very, very much a part of my life in a specific way. She just wanted to see me earn my Ph.D. and literally stayed long enough to do it. She constantly encouraged me to make sure whatever work I pursued would benefit and helps Black people, which is why I pursued interests in Black racial disparities. I considered it full circle to advocate for her as she got older using what I had learned, because a lot of my family didn't see some of the problems she was beginning to have, and if they did, they didn't see them the same way. I had learned new skills to try to help her.

I had been told since my undergraduate degree by faculty advisors when I started research that, "You need to pursue a career in aging." I had my own reservations at the time because I thought it was an incredibly sad discipline. My perception was that working in anything related to Alzheimer's disease and dementia would be very sad. I respected older people for the elders they are and the pillars they are and didn't want to see them in a compromised state. Other than that, I did not think that there was ever really a reason given why I should pursue this, except that I did not think it related to my interests at the time. I have typically not been one to fully disregard the professional advice from mentors, so I kept the premise of training in aging in my forethought.

By the time that I reached my doctoral training, I did the same thing. My dissertation chair said that I should pursue a career in aging as we were working on my dissertation. And when I started to realize the epidemic and the endemic nature of aging within the Black communities with my previously established interest in racial disparities, in Black mental health, this was very much the next way I wanted to go. This became an area in which I can contribute to at a significant level to help my community and hopefully improve clinical knowledge about treatment in Black communities.

Call to Action

For years, I have heard that psychology needs more Black psychologists, from my time in college to right now in this very moment. The discipline needs more people who identify with marginalized groups. And the reason I refrain from expanding it is to say that, separately, we represent a fraction of a fraction of a percent of all active psychologists at any given moment within the United States. The need is still there. But it's not fully on people's minds or interest in diversifying psychology. It's also on the institutions. It's on the practical side. It's on the internship sites. It's on the postdoc sites, on the licensing board. It's on the supervisors at each of these levels of training to be compassionate, and if they don't believe in diversity and equity, at the very least, they need to believe in accessibility. Equality has been legally codified for decades for one and for all, and there are still issues with that. But because it is legal, the very least people could do is to leave the door open. If you don't know what to do with that, or you don't want anything to do with them once we're in, that's on you. Somebody else will. But at least, if you have the keys to opening a door for somebody to have an opportunity, leave the door open at the very least.

I say that from my experience of, I think, looking back and ahead. I've dealt with quite a few people who just didn't want to be a part of my support system, but left the door at least open to let me do whatever it is, and for the better. It worked. I figured things out or encountered people who were willing to take me to the next level. But we could sit here and argue about, from there we'll match how far somebody could go if it had somebody who allowed access and believed in equity. It helps to elevate it. That is where many people who are stewards of training future underrepresented, marginalized, subjugated people will have a reckoning. That will continue to be an issue until the same people are honest about what they really want. So that you admit that you want greater accessibility, diversity, and inclusivity, or you don't.

My Fielding Journey

Well, unfortunately, I think it's a forbidden descriptor of stories that we don't often tell at Fielding, but I believe it may be significant to share. I had applied multiple times to graduate, traditional, brick-and-mortar clinical psychology programs. I had the right GPA. I had the right grades. I had the right letters of recommendation from the right people. I had the right experience. I perpetually had the wrong GRE scores, and unfortunately, that eliminated me every time I applied to graduate programs. The application process is quite expensive, so I never applied to 10 or more schools. It was five to six at best. Ultimately, when I finished my undergraduate degree, I decided not to apply to graduate school and go on a traditional path straight from undergraduate to graduate school. You could argue if that was the best decision to make, considering it was 2008, and given the socioeconomic climate at the time and learning firsthand that the degree that I just earned was not as competitive as I was led to believe during all the years in high school and in college. It was a turning point. So, I really had to figure out what I wanted to do with my life, and I thought maybe clinical psychology wasn't going to be it because I was out, and I was tired.

I eventually talked to one of my mentors at my undergraduate alma mater. He told me to at least get a master's in clinical psychology, which would give me some experience in graduate school because I didn't have the GRE scores to be competitive. So, I did that, but that seemed not to help, either. I felt defeated, and I assumed that my dream of getting a Ph.D. someday in clinical psychology was ill-intended and not for me anymore. I ended up becoming a clinical research coordinator contracted by the Department of Defense, but when I was laid-off after my first year out of graduate school, I switched careers again and trained as a drug counselor at a correctional facility. I pursued licensure as a professional counselor and settled into that as my long-term career. Then, an opportunity to return to clinical research came along, prompting my return to work at a private research firm and in a role as a psychometrist for the facility. After the experience I had earning my master's degree and taking out loans, I decided to quit that job, even though it had great benefits, which was exceedingly rare at the time. Fortunately, I had a parent who could help me and support me, but it was very difficult to maintain that for two years to get a master's degree, and I decided then that if I were to go back to school ever again that I could not quit my job to go to school.

Unfortunately, in many of my job positions, I experienced a lot of educational racism. I would see positions where a master's degree was required and Ph.D. preferred. I met all the criteria, but I didn't have a Ph.D.

I even had a horrible boss who one day said to me, "If you had a Ph.D., you wouldn't have to report to me." I started thinking that maybe I needed to consider the Ph.D. path because I was being overlooked for job positions for one reason or the other.

These experiences and my continued dream of being Dr. Bragg led me to research doctoral programs. I knew about Fielding even when I was in my first or second year in my rural junior college. It always had an asterisk when people would talk about it. Everyone that I spoke to about the program did not know it was distributed learning but had the "online school" reputation. At the time, I was not a fan of online schooling just because of my attention span. Eventually, I decided to take Fielding seriously and learn more about the university. First, I looked to see if they were still accredited, which they were, by the American Psychological Association for clinical psychology. Then, I went to an information session and was pleasantly surprised because Fielding sounded a lot different in a good way than I expected, like it was manageable. I thought about it and decided I could do it and then applied for the Fall 2015 term. The $75 application fee was waived since I attended the information session and applied for the next term. During the application process, I chickened out several times and didn't send in the correct statement of purpose. Each time, somebody would contact me and let me know more about the statement of purpose and give me an opportunity to submit it again. It took me until Fall 2016 to fully submit my application.

And that was it – my Fielding origin story. I'm glad that I submitted my application and went on this journey. Honestly, looking back, I probably should have done it sooner. I was fearful it would be like my former graduate school experiences, but it wasn't. Fielding is no different than other accredited programs, and I knew that it was just what I needed. Sometimes, the path that I need is not the typical path, but I'm also not a representation of the typical student.

I'm Black. I'm from a rural, poor state, the first generation: high school to Ph.D. on one side of my family; college to graduate school on the on the other side. I spoke to several colleagues who have more privilege and more access to resources, and likely more knowledge just based on a lineage of education in their family than I did. Thus, many resources that I needed to be successful are going to be non-traditional. It's serendipitous that I enrolled at the Fall 2016 term, because, quite frankly, I know if I had waited until 2017 then I would have likely talked myself out of it. I would have been upset if I waited another year. I *know* attending Fielding was an important decision and one I should have been more serious about sooner.

Fielding's Advantages

When the pandemic started, other schools had to figure out how to adjust to a virtual learning environment. Fielding was already doing this but had to adapt the number of hours that students can attend virtually versus in person until it was safe enough to restart in-person residency hours. And I like that we were already ahead of the game. We already had the platform and technology in place. It didn't disrupt anything in that regard or anyone's progress with coursework, and I don't think that's gotten the acknowledgment that it deserves.

Fielding needs to be seen as providing a gateway for people that look like me—from marginalized backgrounds—to become psychologists because the APA has had a call to increase that for years. Many people, regardless of their identities, Black or not, are in the same position that I am. They're working to support themselves and others. This is their second or third career. They're going back to school for the third or fourth time, and they can't quit their jobs. I am a single-income and head of household. If I don't work, I don't have a car, and I don't have a roof. Eventually, I did have to quit the job that I had, but I was able to find a job that was more flexible and continue to work there, which was key. I couldn't have done that if I was at a brick-and-mortar institution.

Fielding's Challenges

Fielding still has room to grow when it comes to racial inclusivity and accessibility; however, it's not in the same ways that other universities struggle. I was able to have the space and autonomy to be a part of creating the Black Student Association. I also made my studies Afrocentric because I wanted them to be, but also an issue. I had to create that area of study because it wasn't available.

Very early on in my Fielding studies, I began to infer from faculty and others that Fielding's clinical program was the problem child of the APA— that we're not as watched and celebrated as other institutions that are APA accredited. One of the reasons, in my opinion, is looking at the training inequity gap. Many do not have access to quality, APA-accredited, clinical training at a doctoral level. When I first started, I was told that we had the largest cohort of students that identified of Black people. I believe the couple of other cohorts after that broke those records. You must think about what that means. I could go on a whole soapbox about the reasons why education has been devalued even at the undergraduate level, which has to do with the gap in educational disparities for people that look like me and have a background similar to mine. I think it's important to highlight what it has meant. I was able to pursue and attain a highly prestigious internship, as well as a postdoc in neuropsychology. I did that at a distributed learning institution —the only one that is distributed learning *and* APA accredited. Fielding's model works.

Black Student Association—Call to Leadership

I was the Inaugural President of the Black Student Association, but I don't consider myself a founder. I guess I could be because the group already existed before I came in. It was an affinity group but not a student organization. Leading the BSA was difficult at times. I was a first-year student trying to acclimate to life as a student while working full-time. This is not a unique vantage point, as it's very similar to how other people and student groups have other commitments and obligations. We just don't have the time to do extracurricular ventures, but we make the time to do what matters to us. And this mattered. My mentality was that if no one led the BSA, then the work wouldn't move forward. I didn't want the idea of an official student association to die. I had never gone to a school that didn't have a Black student organization like a Black Student Union or, African American Student Association. Personally, I benefitted from having the camaraderie, fellowship, and alignment with people who look like me. We're normally one of a few in spaces like graduate schools, so having a diverse and inclusive community was important. I wanted to leave the door open for other people. Little by little, we increased membership numbers, but now, it has trickled down. Hopefully, we'll see a boost in numbers once again in the next couple of years. I presume the pandemic is a significant reason why BSA membership has dwindled, in addition to people graduating.

At the beginning, I really didn't see myself as a leader, organizationally or generally. I saw myself as somebody who was willing to maintain the status quo so we could be an organization and promote and advocate for what we felt it was the Black student body needed and wanted. We based out efforts off reports that we heard or our own interpretation of the Black student experience. Since I've graduated, it's been pressed on me that I am a leader, not just by Fielding administrators and staff, but the current Executive Board and their advisors of the BSA and even from President Rogers and Provost Williams—who just joined Fielding. That is very touching because I wasn't trying to lead. I was just trying to help. Of course, that's one element of leadership. I didn't see it as it was a "me" thing. It was very much an "our" thing for whomever wanted to be included in BSA or was thinking about it. I first felt like a leader when Dr. Stephen Ruffins passed away, who was my instructor at the time in my psychoanalytic track. Right after the term ended, he asked me to announce on the BSA portal that it would be the last time he would be at Summer Session. I didn't even have enough time to start planning how we were going to say goodbye to him. He died within a couple of days of me posting that announcement. I remember at the time there were many psychology faculty members retiring, and they had these large, public, corny, inside-joke farewells at the community meetings at Winter Session. Nothing was done when he had passed away. I could understand, maybe from the faculty side, it was too sudden. It was too hard. Right?

However, I wanted to make it known to the Fielding community. It was important to acknowledge that he was the only Black faculty member in the Psychoanalytic track but also to highlight his caring nature. To be so sick and still to be as active as he was, and with BSA at the time, too, was astounding. I pursued setting up an honorary scholarship created in his name, and fortunately, there were quite a few members of BSA at the time that were also touched by his passing and wanted to contribute to the campaigning. We heard everything like "Oh, you know how long it takes to get a scholarship funded?" "We're in the middle of getting an endowed scholarship in the name of somebody else. We're not even halfway to one of our goals, for that matter. This is not going to be something that you're going to be able to do." "It's going to take years." I remember vividly every time I had that and thought to myself, "Okay, yeah, I know that's typically how it works. I'm not that person. I'm not pursuing anything else; this is important, and it'll happen."

We got a fully endowed scholarship created less than four weeks, which from what I understand was *record time*. When the administration made the announcement, we were at Summer Session. I felt very proud that we were able to do that, and I think my aspiration for us to see it through so quickly was the thought that we were not going to take years to fund that because we didn't have years. If it had taken four years to be fully funded, that would have been 2023. We didn't have that time, and quite frankly, Dr. Ruffins didn't have that time. I feel like my passion and manifestation of, "That's not how it's not going to be. Make it happen," lifted it so it wouldn't, and it emanated in terms of how I spoke about it to whoever needed to hear it. I'm grateful for that. I know quite a few students have benefited from that scholarship, too.

I realize now that I led and mentored students who were members of the BSA. In retrospect, now that I've graduated, I realize that I was there for some students who see me as a mentor now. I think that that's another interesting transition and lens in which to view it because I was just simply trying to help. That help came from the fact that I didn't have a lot of the support and help in the ways I needed while at Fielding and other institutions. I'm very much driven by giving what I didn't get and hopefully will help to fill in the gaps for somebody else. I'm very grateful that I was able to touch and inspire the students and faculty alike during my time at Fielding.

It was very difficult at times, and at one point right before the pandemic, I was tempted and convinced I needed to let BSA go because nobody was active with it. It was by me, if I just to do it alone. Then, the new two new cohorts had just come in and started participating more, and they were far more organized. They had far more skills than I did: graphic design and event planning in a virtual space, They took on the initiatives that were created in my time as President and made them recurring, expected calendar events. That is phenomenal. So, I'm glad that the seeds that we harvested in my time grew to be something bigger because that was the goal. Some of us even rallied together to give our dissent about the APA's apology at the annual convention in 2022 and received the prestigious Stuart C. Tentoni Outstanding Professional Development Program Award. We were the first students to earn the award at Fielding. That critical conversation was my last event with BSA before I graduated and such a pivotal moment of my student tenure as a Fielding student. My hope is that the fire and ambition that created the BSA never quells and that it continues to be a support for the Black students, faculty, and staff at Fielding.

Call for Change

I had my own moratorium with my racial identity, in what I term as the *Civil Rights Renaissance 2020*, and it was a huge awakening. I was very much pro-Black before that, but in terms of my own intersectionality or location of racial identity, and how that presents a lot of situations, I didn't see it to the depth that it probably had been occurring. I often didn't speak out or just had silent protest. I'd be wearing a hair bonnet, hat, or mask with a message like, "I Can't Breathe." I wasn't much for the talking. It was the doing and being in a leadership role when more students became active, and seeing how unapologetically Black they were really had inspired me and empowered me (I bristle using that word), but it was maybe validated. I decided I was going to become more vocal and direct in my advocacy efforts and expressions of my thoughts and opinions. I think my experiences in the 2020-2021 school year were what really set me up to have the voice that I needed to be able to say, "No. I want more training, increase the scope of my lens, my framework in DEIA." The "A" for accessibility is vital because if you don't make it accessible, then it's not equitable. We have other questions of belonging that are associated with that. So, I think that the A is the most important part of the DEI framework.

I used to dream of days like this, and I fantasized about being at that internship at CMTP and about one day being at the CTE Center, both at Boston University. I am beyond grateful and proud that I was able to see my vision through from preschool. There have been multiple full-circle moments for me because I honored and answered my calling.

Your Calling

I believe that if you're interested in pursuing a degree, you should do it. There's a lot of rhetoric now that states that a degree is just not as valuable as it used to be. I'm not going to say that there's not some validity to it, depending on each person's own experiences. That is unfortunately very true for some demographics, as we witness with racially marginalized groups. Knowledge is power and getting a degree is not just about being bright, elevating your socioeconomic status, and making more money. It was more about education before income ever was correlated with education. Higher education institutions were places to gain more knowledge. And it still is that. I don't think that you can ever lose in life by gaining more knowledge.

Now, there is so much competition and sources of information. I'd argue that that's a problem that we're seeing. I think that if someone needs to pursue graduate education, in terms of Fielding, if it's an alignment with what they want to pursue, and it meets their needs in ways that attending another university may not have. When it comes to the clinical psychology program, Fielding doesn't get enough credit for actually being a premier institution. It is the only distributed learning program that's APA accredited. That means it's doing quite a few things right. The APA doesn't just generically give that out to people. A lot of institutions, one of which I used to work for, are still trying to pursue accreditation and still have not received it.

People need to get over the stigma of the name of our institution being considered "less." What's in a name? Fielding, at its core, is a social justice-oriented institution. Some still worry about going to a university with a bigger name. I won't dismiss or disregard that that has precedence because elitism, unfortunately, still exists, especially in polar, white supremacism in academia. At the same time, Fielding has what you need to get you where you want to be. You need to have a vision and be unapologetic about speaking it.

Joining Fielding's Scholar-Practitioner Community

How My PhD Degree Launched My Career As An Art Therapist

Maxine Borowsky Junge

Professor Emerita, Loyola Marymount

In 1986 I was 44 years old, Associate Professor of Clinical Art Therapy and Marital and Family Therapy, and Chair of the Department at Loyola Marymount University in Los Angeles, when they told me I would never be promoted to full professor without a Ph.D. (No one seemed to care what kind, only that I had one.) I had always loved learning, and every time I got bored I considered going back to school, but a valued mentor, Dr. Barbara Solomon, told me "Don't go to school unless you know why you're going." Good advice. Now I knew why I was going.

I looked around the L.A. area at university mental health programs of various stripes and found them wanting, very wanting. Running out of possibilities, I decided I could keep my mouth shut long enough to get a PhD at USC, where I had earned a MSW 20 years before. I made an appointment with the dean of the School of Social Work who, after telling me they would like me to go there, said I would need to go to junior college for two semesters to take algebra so I could pass the GRE. I said "I'm too old for that!" I pushed, but the rule held and I said "Then I'm not coming here." And I didn't.

Some years before, I had heard about Fielding from an L.A. psychologist who had been on Fielding's initial regional accreditation site team. She said "Something interesting is going on there." So I decided to make a trip to Fielding's Santa Barbara headquarters to have a look. Staff and faculty I met were smart, funny, and full of life and the well-structured study guides

I read were written in the female pronoun. Like the site visitor before me, I said "Something interesting is going on there." I applied.

While I was driving home on the Harbor Freeway after my entrance interview with Judy Stevens-Long at Cal State L.A., my car was clipped by a truck, sending it into an uncontrollable spin. I went careening across the lanes of traffic, watching approaching cars come at me and expecting to die, and finally crashing into the center divider. The car was totaled; I was unhurt. An omen? About Fielding? I decided it was a good omen that I was still alive!

For a long time I had been saddened at how few people at all, much less academics, were interested in any form of *action* toward change instead of merely studying, researching, and talking and talking and talking. Academics studied and researched. And then they studied and researched some more. Then they talked. I grew frustrated. One said to me "What's the use of doing it, if it hasn't been done before?" "That's exactly why I want to do it," I said. Many of them had never been out working in "real life" at all.

At Fielding I found doers, what they called "scholar-practitioners." The Human and Organizational Development (HOD) program was led by Don Bushnell and Anna DiStefano then. I discovered that the school, program, and faculty had a social justice and action bent and that they really meant it. They asked the tough questions and were willing to go deeply into the dark complex thickets of change. Wow! Another student and I, collaborated with two faculty members to diversify the HOD faculty. We searched out interesting, accomplished people of color and helped them through the unique, personal, and rigorous hiring process. Peter Park was our first. I had found him through a Loyola Marymount pastor that I knew and went to visit him at his apartment to convince him to apply at Fielding.

It's a cliché to say I found a home at Fielding, but I did. I found a sense of place and comfort I'd never known before, nor found since. There is something to be said about fitting in that is deeply satisfying. I loved the intense questioning and arguments that went on. It was safe to open my mouth for once and say what I really thought, as half-formed as my ideas might have been. Hard-wired as a social activist person, sick of all the right words in academia that actually meant very little, I found a true intellectual and practical commitment to change and inclusion at Fielding, a motivation I could admire, respect and, with integrity, be part of.

I had been a visual artist since childhood, a painter, critic, and art historian, and art became part of many of my Fielding projects and papers—such as "Paintings and Drawings in the Spirit of Different Personality Theorists", "Feminine Imagery and a Young Woman's Search for Identity", "The Perception of Doors, A Sociodynamic Investigation of Doors in 20th Century Painting." All of these projects started at Fielding; afterwards they were accepted in peer-reviewed journal articles and later appeared in a book, my favorite of all of them. [i] My art was appreciated and supported more than it had ever been at art school or in MFA work, where the male-dominated philosophy and environment sought to critique and destroy the competition and to ignore women altogether.

I was lucky to have Will McWhinney as my mentor at Fielding. Will taught me confidence in my own far-ranging style and challenged me to expand it into the unknown. The word around Fielding was that Will could be abrupt and scary. It was rumored he had written "bullshit, bullshit, bullshit" on one student's paper. With me he was a constant, gentle guide, and also a pushy one, eager to dump me into the abyss to find the riches there, while he offered me support to climb my way out again. I consider my dissertation, a phenomenological study of visual artists and writers ("Creative realities, the search for meanings") the best work I have ever done. In it I created an important theory of creativity.

Since graduating from Fielding, I have published 10 books. (*The eleventh, An Art Psychotherapist Considers Mass Murders, Creativity, Violence and Mental Illness,* is in process for 2019.) Many of them began as projects at Fielding and all are in its spirit. In 2012 I published *Graphic Facilitation and Art Therapy, imagery and metaphor in organizational development* with a magical Foreword by Charlie Seashore. I believe it was one of his last pieces before his death. Among many things, Charlie taught me the healing pleasures of humor.

With my first book, *A History of Art Therapy in the United States* (1994), I was able to make an important contribution to the profession of art therapy, the first inclusive history of art therapy ever. Sixteen years later, in

2010, *The Modern History of Art Therapy in the United States* was published. It is used as a text in graduate programs across the country.

My other books have primarily been about creativity and art therapy, but in 2016 a very different kind of book, reflective of my social action bent, was published, *Voices from the Barrio: Con Safos: Reflections of Life in the Barrio*. This was the story of the first ever independent Chicano literary magazine. In the late 1960s and 1970s during the movement for Chicano civil rights and school walkouts, I ran an arts and education program "Operation Adventure" in East Los Angeles (before I ever heard the words "Fielding" or "art therapy"), where I met and worked with the writers and artists who put together *Con Safos*. I published a poem in the journal "Upon submitting proposals for federally funded summer programs." My last book, in 2017, *Dear Myra, Dear Max*, was an epistolary about aging with Myra Levick.

After Fielding, I continued teaching at Loyola Marymount University, then Goddard College (Vermont) and Antioch University in Seattle. I teach, supervise, hold many kinds of groups, and mentor students and mental health practitioners in my living room on Whidbey Island, Washington, with the fire roaring and the ferries making their way across Puget Sound outside my window. I have continued to draw and paint, and won "Best of Show" at the Island County Fair for my Mass Murders Triptych, which was exhibited along with the usual paintings of cows, horses, and dogs.

Education should be transformative. Mostly it isn't. At Fielding it was. Although I am not the kind of alumna who comes to reunions, Fielding remains for me a touchstone of how it should be done and how it *could* be done.

By the way, I earned that promotion to full professor at Loyola Marymount and am now Professor Emerita.

References

Junge, M. (2008). *Mourning, memory and life itself, essays by an art therapist*. Springfield, IL: Charles C Thomas.

On Becoming An Axiological Hermeneut

Clifford G. Hurst

Assistant Professor, Ohio Wesleyan University

When introducing myself to college classes or to workshop participants I sometimes describe myself as an *axiological hermeneut*. This gets a mixed reaction of laughter, blank stares, and raised eyebrows. That is what my Fielding experience has done to me. I've become an axiological hermeneut.

Those of you who have studied with faculty colleague Katrina Rogers know that a basic definition of hermeneutics is that it is the art of interpretation. A hermeneut is one who practices the discipline of hermeneutics. A hermeneut will argue that what matters is not so much what process philosophers call the *situation* or what phenomenologists call *lived-experiences* that count for meaning as it is the person's interpretation of those experiences or situations.

Axiology refers to the study of human values. Formal axiology is a particular theory of the evaluative thought structures underlying people's values. I am a student and scholar of formal axiology. Hence, being an axiological hermeneut means that I seek to understand how people make meaning of their lives through the lens of the structure of their values.

A Career Change

My Fielding experience allowed me to make a late-in-life career change. I now find meaning in my work and I hope that, in ways small or large, I am making a difference for good in the world. I am an associate professor of management in the Bill and Vieve Gore School of Business at Westminster College in Salt Lake City. Westminster is a small, private, not-for-profit liberal arts college. I teach entrepreneurship and social entrepreneurship at the MBA and undergraduate levels.

I entered Fielding's HOD doctoral program in September of 2006 at the age of 53, having spent the previous 18 years running my own OD consulting practice. My goal at that time was to become a more theoretically grounded consultant. In my consulting practice I was using an assessment tool known as the Hartman Value Profile (HVP). It is based on the theory of formal axiology, which had first been articulated by the philosopher Robert S. Hartman (1967, 2006). It is a powerful tool, but I knew very little of its psychological and philosophical underpinnings. I wanted to know more. A strong impulse behind my desire to earn a doctorate was to become more knowledgeable about formal axiology. Pursuing this showed me the power of Fielding's adult learning model. Few of the faculty members were familiar with Hartman's work; none were experts in it, but that did not stop them from guiding me in my study of it. I remain especially grateful for the encouragement in this pursuit that I received from faculty colleague Miguel Guilarte, whom I eventually asked to chair my dissertation committee.

By the time I was midway through my studies at Fielding, I had become captivated by a vision of a new career as an academic. I set my sights on becoming a professor as soon as I earned my PhD. I began my academic job search shortly after my pilot study was concluded and was hired by Westminster in the same month that my Final Oral Review for my dissertation was completed. That was in March of 2012. I began teaching at Westminster in August of that year and am now in my seventh year as a full-time professor. Looking back on my time as a doctoral student, the road to my current profession seems straighter in hindsight than it ever did during my five-and-a-half years at Fielding.

Of course, an earned doctorate was a prerequisite for becoming a professor, but the encouragement to publish that I received from my faculty during my years as a doctoral student, coupled with the modeling of what it means to be a teacher of adults, aided greatly in the launch of my new career.

Westminster prides itself on being a teaching college, as opposed to a research university. I am proud of the time I spend in the classroom and proud of the influence that, I believe, I am having upon my students. Two years ago, I developed the curriculum for a new inter-disciplinary undergraduate minor in entrepreneurship, which is proving to be quite popular. I am particularly proud of my part in establishing a social impact incubator at our campus. It was undoubtedly Fielding's emphasis on social justice that allowed me to appreciate the power of using startup business principles to do good in the world.

In addition to Westminster's emphasis on teaching, our business school expects of our faculty a certain standard of scholarly output, primarily in the form of publications in peer-reviewed academic journals. Fielding prepared me well for both roles.

The Beginning

Having applied to Fielding without a master's degree, I was required to demonstrate evidence of scholarly writing. Faculty colleague Dottie Agger-Gupta advised me to take one of my previously published trade journal articles and revise it as if I were submitting it to an academic journal. I followed her advice. Consequently, I was accepted into the New Student Orientation (NSO) that began in September of 2006. Having spent so much time writing that paper as part of my application, I began to wonder what else I could do with it. After attending writing workshops offered by HOD faculty and colleague Judy Stevens-Long at two National Sessions and inviting her to rake my manuscript over the coals a few times, I decided to submit it for publication. It was accepted after minor revisions (Hurst, 2008). This gave me an idea. What if I could use the in-depth portions of some of my KAs as opportunities for subsequent publication? Here again, Miguel Guilarte encouraged me to do this. He guided me through my Knowledge Area (KA) in Human Development, the in-depth portion of which became a manuscript that was eventually published in the *Journal of Formal Axiology: Theory and Practice* (Hurst, 2009). It was a comparison of the Hartman Value Profile with the more widely known Rokeach Value Survey. What I learned in that KA continues to inform my research in value theory today.

A second study guided by Miguel also resulted in an article in the same journal. This was my treatise on "The Non-Mathematical Logic of a Science of Values" (Hurst, 2011). I consider this article to be my most significant contribution to the refinement of the theory of formal axiology to date. A more recent paper entitled, "The Intentions of Axiological Interpreters" (Hurst, 2014), reveals my indebtedness to Katrina Rogers and what she taught me about philosophical hermeneutics during an advanced doctoral seminar on that subject.

For their encouragement of my nascent publication efforts, I remain grateful to Miguel Guilarte, Katrina Rogers, and Judy Stevens-Long, and also to Keith Melville, who demonstrated through his teaching and in his own writing that it is possible to write in a way that is both scholarly and readable.

As soon as I began applying to become a professor, I learned how much emphasis hiring committees place upon publications in peer-reviewed journals. Without the three papers I had published as a doctoral student I doubt that I would have been hired to a permanent teaching position at a four-year college or university. The subject of my dissertation aided in my job search as well. And it allowed me to envision a future research stream that is gradually coming to fruition.

Most Recent Publication

Since my appointment as a professor, I have published several additional articles and reviews in the *Journal of Formal Axiology*. Eager to expand my writings about formal axiology and the HVP into more of the mainstream of management literature, I was delighted when my article entitled, "An Axiological Measure of Entrepreneurial Cognition" was accepted this past fall by the *International Journal of Entrepreneurial Behavior and Research* (Hurst, 2018). This latest paper is a direct outgrowth of a stream of research I had begun with my dissertation.

What's Next?

Having spent much of the past 10 years studying the deep-seated evaluative thought patterns of entrepreneurs, I am now turning my attention to a study of how undergraduate college students think. I seek to answer the question: "Do we, as educators, impart any lasting, meaningful, and positive impact upon students' developing cognitive patterns?" Given that Fielding, too, prides itself on providing its students with a transformative education, I would also like to partner with Fielding to extend this study to doctoral students and attempt to measure how their deep-seated cognitive patterns change or fail to change over the course of their graduate studies.

Shortly after graduating from Fielding, I was invited to serve on the board of the Robert S. Hartman Institute of Formal and Applied Axiology (RSHI), a 501(c) 3 not-for-profit organization. I currently serve as the Vice President of Research and as editor of the *Journal of Formal Axiology: Theory and Practice.*

During the summer of 2018, I received a Gore Summer Research Grant from Westminster College that allowed me to take two undergraduate students to the University of Tennessee where, for 10 days, we dug into the Hartman Archives at the Special Collections Library there. Hartman had been a visiting professor of philosophy at Tennessee when he died, unexpectedly and too young, at the age of 63. Although Hartman was a prolific writer, only one book of his was ever published in English in his lifetime. Throughout his career, he had kept copious records of his lecture notes, essays, speeches, and numerous drafts of various journal and book manuscripts. More than 100,000 pages of unpublished papers, mostly in the form of typewritten carbon copies, are stored in those archives. Since Hartman's death in 1973, the Institute has published two of his book-length manuscripts, but much of what Hartman wrote remains unread and unpublished. I am currently developing a proposal to the Board of the Institute that we undertake to systematically transcribe, edit, and publish a much larger selection of Hartman's work. The world today needs Hartman's ideas.

Hartman's Body of Work

The more I study Hartman's body of work, the more admiration I have for the depth and breadth of his thought. Hartman did much more than just develop a value theory. In 1947, he founded the Council of Profit Sharing

Industries (Hustwit, n.d). During our time at the Archives, we discovered a manuscript written circa 1958 entitled: "The Partnership Between Capital and Labor," which lays out Hartman's belief in this new form of capitalism based on partnership. I intend to transcribe, edit, and publish the introductory portions of that manuscript soon.

Hartman was a founding member of an organization of concerned scientists against nuclear proliferation and wrote extensively about the threat of nuclear annihilation and how, through developing a science of value, we may be able to avoid a nuclear war. It is for this work that he was nominated for the Nobel Peace Prize in 1973. His warnings from that era are even more important to us who are living today.

Hartman was also an early member of the Association of Humanistic Psychology, founded by his close friend Abraham Maslow, and other thought leaders who are well known to Fielding people, including Virginia Satir, Carl Rogers, Gordon Allport, and Rollo May (AAHP.org). During our archival research, my students and I uncovered additional writings by Hartman about humanistic psychology and its relation to philosophy.

Summary

In summation, I applied to Fielding in part to begin to understand more fully the theory of formal axiology. I've learned a great deal about it since then and I continue to learn. Today I am leading the effort to bring more of Hartman's work to the light of day. I serve as editor of the only peer-reviewed journal dedicated to the refinement, expansion, and application of that theory. I did not enroll at Fielding intending to become a professor, but now that I am one, I realize that Fielding led me to my true calling. I am increasingly becoming able to bring formal axiology into my classrooms, in hopes of stimulating a new generation of value theorists who can—through this knowledge—make this world a better place. The world needs a new generation of axiological hermeneuts.

References

Hartman, R. S. (1967). *The structure of value: Foundations of scientific axiology.* Eugene, OR: Wipf & Stock.

Hartman, R. S. (2006). *The Hartman Value Profile (HVP) manual of interpretation,* 2nd Ed. Knoxville, TN: Robert S. Hartman Institute.

Hurst, C. G. (2008). Sustainable telemarketing? A new theory of consumer behavior. *Direct Marketing: An International Journal, 2*(2), 111-124.

Hurst, C. G. (2009). A meaningful score: Hartman v. Rokeach. *Journal of Formal Axiology: Theory and Practice, 2,* 79-96.

Hurst, C. G. (2011). The non-mathematical logic of a science of values. *Journal of Formal Axiology: Theory and Practice, 4,* 1-12.

Hurst, C. G. (2014). The intentions of axiological interpreters. *Journal of Formal Axiology Theory and Practice, 7,* 1-10.

Hurst, C. G. (2018). An axiological measure of entrepreneurial cognition. *International Journal of Entrepreneurial Behavior and Research.* Advance online publication. DOI: 10.1108/IJEBR-05-2018-0337.

Hustwit, W. P. (n.d.) The father of profit-sharing. *Wooster Magazine.* Retrieved from: http://www.axiometrics.net/Wooster.htm.

My Transformational Journey From Practitioner To A Scholar-Practitioner

Gary Wagenheim

Vice Chair and Treasurer, Fielding Board of Trustees

Adjunct Professor of Management

Beedie School of Business, Simon Fraser University

My Fielding learning experience transformed me from a practitioner to scholar-practitioner. As Robert Quinn (1996) wrote, "Deep change is different than incremental change in that it requires new ways of thinking and behaving. It is change that is major in scope, discontinuous with the past and generally irreversible."

In the classroom, I changed as a teacher. In the office, I changed as a consultant. I have a greater breadth and depth of content knowledge, a keen awareness of my ontological and epistemological approaches, and a deeper level of understanding of client and learner needs. I discovered that becoming a scholar-practitioner is more than merely choosing a culture of inquiry for research or a model for consulting; it is integrating inquiry as a lifelong practice. My journey to becoming a reflective scholar-practitioner was about transforming my consciousness, changing my mindset, illuminating my self-awareness, being knowledgeable and informed by theory, and changing from being a consumer of knowledge to a producer and purveyor of knowledge.

My Graduate Education

My career was not a predictable path nor a straight line. I started a clothing store at the age of 24 with no money and no experience in retail. That store was successful, so I expanded to a chain of stores and eventually sold it to employees when I was 37. As I was winding down my business, I studied for my MBA because I was unsure of what to do next and thought I would figure it out in school. In the last year of the MBA program, I did figure it out, as I started a consulting firm and taught part-time at two community colleges and a liberal arts college. I loved both teaching and consulting. Upon graduation, I searched for a faculty position, mainly at community colleges and a few universities. To my surprise, I was hired at a Big Ten University. Fortunately, they were searching for a scholar-practitioner and I fit the bill, at least the practitioner part. I was hired as an assistant professor on a tenure track without a PhD, and rose to the rank of full professor, still without a PhD.

While I had been in the field of higher education for a long time, the demands of teaching, scholarship, and service at a major university paradoxically left little time for advancing my own education. The sound of the tenure clock ticking led me to choose the path of tenure over education, and led to the postponement of studying for a PhD. Much like going for my MBA as I was exiting business, I went to Fielding for my PhD after resigning my position at Purdue and moving to Vancouver, Canada to marry. I went for both graduate degrees for the same reason. I was interested in learning and deep personal change; I was not interested in instrumental learning or credentialing. I aspired to know more, to be more, and to do more with my life in teaching and consulting. I wanted to make contributions to the field and transfer that knowledge to students and clients.

As a lifelong independent learner, my approach closely follows Kolb's (1984) experiential learning model. I am an active experimenter who jumps into a learning experience cold, reflects on the outcomes, seeks additional information and theories to inform my learning, and then applies that new knowledge to solve a problem. I then follow a cycle of practice, reflect, and modify until I develop the skill to the best of my ability.

In Fielding's andragogy (Knowles, 1980) my experience, independence, and action-oriented learning style were acknowledged and supported. Rather than change my learning style to fit Fielding, Fielding encouraged me to use my natural learning style. In this way, Fielding's student-centered model perfectly filled my learning needs.

As a mid-career professional with a busy international consulting schedule, Fielding's flexible distributed education model afforded me the opportunity to study while I continued working. In addition, the student-directed approach allowed me to study the specific topics I taught, topics where Fielding faculty had expertise, while developing myself as a scholar and practitioner.

My Transformation

So how did this transformation evolve? It was a combination of exploring the subject matter combined with reflecting on my personal development that enriched my learning and deepened my change. My exploration of knowledge expanded, which led to more reading, more thinking, and more writing, resulting in more questions than answers. Of course, this created a certain emotional tension and frustration that ultimately blossomed into my maturation as a scholar. I eventually realized that asking the right questions was more important than having the right answers. It was the process of getting lost in the knowledge that facilitated the development of my inquiry.

Fielding's faculty capably served as guides, always leading with questions, occasionally adding content, focusing me on the process of self-learning. Also, the Fielding learning model of knowledge areas addressed both ends of the theory-practice continuum. Studying at three distinct yet connected levels—overview, in-depth, and applied— for each knowledge area yielded the deep learning I craved.

The faculty encouraged me to survey the width of a field in an *overview,* which meant reading numerous books and countless journal articles on a given topic, all the way back to the classics, then picking a specific element of the field *in-depth* that I wanted to explore in a robust and deep way and, lastly, to do an *applied* level where I was required to use my knowledge in practice in my teaching or consulting. I came to understand how theories and fields develop, to understand the tenets upon which that knowledge is built, and to see the benefits, controversies, and flaws in the knowledge. I began to engage actively in the discourse and to think about how to make contributions to my chosen field.

In addition, learning contracts for each knowledge area contained doctoral competencies—that is, critical thinking, scholarly writing, and a scholar-practitioner mindset—that I wanted to develop along with knowledge of the field. In this way, faculty members assessed my work on a given topic while providing feedback on the doctoral competencies I was working to develop. I also did a self-assessment in each knowledge area, which simultaneously honed my reflective practice skills.

How I Am Different as a Scholar-Practitioner

Fielding encouraged me to adopt an interdisciplinary perspective combining theories of personality, social psychology, human development, learning, motivation, and leadership that formed the foundation for enriching my work. It was not always obvious how to combine these fields to produce an integrative way of knowing; however, in the struggle I found more learning. At first, I simply sought to use and understand these perspectives separately; however, it was as I slowly learned to integrate them that I clearly saw different views and discovered better solutions. This eventually led to an inquiring learning cycle of framing, naming, and reframing of problems that produced better knowledge and effectiveness in my teaching and consulting.

I explored the broad spectrum of theories, gained more depth by focusing on specific topics of interest, and, most of all, applied my new knowledge in my consulting, writing, and teaching. The learning model at Fielding facilitated this learning development.

So while I was integrating knowledge from interdisciplinary perspectives in my PhD, I was doing it in my lifelong personal development journey, too. I have always sought to integrate my life in ways that allow me to grow as a person and contribute to the community through education, business, and volunteerism. I love being with and helping people. I really view ambiguity and change as opportunities for learning. Certain personal core values—

independence, hard work, flexibility, and honesty—allow me to see many possibilities and few roadblocks in life. I try to balance my life so that what I do for play I also do for work, creating a professional life and personal life that are truly integrated. I am coaching and teaching when talking with friends in a coffee shop in much the same way I am with students in a class. Now this was true before Fielding, but what is different is how I manifest my transformation into scholar-practitioner in the same endeavors after Fielding.

I was reading books on leadership before I ever dreamed of matriculating into an MBA program; counseling employees long before I discovered the discipline of organizational behavior; and training employees before I knew the meaning of the word pedagogy. I was doing all of this intuitively, doing it because it was my temperament. I was not knowledgeable about what I was doing. What I learned in my PhD program at Fielding were the theories to better inform and improve my work. Kurt Lewin's (1951) maxim captures it best: "There is nothing so practical as a good theory." Theory really does inform my professional practice; it provides vocabulary, explanation, and frameworks for action. Theory is the scholar I now bring to my practitioner.

My own personal growth combined with subject matter knowledge learned at Fielding directly informs my work in creating innovative pedagogy to teach in MBA and executive education leadership programs. I transfer theory to practice and practice to theory in my research and contribute to the field of leadership through journal articles, conference presentations, teaching, and consulting. I use my Fielding education whether I am teaching students in an MBA class in Vancouver, facilitating a team of executives at a retreat in Helsinki, coaching skiing on the slopes of Whistler, writing an article for an academic journal, or participating in a Fielding Board of Trustees meeting in Santa Barbara.

As an educator teaching in graduate programs and an organizational development consultant working with senior managers of international organizations, I constantly utilize my Fielding education to inform my practice. Graduate students and senior managers, as discriminating consumers of knowledge, expect lessons grounded in theory and often ask for references or divergent theories. Their expectations of a graduate education are considerably higher than what they find in best-selling business books or trade magazines, which often rely on anecdotal rather than theoretical data. These students are critical evaluators of information and want to know not only the theory that supports the lesson, but the research behind the theory.

The Fielding learning model facilitated incorporating pertinent theorists into my research and eventually into my teaching and consulting practice. One of the key aspects of my teaching and consulting is helping students and managers understand the connection between theory and practice, as a generative way of increasing both their knowledge (knowing) and effectiveness (doing). Theories are useful because they help provide explanations for our actions, create vocabularies for discussion, frame our issues, and serve as catalysts for reflection.

I based my Fielding learning practice on constructing an understanding of theories from multiple perspectives that informed and influenced the field of human and organizational development, and that can be incorporated into my teaching practice. My maturation as a learner moved along the continuum from dualism to relativism, from single perspective to multiple perspectives, from one truth to many truths, which is to say I became a more effective teacher and consultant by becoming a more effective learner at Fielding.

The real magic of the Fielding education model was helping me navigate my own development as a scholar-practitioner. I really do see the world differently, ask different questions, and generate different and, I hope, better solutions. For me, becoming a scholar-practitioner is more than merely choosing a culture of inquiry that seems interesting or effective for research purposes; it is integrating my life with inquiry as a lifelong practice. The Fielding experience allows me to fully immerse myself more in my life in ways that produce harmony and integration.

Fielding helped me cross the learning chasm from passive patron of existing knowledge to active creator of new knowledge, which marks the definitive migration from practitioner to scholar-practitioner. Transforming from practitioner to scholar-practitioner fundamentally changed my life, shifted my worldview, and forged a perpetual curiosity for acquiring knowledge that motivates me to cultivate a spirit of inquiry as a way of being—all of which is to say that Fielding transformed me to a higher level of consciousness.

Every step in the Fielding education model, from application to graduation, values human development as the core tenet. An interesting double-loop learning concept (Argyris, 1993) forms the basis of the Fielding model, so while students study *about* human and organizational development they are engaged in a model *of* human and organizational development. Stated another way, Fielding practices what it preaches in educating and developing scholar-practitioners. There is congruence between espoused and actual learning in the Fielding education model, and my transformation is yet another example in a long line of alums with the same transformative experience.

References

Argyris, C. (1993). *Knowledge for action: A guide to overcoming barriers to organizational change.* San Francisco: Jossey-Bass Publishers.

Knowles, M. S. (1980). *The modern practice of adult education: From pedagogy to andragogy.* Englewood Cliffs, NJ: Cambridge.

Kolb, D. A. (1984). *Experiential learning: Experience as the source of learning and development.* Englewood Cliffs, NJ: Prentice Hall.

Lewin, K. (1951). Problems of research in social psychology. In D. Cartwright (Ed.), *Field theory in social science: Selected theoretical papers* (pp. 155-169). New York: Harper & Row.

Quinn, R. E. (1996). *Deep change: Discovering the leader within.* San Francisco: Jossey-Bass.

The Currency Of Voice

Carrie A. L. Arnold
Principal Coach and Consultant
The Willow Group

In a recent conversation with a client organization, I asked the director of organization development to share a little bit about a female client with me. He responded by saying she is highly regarded, with a well-respected voice. His answer was genuine, quick, and unrehearsed, as the main topic of our conversation was less about the female leader and more about the organization dynamics I needed to understand. What a remarkable compliment! It is one most, if not all, women in leadership aspire to hear.

Rebecca Solnit (2017), an American writer and contributing editor at *Harper's Magazine*, recently quipped, "The right to speak is a form of wealth that is being redistributed." In the past, simply holding a leadership role was the only form of currency needed; this is no longer true. It is those with a valuable voice that carry the highest degree of exchange, and it is wealth that can be lost or gained depending on the effort made to be heard. As counterintuitive as it seems, occupying a leadership position does not automatically bring the right to speak. When the elements of race, gender, sexual orientation, national origin, religion, or other personal characteristics are considered, this figurative wealth can be reallocated to groups that hold a higher degree of privilege or status.

As a woman wrestles to gain access to authority, status, and leadership, she cannot lose sight of the need to protect her most valuable asset—her voice.

When I began my doctoral journey at Fielding Graduate University in 2014, I wanted to study the linguistic moves made by leaders that inspire followers. I sought to understand their metaphors, cadence, story, and use of speech acts. I had seen and heard multiple examples of language that did not work. Leaders can overuse the same patterns or catchphrases until they become a behind-the-scenes mockery. I also saw cases of leaders who used language choices that became adopted, quoted, and leveraged. Followers mimicked, not out of disrespect, but out of passionate acceptance. Something was said that counted and, despite how basic the rhetoric, it resonated in ways that spread. Words matter, and I wanted to make sense of the relationship between them and the leader.

Unfortunately, just as trying to wear a pair of shoes that do not quite fit every part of the foot appropriately, something kept rubbing me wrong regarding my topic of interest. I realized I could "dissertation" my way through the speech patterns, leader linguistics, and powerful metaphors of individual executives but never make a difference with those who do not speak with a level of purpose and effectiveness. I first needed to understand what kept leaders so muted, muffled from all the same language choices and rhetoric, so silenced. Thankfully, I had supportive faculty and students at Fielding that were patient with me as I grappled with the needed research question.

This shift, or the flipping of the topic, gave me a chance to refocus on a nuanced angle that has not been given much attention within scholarly leadership conversations. There is a growing body of research on *employee* voice and silence, but there is little to none on the idea that leadership could and does feel silenced. I decided to explore this subtle distinction, and I set out to better understand the female leader and her passage from feeling silenced to feeling heard. I finished my PhD on the silenced female leader in 2016 and realized I was far from finished. My sample size was enough to earn a doctorate in Human Development, but I was not satisfied that I had enough to understand the phenomenon of female leader silencing entirely. In my Fellow role with the Institute for Social Innovation, I tripled the sample size of women, and I continue to study and collect stories as I speak on this crucial topic.

With the support of Fielding, here are a few things I learned about the silenced:

First, it was easy to find women interested in being part of the research. More hands raised than I had time or ability to interview. It was not a challenge to find participants. The difficulty was finding female leaders who could talk about their recovery. Far too many women in leadership currently feel silenced. Finding those who could speak to the journey to valuable voice became not just difficult, but a finding in and of itself.

Second, when women in leadership feel silenced, they often feel sick. It became clear to me after dozens of interviews that the experience of silencing impacts women like a virus. They feel compromised cognitively, emotionally, spiritually, physically and, of course, their leadership is not at its best when they do not think they have the agency to speak.

Third, silencing in leadership is rarely about sex. It is essential to make a distinction between "breaking the silence" specific to sexual harassment and assault as opposed to the leader silencing that is pertinent to my research. Women and men are breaking silence around the "casting couch" experience they had to endure at a younger age with high-ranking privileged people. This phenomenon is often true of younger women who are entering into professional roles. My research was less about harassment or assault, and more about the damage women in leadership experience when they feel psychologically silenced.

Here the silencers do not have a consistent profile. Female leaders can feel silenced by board members, peers, bosses, direct reports, customers, and a variety of different stakeholder groups. Sometimes the silencers are specific, with names and profiles provided. At other times, the silencers are systems that do not work for one-half of the population. Equal numbers of men and women hold middle management positions. Unfortunately, women often plateau at this level and are not promoted to higher levels of leadership for which they are capable. Systems that favor men are institutional, tangled, and difficult to shift.

Fourth, there is also a finding that women silence themselves to maintain a relationship with their organization. Often they are the primary wage earners in the family and carry a strong sense of responsibility that may keep them from the confidence to make job changes when they begin to feel suppressed. Staying and suffering is an adverse finding in the research.

Last, the ways in which women in leadership feel silenced varies. We often wish we could categorize all of the negative issues to identify and then eradicate them from reoccurring. However, like any form of microaggression, these issues are individualized. What feels egregiously silencing to one female leader may feel like a slight paper cut to another. Eye rolls, disinvites, raised voices, name-calling, talking over, public shaming, discrediting, lack of eye contact, ignoring, excluding, or any variety of marginalizing behavior can have varying degrees of impact. The most important finding was not how the silencing occurs. Instead, it is important to note that women silence other women just as often as men silence women. Many participants in my research argued that feeling silenced by a female is often more painful and acute than anything experienced by men.

The research that explored the silencing was dark. The stories were hard to hear, hold, and put in print. After a period, I had to wonder if I would ever quite capture the light, as it seemed so fleeting. I needed to hear how women improved. Did they recover? Who helped? What helped? How long did it take?

With encouragement from my Fielding dissertation committee to go deeper, here is what I learned about voice recovery.

It takes time. For those that did recover, on average women explained the healing process as lasting up to two years. Once they reached true recovery of voice, they were still susceptible to feeling silenced, but they had a "never again" attitude and were able to regain voice faster with setbacks.

Second, women said that men were not always part of the problem, but they were, more often than not, part of the solution. Having healthy, respectful, and good male champions makes an enormous difference for women experiencing silencing. Knowing they had a man in their corner who would support them was crucial to healing.

Third, women healed when they found care and community. I have learned the hard way that many women have an allergy to the term "self-care." When self-care is the solution, women automatically think of healthy eating, exercise, and weight management. No one refutes that these are all important and necessary for good living. However, this is not the type of care that creates healing when one is silenced. When women are with others who listen and share equally, this is care. Too many times, women who feel silenced are the designated listeners in their leadership or social circles. They need time to speak and be heard.

When women can be with other generous women who share a leadership context, this is care. Leadership is a lonely role, and so few women find themselves in senior positions. Peer groups and community are often hard to access. Executive women need to discover or create communities of practice with other executives. Not every female friend will be able to understand the other's experience in leadership.

Last, when women begin to speak up on behalf of other silenced women, this is care. Healing from silencing can happen when women ensure that they do not become silencers themselves. Giving voice to those who are stifled or suppressed is often the antidote to enable female leaders to stay in healthy places of valuable voice.

Thus, self-care is not the word I use now when I talk about recovering from feeling silenced. Instead, I go back to the compliment I wrote about in my first paragraph. Women need to examine their ability to have self-regard—to regard themselves as having agency, authority, and influence. When we view something highly, we compliment, listen, spend time, enjoy, and appreciate. Women who find and cultivate self-regard are more likely to recover from silencing experiences. Then, as they heal, they need to nurture and support their own sense of valuable voice.

Finally, as a Fellow and Fielding alumna, I have learned that voice alone is never enough!

Anyone can make an utterance, expression, or declaration. We all use speech, but we do not all use it with a degree of effectiveness. As female leaders move away from their silencing experiences and embrace the voice that is inherent in their leadership roles, they need to balance purpose with efficacy. They need to understand what is heard and how. They need to know when to leverage declarative language that is assertive and action-oriented with language that is effective and contextual, filled with metaphor or story. Just finding their authentic voice is rarely sufficient.

They need to discover what is authentic and then be able to pivot and access all the degrees and shades of rhetoric, discourse, and language that needs to be heard from the platform of their leadership role.

Understanding silencing and voice is a journey that is taking me back into some of my original interest in leadership linguistics. How do leaders speak in ways that are heard? What makes people engage and follow versus disconnect and barely comply? In this day, where leadership is so riddled with complexity and ambiguity, how are we leveraging our ability to speak? How do our words create transformation in ourselves and others? Fielding Graduate University not only helped me find my voice, but has also prepared me for this lifelong work and research that does not end with a graduation ceremony. As women find voice with currency, they pave the path for everyone to find a voice, which is essential in our collective pursuit of a just and sustainable world.

References

Solnit, R. (2017). Silence and powerlessness go hand in hand—women's voices must be heard. *The Guardian*. Retrieved from https://www.theguardian. com/commentisfree/2017/mar/08/silence-powerlessness-womens-voices-rebecca-solnit

Maintaining The Garden

Episodes In Sustainability And Organization Development

Julie Smendzuik-O'Brien
Institute for Social Innovation Fellow

Laced throughout the learning plan I drafted at the beginning of my doctoral journey at Fielding Graduate University was the image of a garden in which my scholarship and learning would grow. Before enrolling at Fielding, the garden as metaphor for both creation and stewardship had been with me through formation in my religious faith, while coaxing the growth of reluctant vegetables with my father, and during my study of hunger in the world—an introduction to global systems of politics, economics, foreign aid, development in its many forms, and the dilemmas wrought by the Green Revolution.

In this essay, I discuss three experiences with the garden and its changes, characterized as past, present, and future, to show a few of the impacts my PhD studies have had. The past experience was a small research project conducted in 2008 that resulted in changes for sustainability. The second is my current experience on the board of the Organization Development and Change (ODC) Division of the Academy of Management, on which I have served since 2013. The third is an exposition of where I have been taking my research and practice since completing my doctorate in 2017, specifically with efforts related to a major watershed in my region of the United States with my faith congregation to better understand issues of climate change and sustainability, and with internal organization development practitioners who are working with sustainability changes.

For the *praxis* or *applied* dimension of my social change knowledge area, I investigated a climate protection agreement entered into by mayors throughout the United States (see https://www.usmayors.org/mayors-climate-protection-center). The originator of this mayors' agreement, the mayor of Seattle, Washington, had a problem with cruise ships that would leave their engines running while moored in the city's harbor. Because the engines were fueled with diesel, serious air-quality issues arose for Seattle. The mayor and other city leaders decided to invite the cruise ships to use the city's electrical grid to maintain power rather than emit black diesel smoke, which was also not only affecting human health but was also melting the snow pack in the nearby mountain range, a major source of water for the city. This resolved the air-quality issues of the city and prompted the mayor to consider whether other U.S. cities could make some difference in climate change by taking initiatives in their own areas. No leadership was coming from Washington, DC due to the reluctance of the George W. Bush administration to sign the international Kyoto Protocol for various reasons (see, for example, Hovi, Sprinz, & Bang, 2010).

With this background, I became curious whether cities in my home state of Minnesota were involved in this climate protection effort. On a list of engaged cities, I found to my satisfaction that the state's two major cities, Minneapolis and St. Paul, had signed the agreement. Upon further investigation, I found that these two cities had been involved in climate-related activities for cities sponsored by the United Nations for a number of years. Because I lived in one of the suburbs, however, I decided to check on their involvement as well. I found that eight of the suburbs of Minneapolis-St. Paul had signed the mayor's protection agreement, and I wondered how they were implementing it. I decided to research the motivations for signing and ask about activities related to climate protection in suburbia. Because this was going to be a research project involving human subjects, I had to gain approval of my survey instrument and my research approach from the Institutional Review Board (IRB) at the university. Upon receiving approval from the IRB, I proceeded to contact the eight suburban cities and to interview city staff members about the two areas noted—motivation to sign the agreement, and actions that the cities were taking. One of my findings was that my own suburb was not a part of this nationwide effort. So after I submitted my paper to my Fielding faculty assessor, I decided to contact my home suburb to share my results with the city planner.

The planner and I arranged for me to present my research to the city council. It was a very long council meeting; I was at the end of the agenda and began my presentation at about 11 p.m. My results were challenged by one council member who thought that research meant conducting an experiment rather than the social science research that I recommended. Ultimately my mayor signed on to the mayors' climate protection agreement. In 2014 Maplewood was recognized for its sustainability efforts (City of Maplewood Minnesota, 2014, September), and in July 2018 the city was awarded the Green Step Cities/Step 5 Award by the Minnesota League of Cities (https://maplewoodmn.gov/1003/GreenStep-Cities). The city planner told me on more than one occasion that my research was the spark that prompted the city to take action. The time from when I first presented my research to when the city received awards, however, was six and 10 years, respectively. These are indicators of how long change may take.

The second example of using my doctorate to good effect is my current involvement with the Organization Development and Change Division of the Academy of Management, a scholarly professional organization with over 20,000 members worldwide whose work has influenced the field of management for decades. The ODC Division has about 2,000 members. In 2013 my name was submitted by a fellow Fielding student to serve as a student representative on the board of the ODC Division. I was honored to have my name submitted, and further honored to be accepted as the student representative that year. The membership of the ODC Division was aging, and a recent self-study by the division showed a need for improvements in recruitment and other areas. I was excited by the potential to contribute.

One of the major changes was the need to create bylaws for the division, and to identify more clearly the roles of both elected and appointed board members of the division. A new position created in the bylaws was for an appointed membership engagement coordinator. Because no other board members were interested, I volunteered to serve as the membership coordinator for the division. This was an opportunity to help facilitate organizational change for a significant professional association within my discipline of organization development and change. In the years since that appointment, I have analyzed membership data, created newsletters, worked with board members to engage members at the annual meeting each August, offered workshops for students to explain how the Academy functions, and have been the advocate for division members in both the scholarship and practice of the field of organization development and change. My work has been acknowledged and endorsed by fellow board members. I have been reappointed three times to additional two-year terms through July 2020.

The benefit for me first as a doctoral student and now as a PhD graduate is the opportunity to see the workings of a scholarly organization firsthand and to actively participate in shaping its programs. I have learned intimate details of how the annual international conference is staged and have successfully submitted designs for five professional development workshops, served as a paper-session chair, chaired a symposium on the education of scholar-practitioners in organization development and change, and have frequently served as a reviewer of papers submitted for the program. I have had less personal success with submission of scholarly papers, but I persist.

For the future, three areas of endeavor are emerging. In January 2018, I was elected to the board of the North Woods and Waters of the St. Croix Heritage Area (NWW) regional watershed program. The St. Croix River, designated a Wild and Scenic River by both federal and state agencies, is situated between Minnesota and Wisconsin in the upper Midwestern part of the United States (see https://www.rivers.gov/rivers/st-croix.php).

I joined an ongoing effort to create a heritage area for the St. Croix Watershed and to seek federal designation under the US Department of the Interior's National Park Service. Designated heritage areas are regions of the United States that contributed significantly to the development of the country. Local citizens began an effort to designate the St. Croix River Watershed one of these heritage areas because of the importance of trade waterways, kinship and treaty relationships with Native Americans, significant lumber contributions to the built environment, the variety of European immigrants who came to the area, and the relationships between immigrants and Native peoples.

In the late eighteenth and early nineteenth centuries (1787-1803) this part of Minnesota and Wisconsin was in the vast, unsettled Northwest Territory of the United States. It was for many years off the "beaten path," that is, not on the more frequently used trails to the West, so relationships between native peoples and European immigrants were more cordial than elsewhere in the country. Swedish and French immigrants worked side by side with native peoples to fell the forests, build homes, and trade for needed items. The area is important to U.S. heritage not only because of this peaceful relationship between immigrants and native peoples but also because of the profound economic impact of lumber from the area. After the great Chicago fire in 1871, lumber from this part of Wisconsin and Minnesota was sent to Illinois to rebuild that major Midwestern city. So extensive was the logging for this and other projects that land in the St. Croix River watershed was essentially denuded, and the area experienced severe natural resource issues such as erosion and fires. This led the people of the region to establish conservation measures to restore forests and today, in 2018, the region boasts a sustainable forest industry. Other benefits of the conservation effort include recreation and tourism.

The region was the also the birthplace of the first Earth Day in 1970, due to the cooperation of national legislators from the area, Senator Gaylord Nelson of Wisconsin and Senator Walter Mondale of Minnesota. While it is not a national holiday, citizens throughout the United States often acknowledge the day with celebrations and activities about the value of our earthly home and our planet's natural resources. For much of my career I worked in agriculture and natural resources management, and I wrote my dissertation in part about sustainability issues not only in the United States but also globally. By applying my experience as well as the skills learned through my doctoral program I believe I can contribute to the sustainability of my part of the United States. I have an opportunity on this board to offer my expertise in research and practice to foster social change and ongoing civic engagement to enable residents of the area to support designation of the heritage area and to then benefit from possible economic developments, pride of history and place, and increased protection of natural resources.

Another arena in which I hope to make some difference regarding sustainability issues is within the Catholic community. About 600 institutions in the U.S. Catholic community have signed on to a Catholic Climate Covenant in response to the serious reports of climate change and potential impacts on people, property, and the planet. Many have signed this Catholic climate agreement, but as yet the leader in my local church community, the archdiocese in which I live, has not yet signed it. I hope to be among those trying to persuade the bishop to engage in this important global issue.

Last of my emerging activities, I am honored to have been named an ISI Fellow of the Institute for Social Innovation at Fielding. My project is to develop and advance a model for internal organization development practitioners related to sustainability changes within their organizations. I am a member of the Minnesota Organization Development Network's program committee, where I am committed to advancing that idea. I have been invited to participate in national conversations occurring in 2018 and 2019 about the future of the profession of Organization Development and Change, where I plan to promote this idea as well.

As I reflected on what I might highlight in this essay, I realized that some things have persisted for me from my post-baccalaureate days through my doctorate at Fielding. Important to me are the roles of faith and belief in the potential for good stewardship of the earth and its resources. Another is my ability to learn from my experience and to apply past successful efforts to new efforts for organizational and social change. Last is the recognition that through my work at Fielding Graduate University in this PhD program and in writing my dissertation, I have found a more distinctive voice. I plan to use that voice to do what I can to address climate change, to encourage the belief of my fellow humans about the beauty and importance of maintaining our earth and, with humility and persistence, to make a genuine difference that will benefit many.

This institute: https://www.ncronline.org/news/environment/nearly-600-institutions-back-catholic-climate-declaration has been deemed by leaders in our field as a major milestone in its development.

References

City of Maplewood Minnesota. (2014, September). Maplewood recognized for environmental sustainability efforts. *Maplewood Living*, 1. https://issuu.com/maplewoodmn/docs/2014/63.

Hovi, J., Sprinz, D. F., & Bang, G. (2010). Why the United States did not become a party to the Kyoto protocol: German, Norwegian, and US perspectives. *European Journal of International Relations, 18*(1), 129-150. Doi: 10.1177/1354066110380964.

How Fielding Has Shaped
My Professional Life

Timothy K. Stanton
Senior Engaged Scholar
Ravensong Associates

In 1977 I accepted an appointment to the directorship of the Field Study Office in the College of Human Ecology at Cornell University. In this role I provided academic leadership and administration of a small, interdisciplinary undergraduate program that engaged students in intensive service-learning in New York City, across North America, and in the local Ithaca, New York area. There were four of us on the faculty. We were "extradepartmental," located under the college dean outside of and, in some ways competitive with, the college's academic departments.

When I took this job, I had a master's degree in education from San Francisco State University. My only higher education experience was as a part-time adjunct behavioral sciences instructor in a community college district. My main occupation then was organizing young people to engage in civic and community activities aimed at providing needed human services and desired social change. The four of us faculty members in the office quickly developed our programs into nationally recognized innovations in academically accredited, service-based experiential learning. It seemed that the more successful we were in attracting and serving students and our community partners and gaining national recognition, the more we were attacked by our more conventional, department-based colleagues for whom experiential learning was both "too touchy-feely" and "lacking in subject matter." The department chairs were continually after the dean to close us down and divide our budget among them.

One day the dean invited the four of us into his office and said, "I have a problem. You need to get your proper credentials." At the time only two of us had terminal degrees. One had a PhD in community development; the other had an EdD in education. The other "two of us" were me and the fourth colleague. The dean said, "I will help you do this as much as I can in terms of time off and some modest financial support. You need to get going right away, as I can't hold off the critics of your work much longer."

At about the same time a postcard arrived unsolicited in my mailbox announcing first-time accreditation for the Fielding Institute. I had not heard of Fielding, but I found the information about it on the card—a graduate school for mid-career professionals with an interdisciplinary curriculum in human development—immediately attractive. Until Fielding entered my consciousness the only feasible alternative route to a PhD I could see was Cornell's employee degree program. This was not attractive to me, because there were no degrees offered outside my college that deeply interested me and could potentially motivate me to pursue and complete doctoral study. The degrees offered within my college, while interesting and potentially motivating, did not appear feasible politically. How was I going to study and be assessed by colleagues with whom I was simultaneously fighting for budget and academic respectability?

Attracted by its interdisciplinary curriculum and its andragogical approach to graduate study, I applied to Fielding and, fortunately, was invited to attend what was then an ACW—Admissions Contracting Workshop—in Santa Barbara. What I found there was an amazingly diverse, friendly, supportive cohort of like-minded students; intellectually exciting, supportive faculty members, or rather mentors, some of whose work I was familiar with and used in my Cornell teaching; and Don Bushnell, who became my main advisor, mentor, and guide to "over the wall" recreation at La Casa de Maria in Montecito. I immediately signed up and began my studies, joining a New York City cluster group advised and hosted by faculty colleague Jeremy Shapiro.

Perhaps most compelling to me about Fielding, and what became most valuable about it, was the encouragement I received from faculty and advisors to craft my knowledge area, contracting in such a way that my work-

work was my Fielding work. This was important financially, as I needed to maintain my full-time employment. In addition, it enabled me to pursue my studies in ways that exposed me to new theories and knowledge and to apply this learning to papers I was writing for publication, assignments and examination exercises I could use in my courses, and personal exploration of areas of interest I had yet to contend with at that point in my life. My discovery of this approach to graduate education, or rather its discovery of me via the mail at just the right moment in my professional life, was one of the most important gifts I've received. It enabled me to deepen and advance my work at Cornell and later at Stanford University, where I spent 30 years directing and teaching in both undergraduate and graduate programs on the main campus, in the medical school, and in Cape Town, South Africa. For this discovery of or by Fielding and my experience of the university and its marvelous community, I am eternally grateful.

How specifically has Fielding shaped my professional life? It guided me in the exploration of fields (e.g., systems theories) in which I had great interest but lack of in-depth knowledge, knowledge I could share with my students and apply to my understanding of my world, as well as the social policy problems with which I was engaged and in which I engaged my students. It exemplified an approach to and process of enabling self-directed, critical learning to which I aspired in my own teaching. It exposed me to professional work in fields related to mine of which I was ignorant.

For example, in 1984, about midway through my Fielding studies, I took sabbatical leave from Cornell to focus on my Fielding work in the San Francisco Bay Area. Faculty colleague Don Bushnell suggested that I undertake a part-time internship during that year with Pacific Gas & Electric Company's Organization Planning and Development Department. This turned out to be one of the most intense, challenging, and rewarding experiential learning experiences I have had. I acquired skills and knowledge that tempted me to leave higher education and join the OD field. Ultimately it made me both a stronger university administrator and a much better teacher.

I joined the Bay Area cluster when I came back to San Francisco from Cornell and continued with them until completion. A highlight was our work with faculty colleague Frank Friedlander to craft an "overview" seminar for ourselves in the systems theory knowledge area. It was a deeply collaborative effort, with each person taking a theoretical area to research and present during our two-day seminar. Those days were hugely enriching and exciting, both intellectually and personally. I remember returning home after we concluded thinking "that's what education should be about!"

Don and faculty colleague Malcolm Knowles encouraged me to craft a dissertation that could be integrated with my Stanford-based work with a national organization, Campus Compact, which was promoting civic engagement and service learning. It became a year-long follow-up study of faculty members who had participated in a week-long, national service-learning curriculum development institute I and others offered at Stanford for the Compact.[ii] My study was most interesting and rewarding in that it enabled me to observe first-hand and analyze the experiences of these faculty members on their campuses as they attempted to design and offer courses in what were then hostile environments for the kind of teaching we were promoting. It led to my researching and writing the first and only history of my field's first 30 years via an oral history focused on its early "pioneers" (Stanton, Giles, & Cruz, 1999), and numerous additional publications.

My dissertation and, actually, most of my Fielding experience deepened and cemented my commitment to what was then a nascent, embattled field. It was a building block in my leadership abilities, dedicated to further developing this field, installing service-learning pedagogy in the core academic mission of Stanford and at numerous other North American and international higher education institutions. In my post-Stanford retirement life I have established a small, international consulting firm that continues to work these issues with universities around the world, drawing on much of what I learned and developed at Fielding, including my time at PG&E.

I could go on, but will close with one quick anecdote. At Stanford I often had PhD students working with me on various projects. Occasionally we would compare notes on our experiences of pursuing our degrees and dissertations. Without exception these students would almost salivate at the opportunities I had: to direct my own studies with supportive advising and integrate them with my Stanford work; to create my own courses with fellow students in my San Francisco cluster group; to experience the kind of nurturing, mentoring, and recognition I received from my dissertation committee members and external examiner. Stanford at the time may have had a broader reputation and higher status in the academic world, but these students were convinced that I was getting a better and more humane education, with which I had to agree. Thank you, Fielding!

References

Stanton, T., Giles, D., & Cruz, N. (1999). *Service learning: A movement's pioneers reflect on its origins, practice, and future*. San Francisco: Jossey-Bass.